Publisher and Creative Director:
B. Martin Pedersen

Chief Visionary Officer:
Patti Judd

Design Director:
Hee Ra Kim

Designers:
B. Martin Pedersen
Hee Ra Kim
Hiewon Sohn

Associate Editor:
Colleen Boyd

Contributing Editor:
Patti Judd

Publisher's Assistant /Designer:
Claire Yuan Zhuang

Writer:
Maxim Sorokopud

Interns:
Maggie Herrera
Lauren Letarte
Ella York

Japanese Advisors:
USA: Tochiaki & Kumiko Ide
Japan: Taku Satoh
Sakura Nomiyama

Chief Executive Officer:
B. Martin Pedersen

Cover Image:
"USM," designed by
David Carson

Published by:
Graphis Inc.
389 5th Ave., Suite 1105
New York, NY 10016
Phone: 212-532-9387
www.graphis.com
help@graphis.com

ISBN 13: 978-1-954632-32-5

Dear Graphis Readers,

Welcome to another edition of *The Graphis Journal*, where creative powerhouses and boundary-pushers across design, advertising, photography, and beyond come together to ignite your inspiration.

DESIGN: David Carson is the rebel of graphic design, a legend who shook up the industry from his days at *Ray Gun* magazine to his current work for The Macallan. David doesn't follow the rules—he reinvents them, showing the world that bold, non-traditional design can shape generations to come.

Ron Taft makes his return in this issue, diving deep into how his love of music influences everything from his design approach to his philosophy on collaboration. Ron's work will make you feel something, and that's what truly makes him a Graphis Master.

ADVERTISING: Jeff Goodby and **Rich Silverstein** of **Goodby, Silverstein & Partners** have never been ones to play it safe. Together, these Graphis Masters reject the status quo, fusing graphic design and editorial aesthetics to create timeless, groundbreaking work.

PHOTOGRAPHY: From the New York Comic Con to editorial shoots, **Colin Douglas Gray**'s lens captures the soul of his subjects, making him a must-watch photographer.

Lindsay Siu brings stories to life with her camera. Her unique perspective as a first-generation Chinese Canadian shines through in her advertising, portraiture, and entertainment photography, with every image reflecting her commitment to sharing the narratives of others.

ART/ILLUSTRATION: SEAN & EVE blur the lines between typography, illustration, and CGI in a way that will make you question what's real. Their hybrid techniques bring together both digital and analog elements, making them a duo that consistently elevates their craft.

EDUCATION: Simon Johnston isn't just a designer; he's a thinker. Dividing his time between teaching at the **ArtCenter College of Design** and his personal practice, Simon teaches how to verbalize the visual, taking creativity to intellectual heights.

PRODUCTS:
Cars: Imagine a superhero flick in which the DeLorean's cool cousin, the **Bugatti Tourbillon**, swoops in. Sleek, screenless, and ultra-modern, this car is as timeless as it is futuristic. Then there's the **Eli Zero** from **Eli Electric Vehicles**—think Smart car, but even better. It's a perfect mix of agility, minimalism, and style.

Boats: The **Venus Speedster X** by **Seven Seas Yachts** takes us back to the mid-20th century with its looks, but don't be fooled—this modern-day marvel is outfitted with all the high-tech features you could dream of. Or, if you're feeling adventurous, **Pontos**'s **Packable Kayak** offers a lightweight, compact, and efficient design, making it easy to bring along for any adventure.

ARCHITECTURE: This issue highlights architectural designs that transcend form and function, from the windswept shores of **Whistling Wind Island** by **Akb Architects** to the timeless charm of **Jan Henrik Jansen** and **Marshall Blecher**'s **Nieby Crofters Cottage**.

Stay inspired. The creative future is right here in these pages.

B. Martin Pedersen
Publisher & Creative Director

We extend our heartfelt thanks to the international contributors who have made it possible to publish a wide spectrum of the best work in Design, Advertising, Photography, and Art/Illustration. Anyone is welcome to submit their work to the portfolio and award competitions at www.graphis.com. Graphis is not liable or responsible for any copyright infringement on the part of any individual, company, or organization featured in Graphis Journal and will not become involved in copyright disputes or legal actions. Copyright © 2025 Graphis, Inc. All rights reserved. Jacket and book design copyright © 2025 by Graphis, Inc. No part of this journal may be reproduced, utilized, or transmitted in any form without written permission of the publisher.

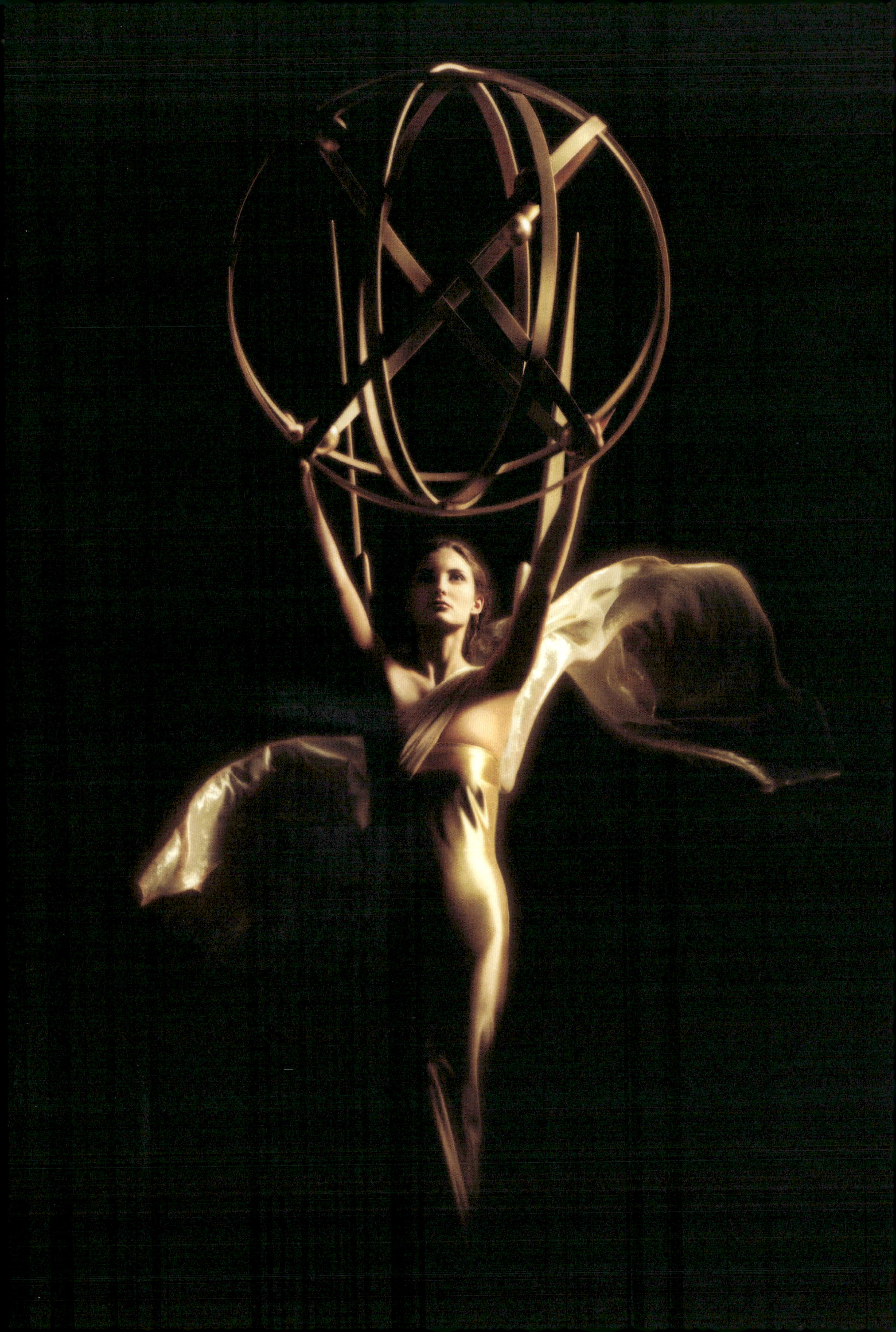

Contents

(Opposite page) 51st Emmy Awards Poster. Photography & Design: Ron Taft

Colin Douglas Gray is an artist and photographer based in Atlanta, Georgia. His diverse body of work includes images of A-list actors, pop stars, fashion icons, religious leaders, cosplayers, and the homeless. Colin's work captures the essence of his subject, and he prides himself on being able to connect with a subject within moments and reflecting that connection back through the final image.

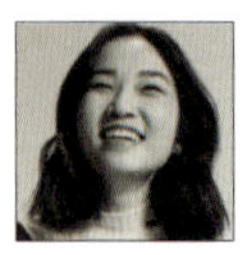

Introduction by Hadley Stambaugh

Hadley Stambaugh combines her fascination with the human spirit and the natural world to create a unique sense of movement and light in her photography. Her work has many subjects, from portraits of A-list actors and fashion icons to still life, everyday students, and their creations. After graduating from the Savannah College of Art & Design, she split her time between her hometown of Pittsburgh, New York City, and Savannah. The time spent between city and rural landscapes allowed her to cultivate a unique aesthetic that mixes the urban fashion influences of New York City and the calming beauty of the low country, her current home, Savannah. Currently, Hadley is the creative director of photography for her alma mater, but she will forever have the eye and heart of a photographer.

Lindsay Siu is a Vancouver-based photographer and director specializing in advertising, portraiture, and entertainment. Her thoughtful imagery conveys a distinct vision, combining the nuance of fine art photography with the clarity and purpose of commercial art. Some of Lindsay's clients include ABC, CBS, NBC, Netflix, Nickelodeon, Paramount, Pfizer, *The New York Times*, *The Hollywood Reporter*, Toyota, and Warner Bros. Studios. Lindsay has been recognized internationally for her work by American Photography, Graphis, The One Show, *Applied Arts*, *Communication Arts*, and *Lürzer's Archive*'s "200 Best Photographers Worldwide."

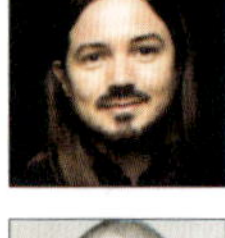

Introduction by Jocelyn Wong

Jocelyn Wong is a designer and art director based in Vancouver, Canada. After graduating from Capilano University's IDEA program, she has worked with many agencies, including Cossette and Camp Pacific, and currently works with the fine folks at Here Be Monsters. Her efforts on various brands and project types have earned her industry awards and recognition from Graphis, the Association of Registered Graphic Designers, *Communication Arts*, and *Applied Arts*. She strives to continue learning and honing her craft with each new project and prioritizing making things people care about. She also would like you to tell your dog she said hi.

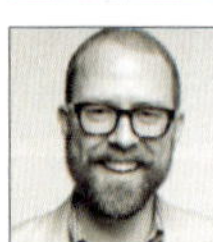

Sean Freeman and Eve Steben's studio is a creative powerhouse known for its innovative and multidisciplinary approach to visual communication—with an award-winning portfolio widely recognized in visual arts features and campaigns worldwide. Their creative process is characterized by a dynamic fusion at the intersection of digital and analog worlds, resulting in tactile, contemporary, and timeless artwork. Driven by a passion for image-making and visual storytelling, Sean and Eve seamlessly blend design, textures, craft, and art experiments to produce compelling hybrid work mixing typography, illustration, photography, and CGI—with a keen sense of balance between form and function.

Introduction by Marshall McKinney

Marshall McKinney cut his teeth in trade journals before earning a master's degree in journalism from the University of Mississippi. Upon graduation, he moved west and landed in *Outside* magazine's art department, a three-time ASME National Magazine Award winner for general excellence. From there, Marshall honed his craft at a number of national magazines, redesigning brands and collecting experiences in the travel, style, food, and sports categories before finally settling down in Charleston, South Carolina, to launch *Garden & Gun* magazine. As founding art director, the brand has gone on to amass much critical acclaim, along with several top honors, including the Society of Publication Designers' "Brand of the Year" and two ASME National Magazine Awards for general excellence, among others. Recently, Marshall left his post at *G&G* after 16 years to freelance, consult, and tinker with brands and projects when he's not coaching his son Wiley's basketball team or getting hip-deep in his garden.

(Opposite page) Chris Francis for SCAD FASH, Savannah College of Art & Design. Photo by Colin Douglas Gray

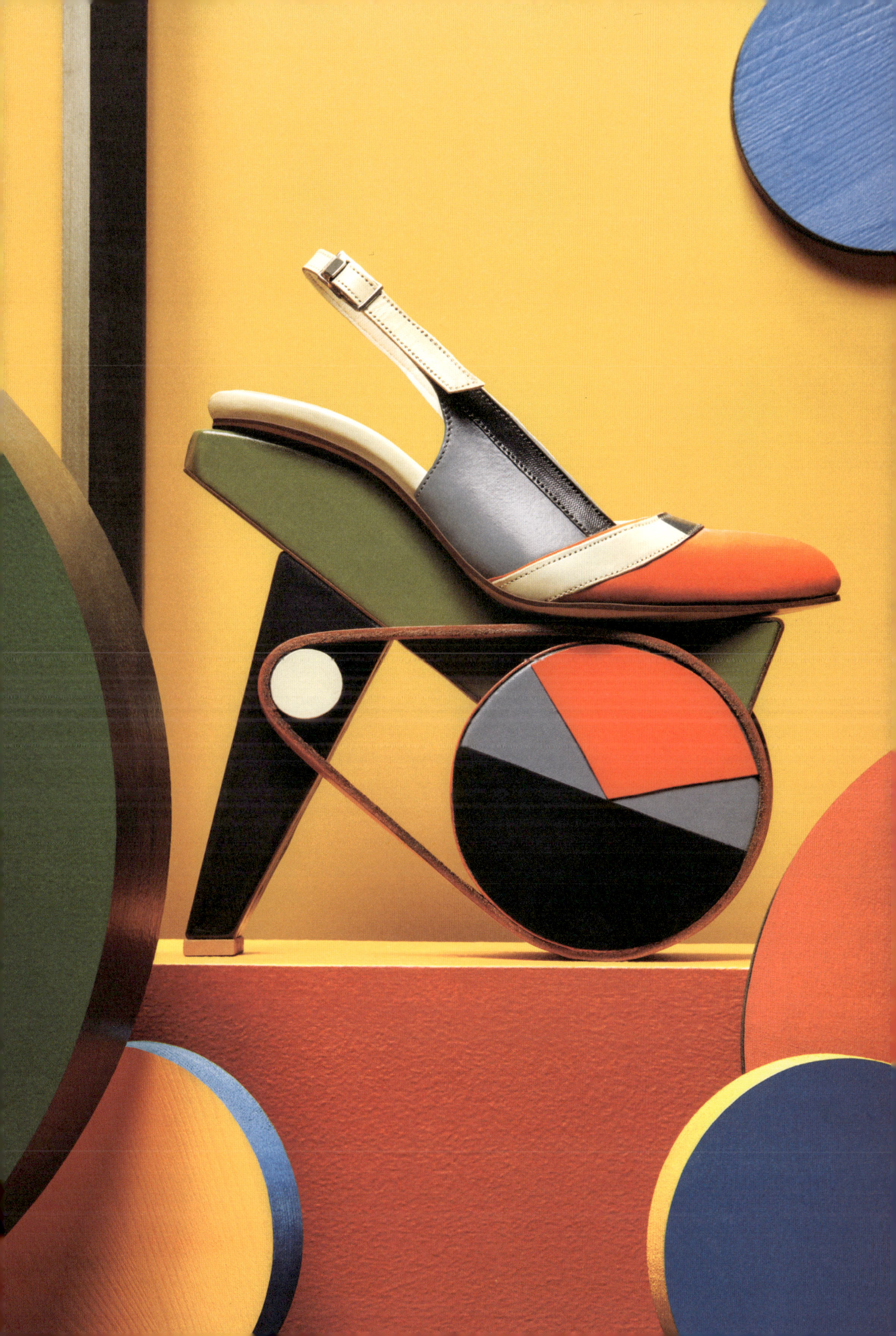

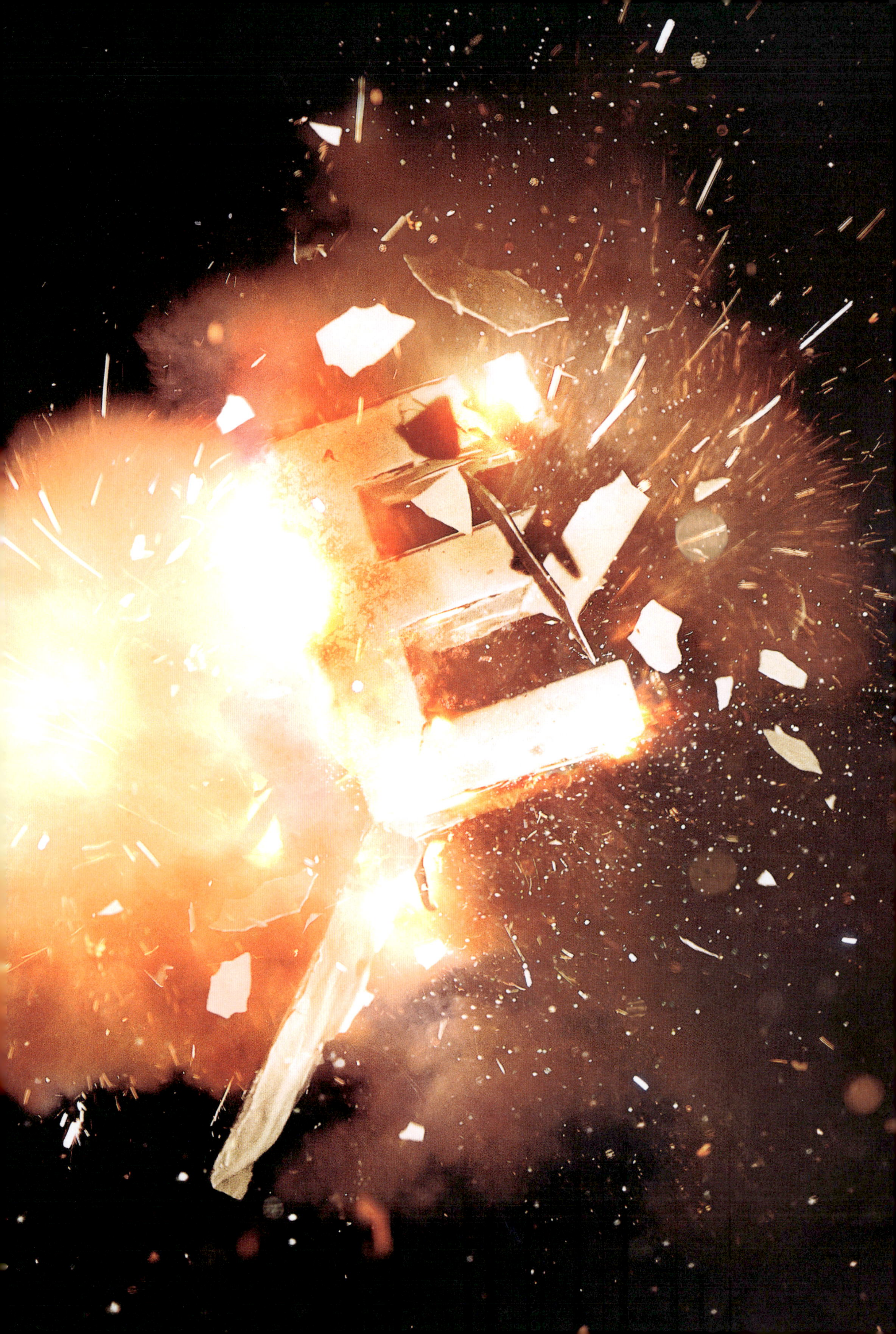

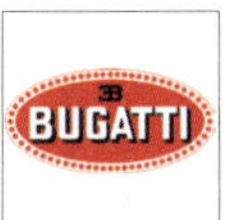

(Opposite page) Client: Self-initated/Personal Project. Project: Describing Words, E for Exploding. Design Firm: THERE IS STUDIO
Typographer: Sean Freeman. Model Maker: Eve Steben. Photographer: Jane Stockdale. Pyrotechnics: John Evans. Post-Production: Sean Freeman

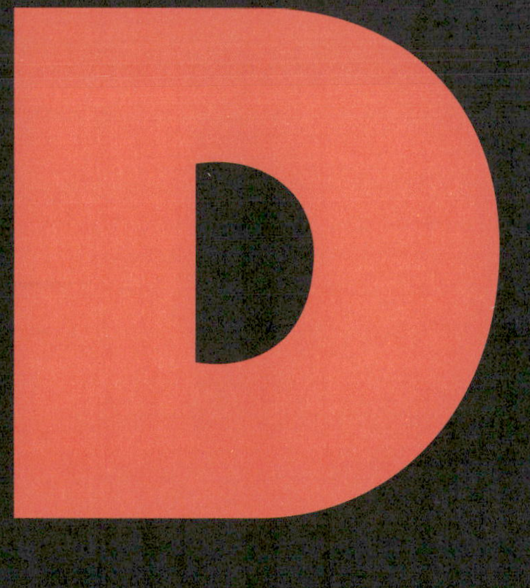

DESIGN

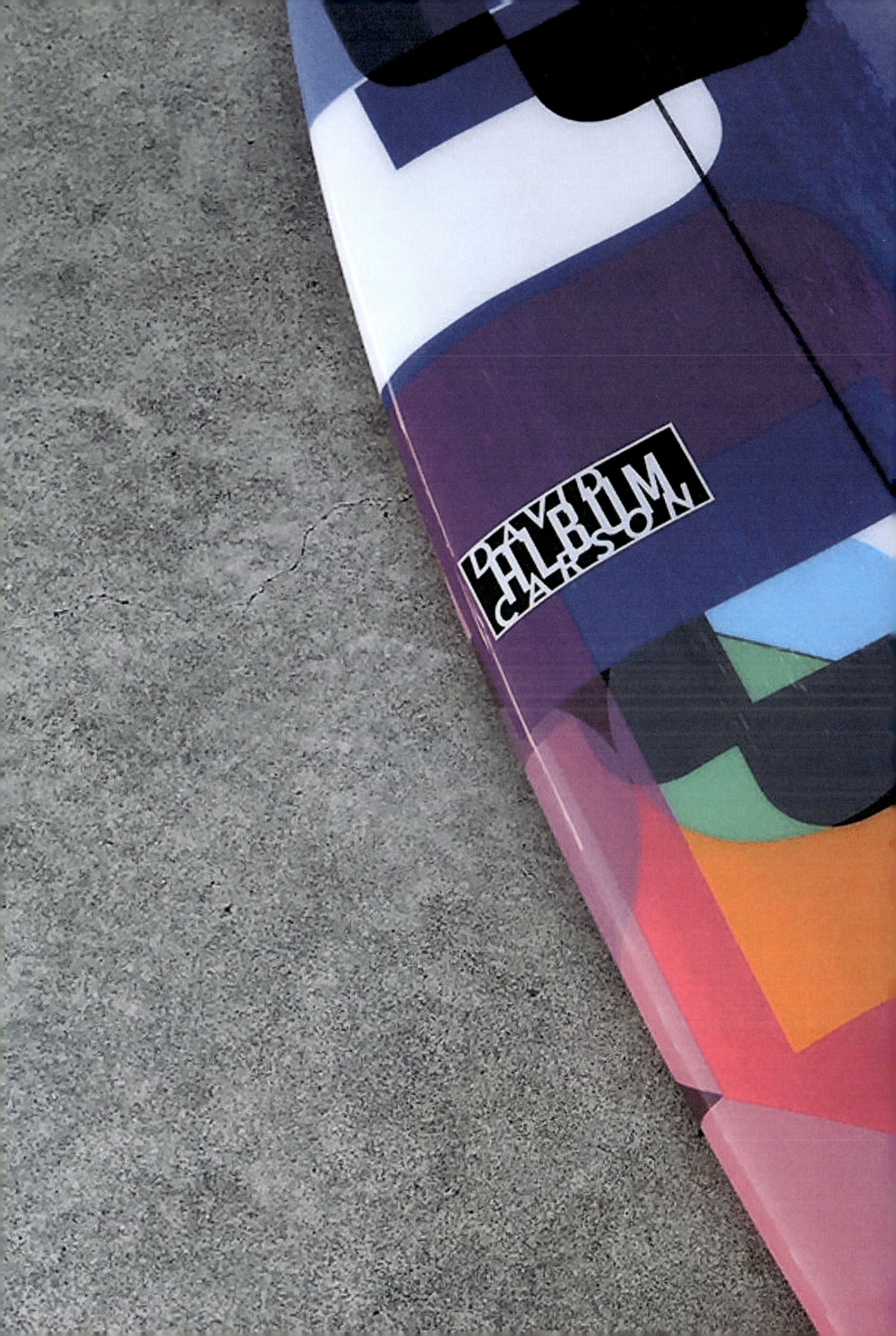

ALBUM
CARSON

David Carson: Breaking with Tradition

DAVID'S WORK SWELLS AND SURGES AS IF CARRIED BY INCOMING WAVES OF FRESH INSPIRATION. UNDERCURRENTS OF MODERNISM PROVIDE THE ULTIMATE FRISSON.

Véronique Vienne, *Author & Professor, Paris College of Art*

DAVID CARSON IS THE PAGANINI OF TYPOGRAPHERS.

Ed Fella, *Graphic Designer & Artist*

EVERY REALM OF HUMAN EXPLORATION NEEDS PIONEERS. DAVID IS AN INTREPID VISIONARY WHO OFFERS THE IMAGE-MAKERS HE COLLABORATES WITH THE FREEDOM TO DISCOVER SOMETHING NEW ON THEIR CREATIVE JOURNEY.

Matt Mahurin, *Illustrator & Photographer*

COMMISSIONING AND UNDERSTANDING DAVID CARSON ARE BOTH COMPLEX THINGS, AND, IN EQUAL MEASURE, BOTH MAKE HIM A TRUE MASTER OF GRAPHIC DESIGN.

Rob Longworth, *Co-Founder & Creative Director, Human After All*

DAVID IS THE REIGNING PICASSO OF THE INTERNATIONAL GRAPHIC DESIGN COMMUNITY.

B. Martin Pedersen, *Designer & Creative Director, Graphis Inc.*

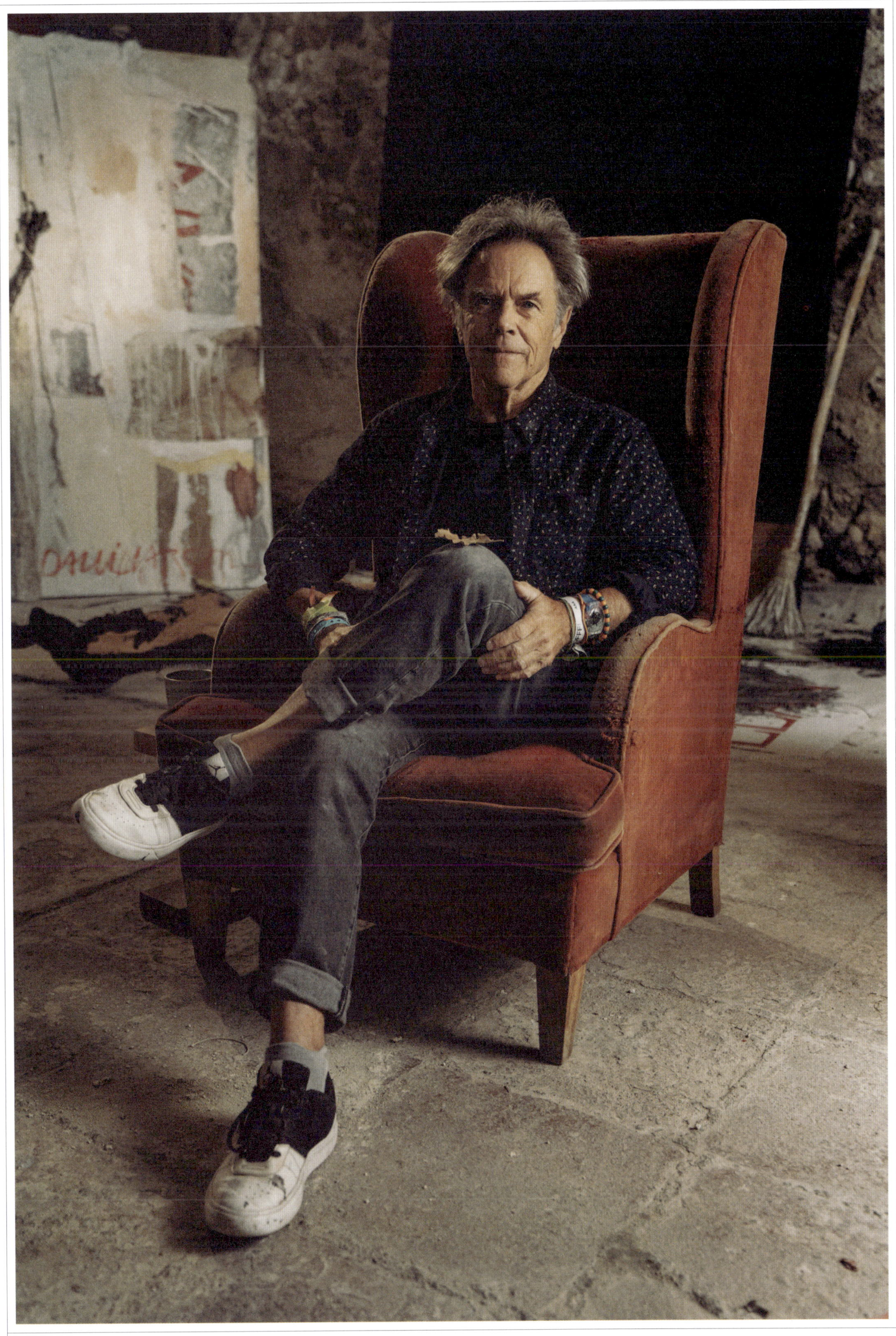

David Carson. Photo Courtesy: The Macallan & David Carson Design

One fateful day, David Carson, a seasoned surfer and high school teacher intrigued by the idea of graphic design, walked into our School of Art workshop at the University of Arizona to investigate. David immediately dug right in, and despite being older than his classmates, he embraced the opportunity to learn about design with a youthful vigor. The fates had indeed smiled upon the world of graphic design. In my classes at the U of A, I taught my students to approach problems critically, clearly, and creatively, looking beyond obvious solutions. David embodied this approach to study the problem effortlessly. Then, upon seeing the design awards I had received during a visit to my working studio, he exclaimed, "You mean you can win awards for this stuff!?" A spark ignited within him, and he discovered his passion for design. David pursued his newfound skills and aptitude with unwavering determination. Using powerful computer programs, David embraced innovative technologies and experimented with deconstructing words, sentences, and page structure. He once designed a full spread for *Beach Culture* magazine "all black" for an article on surfing blind. His radical approach to conceptual design as an integral art element challenged traditional design rules and helped define a new era of graphic design, inspiring an enthusiastic following. David's work, particularly his groundbreaking layouts for *Beach Culture* and *Ray Gun* magazine, had a profound effect on countless designers and students worldwide. His legacy is a testament to the power of his passion, creativity, and willingness to challenge conventions. He really is a wizard of graphic design.

Q&A: David Carson

David, take us back to the beginning. What was that pivotal moment in your career that flipped the script and shaped your design philosophy?

I can't think of one pivotal moment philosophy-wise; it was more like a couple of pivotal moments early on. I taught at a small private school in southern Oregon; my first year, I had grades 1-12 all day in one room. While there, I received a request to post a postcard for the high school students about a two-week summer workshop on something called "Graphic Design." It was the first time I remember even hearing the term. I read what they would be doing during the workshop at the University of Arizona and thought, "Hmmm, that's a career? You can do that for a living? Sounds creative and fun."

I've always been interested in photography, setting up darkrooms in my mom's kitchen and stuff, but not graphic design. I didn't even know the term. I called the program and asked if I could attend as a teacher, and they said no problem. At the start of the summer, I had already arranged a summer job, so I informed them I would need to leave for two weeks in the middle of summer, and they told me that if I backed out and left, there wouldn't be a job when I returned. Something told me I needed to take this class, which I did under the instruction of the amazing artist, designer, teacher, and friend Jackson Boelts. Jackson had a huge impact on my decision to enter this field. After that workshop, everything changed, and I never looked back.

Who were your early design heroes, and how have their influences morphed over the years?

As a result of having no formal training, I didn't know much about design history or influential designers. When I first entered the field, I'd never studied anything related to graphic design, so I didn't have that reference to pull from. I've always been a somewhat quiet observer of all things visual. The first art poster I ever bought was a Rothko print for my college dorm room, but it's hard to point to a specific person or design philosophy that inspired me. I'm a huge fan of Ed Fella, some early Bauhaus posters, and some Dada and Brutalism work. Type artists I was drawn to included experimental Swiss designer Hans-Rudolf Lutz, who I took a workshop with in Rapperswil, Switzerland, at the very start of my career. I also briefly studied with Swiss designer Jean Robert, who designed all the original Swatch watches in the '80s.

Further name-dropping: I consider it a badge of honor that Wolfgang Weingart banned me from appearing on campus at the Basel School of Design. He later showed up unannounced at a student critique workshop I had just given in Lausanne, Switzerland. I met Massimo Vignelli during one of my first speaking gigs in Brazil, and he later surprised me by showing up at an opening exhibition for my work and new book in Venice. He was great! You don't have to love someone's design approach to like them as a person. Tibor Kalman introduced me to grappa and the proper way to drink it in his tiny hotel room in Italy.

Your work is famously known for smashing traditional design norms. How do you ride that fine line between chaos and structure in your creations?

My design journey was unconventional. I never learned all the things designers aren't supposed to do, which I think actually helped me. I just did what made sense to me. It also helped that I had platforms open to, and to some extent, demanded a certain level of an experimental approach.

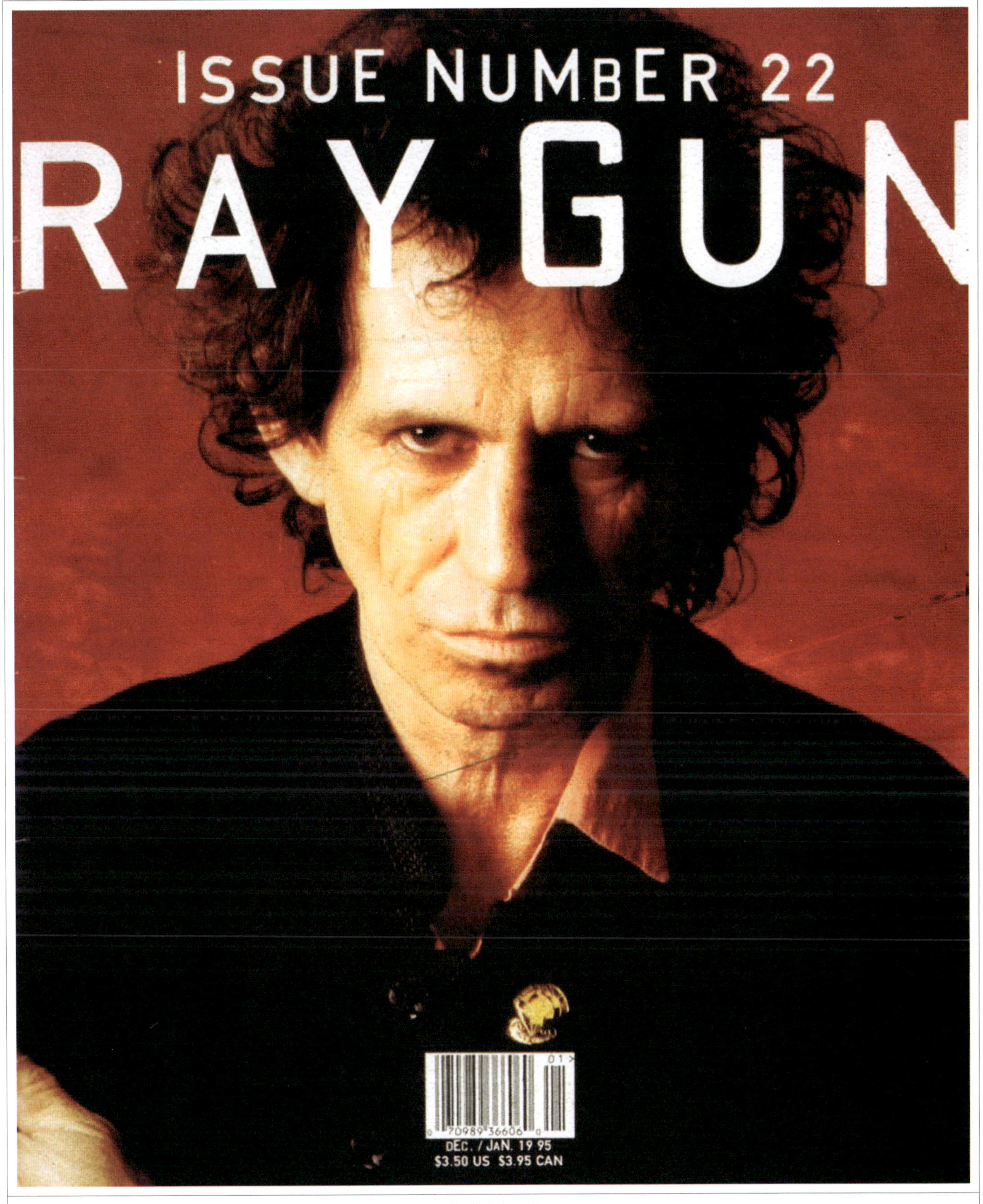

Ray Gun Magazine

My career began as an unpaid intern pasting up quarter-page ads for *Action Now*, a magazine born after the original *Skateboarder* magazine folded. I later designed *TransWorld Skateboarding* magazine at night for three years while I taught high school sociology during the day in Del Mar, California.

In many ways, that was my schooling, trying to sort out this thing called graphic design, magazine flow, colors, type spec'ing, X-acto blades, wax, losing commas on the underside of T-squares, ordering type, and waiting two to three days until it was delivered to see if what you had spec'd actually worked.

Next was the launch of *TransWorld Snowboarding* magazine, then an abrupt decision to exit teaching and move to Gloucester, Massachusetts, to design Billboard Publication's *Musician* mag for one year, and next was a brief stint at *Self* magazine in NYC under the wonderful Véronique Vienne. I left when I heard a rumor that a magazine called *Beach Culture* may be starting, and I quickly moved back to California.

Then, after three years and 30 issues with *Ray Gun* magazine and after relocating my studio to 20th Street in NYC, I designed the adventure lifestyle magazine *Blue* for a couple of issues, assorted special issues and covers from *Form* magazine to Japan's *Idea*, special issues of *Big Magazine*, *Metropolis*, *Trip* magazine from Brazil, *Speak* magazine, and one for Armani. I was flown to Milan to present the entire magazine to Giorgio Armani. Later, I did some catalogs and ads for Burton Snowboards and Quiksilver.

Give us a peek into your creative process. How does a spark of an idea evolve into one of your iconic designs?

I read the brief, look at all the material I'm given, listen if it's music-related, and then think, "What would that look like?" while keeping in mind the audience, client, product, competition, and any other thoughts and feelings generated from my exposure to the brand.

You've got a background in sociology. How does that color your approach to graphic design?

Yes, my college degree was in sociology, where I graduated with "distinction and honors." I think that's why I was first attracted to editorial design. Taking stories about people or events and interpreting them through design was much more interesting to me than, say, designing toothpaste boxes, and it helped that I was interested in the subject matter. Part of my approach has always been, "Why not? Why can't we try that?" Type and columns in gutters, bleeding off the page, changing fonts in the same article, columns touching, articles continued on the front cover instead of the back, columns not being columns but their own unique shape... Of course, some of that had already been done, but it was all new to me. Later, software began making those decisions for the designer. And now, all those rules are followed "to a T" by software, and the result is often generic, safe, decent, predictable, professional, and forgettable.

What fuels your fire and keeps you inspired in your creative journey?

I'm just naturally curious and observing everything around me. Always. Maybe too much sometimes. Also, every brief is unique, and after reading or listening to it, I'm sent in a specific, unique direction. The variety of jobs also helps, as they all need their own unique design voice and interpretation.

Ray Gun magazine is a cornerstone of your legacy. Spill some behind-the-scenes stories or challenges you faced while crafting its look and feel.

Overall, I'd say the challenges were minimal. The publisher brought me in because he liked my work at *Beach Culture* magazine, which I still feel is some of my best magazine work. There were just six issues, done on artboards with tissue and instructions. No one had to approve the design.

The mag itself had no grid or system; every page and article was a new design assignment based on its content. I just did what made sense to me for each article. Some of it worked, some of it didn't. Design writer, critic, and overall great human Ralph Caplan said I was "experimenting in public." Each month was a new issue of experimentation, with no way to delete or change any of it. There also was no immediate feedback, as that would only come in the occasional letter or snail mail someone might send weeks later, at which time I was heavily absorbed in the next issue.

Whenever I got a new issue back, I had three quick tests of that issue: weight, touch, and smell. Did it feel too light and that we were going out of business? Did the cardboard subscription page insets make it feel heavier and that we were doing well? And the smell. Something about the smell of a

brand new, never-opened issue I enjoyed. Finally, was the cover stock too glossy, a good weight, or a good matte finish?

And then I'd start looking at the design. There was no preview on a screen to make sure everything was correct, and we often didn't even get "blue lines"—an odd paper edition printed only in blue—the last chance to make corrections. It was strange paper, a bit like old fax paper. These faded away when left out in the light, btw.

It helped that my studio was in Del Mar, and the rest of the *Ray Gun* staff was in Los Angeles. When you hire people for what they do, you need to get out of the way and let them do it. This was the case with *Ray Gun*. With a very popular section of each issue, "Sound in Print," I gave illustrators and photographers total freedom to interpret songs however they wanted, including picking the song. With *Beach Culture* and *Ray Gun*, I worked with some of the best illustrators in the business, like Matt Mahurin, Craig Frazier, Henrik Drescher, Paul Davis, Milton Glaser, Marshall Arisman, Gary Baseman, Anita Kunz, and so, so many others. Michael Stipe from R.E.M. submitted his photography and loaned some very early computer self-portraits he had done.

Take us on a tour of your favorite projects. What makes them stand out in your eyes?

Beach Culture magazine, Nine Inch Nails, The Macallan, the Aljada Skatepark in Dubai, and Stussy.

Beach Culture magazine: We did six issues in two years, just me and editor Neil Fineman working out of the warehouse at Surfer Publications. Gas and lunch money concerns were part of the process. It was a 24/7 commitment on my end, a true passion project. It was really my first work that started getting some attention. Apple based a two-page ad on the work generated in *Beach Culture* magazine. It was an extreme time of experimenting, growing, and stretching while having the opportunity to use some of my favorite photographers, illustrators, and font designers worldwide.

Nine Inch Nails: Just an all-around great project. I was asked on a phone call to send my portfolio to an address in upstate New York. It was very secretive. Days later, I got another phone call asking me if I could fly to New Orleans to meet with Trent Reznor to discuss the design and photography of his new album and tour. I said yes. He played me the entire double CD in a small room in a former funeral parlor they had taken over. I was pretty sure I had ruined my hearing forever during this listening experience… I also somewhat naively took notes of each track, and Trent later politely listened to all my comments :). After that, I designed the CD packaging and all related materials. Later, they flew me down to Bob Marley's old recording studios in the Bahamas for final cover approval before they headed off to tour Europe. This experience led to also designing the follow-up album, *And All That Could Have Been*.

The Macallan: One of my top working projects continues to be The Macallan. I've been getting to know this luxury brand personally at their distillery in Scotland and interpreting what they do. And what they do is art; they are creative and very down-to-earth folks. They allowed me to dive more into my fine art side, with my own label bottle in 2022 and a lot of new work coming in 2025. I'm especially proud to have also redesigned their logo and branding—the first redesign in almost 20 years released in 2024.

Aljada Skatepark: It was a unique experience to design Dubai's largest outdoor skatepark art and graphics, with two trips to Dubai and meeting so many great people. As a sociologist, observing and meeting the many diverse groups involved, including skaters at the park, was fascinating.

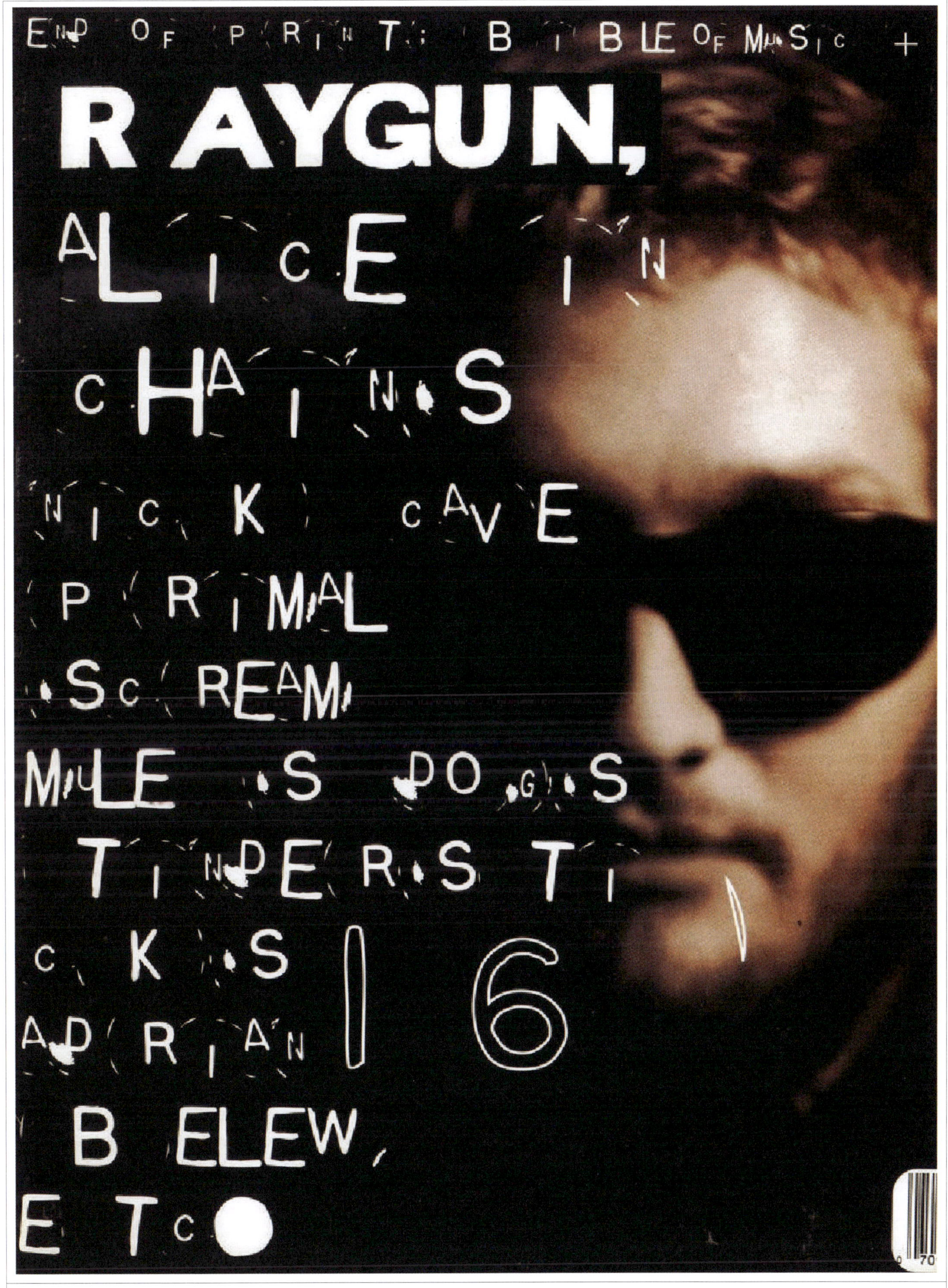

Ray Gun Magazine

Stussy: Shawn and I go way back; I had him contribute to a *Beach Culture* magazine issue. Although he's not involved anymore, the current brand remains enormous worldwide. They sent me all the archives of all the ads over the past 25+ years and let me play. We ended up with a collection of four designs for hoodies and tees, a collection that dropped in spring 2024 and quickly sold out worldwide.

You've inspired legions of designers. What's your take on the current state of design education and the new wave of talent entering the field?
I'm encouraged. There seems to be a hint of experimentation again. Design students often send me work to look at or comment on, and it's refreshing to see them pushing themselves more again—not relying solely on software to do their design or thinking. I recently judged a student poster competition in Japan on the theme of "Peace." There were thousands of entries from around the world, and some amazing work was displayed. I also look forward to judging *AI Art* magazine's first art and design awards in 2025.

Every creative faces criticism. Share an instance where you faced significant pushback on your work and how you navigated it.
I did a lot of work as a visiting artist at 72andSunny in LA. Some of my best work for very large companies was never even shown to the client, which was frustrating. Beats headphones passed on a ton of work I had done, and it seemed like it was happening until the top person who could kill it did. People who hated my work didn't and don't come to me, so I may have fewer battles than many designers. I always show a lot of ideas and directions I think could work, which seems to keep any pushback at a minimum. There's always something they can like or react to and then a direction I can tweak.

Of course, I don't show anything I don't like; they will pick it for sure, and it may follow you for the rest of your career. Just show work you think is better than what they currently have, and, with some tweaking, can get even better and do what they need it to do. Everyone has to find their own way of dealing with criticism; we all get it. I tend to look at the work of a person criticizing mine. If I like what they do, I'm more likely to consider what they complain about. I'm not so concerned if they can't or don't design. It's definitely part of our world, and don't mistake design work criticism for personal criticism. Someone may not like your work, but they are not attacking you personally (although sometimes they do).

You're quite the globe-trotter. Do your travels influence your work and worldview?
It doesn't directly, but it's good for the mind to visit new places and have new experiences. Early on, I always thought I had the best job in the world, being flown all over the globe with a tray of slides to show and talk about my work while meeting interesting people and seeing the world. I recently had that same feeling all these years later.

Surfing is clearly a big part of your life. Does catching waves shape your creativity?
Not directly. The two times in my life when I feel I'm most in the moment are surfing or designing. I'm totally in the moment when riding waves or when I'm in what I call my zone, which kicks in while designing—music on, coffee, and a zillion versions of whatever I'm working on. I love, and on some level, need that focus in what can be a rather nomadic, chaotic life.

Living in the Caribbean sounds like a dream. How does island life feed into your creative spirit?
Well, you know what they say about calling someplace paradise... I always enjoy being near the sea or nature in general. First thing in the morning, I try to get outside and feel the sun on my face, the wind and rain, whatever. I don't get any work done if the surf is good, and less pretty cities may be better sometimes for creative inspiration without distraction. But inspiration can come from anywhere at any time, and I generally work fine wherever I have my laptop, often at various coffee shops, garages, motel rooms, porches, and cobblestone beaches around the world.

How do you balance your career with family life? What lessons do you hope to pass on to your kids?
Well, I have never been accused of living a particularly balanced life. However, I'm not sure I totally agree; I remember reading somewhere what someone said about a balanced life: "What a boring concept." Which I thought had some truth in it...

My kids are 26, 24, and 9—Luke, Luci, and Carson. I would encourage them, and hope I still do, to do what they love doing, do that thing they would do even if money weren't an issue. Explore, say, "Yes." Stay active, and live where you feel happy. Stay in touch with friends and relatives. Don't work at jobs you don't enjoy. My youngest, Carson, says he wants to be a graphic designer when he grows up and has already had an art show featuring his collage work. My daughter, Luci, is an amazing graphic designer—she definitely has "the eye," and my son Luke, who is so multi-talented in everything creative or design-related, is really dialed in. Great things are in the works for all of them. I'm positive.

What's a typical day in the life of David Carson, from the first sip of coffee to the final piece of torn paper or design tweak?
No such thing. Sometimes, if I get up in the middle of the night, I might adjust a collage on the floor just a tiny bit as I walk by. I don't make a huge, if any, distinction between play and work; it just blends together, keeping you from watching the clock and waiting for "holidays."

If you weren't a designer, what would you be doing with your life?
I really have no idea. I found my thing, and I'm lucky I did. I was okay as a teacher but wasn't passionate about it. And you need to be in whatever your life work is. I could do it, the hours were good, and I had more time to go surfing, but those aren't the reasons to go into teaching. Growing up, I was always introduced as the shy one in my family, and that was true. But I was always super observant, and I've been able to pretty much pour my heart and soul into what I do without trying to or forcing it.

When I'm in my design zone on a project, time flies by. I guess I enjoy nature somewhere—maybe painting. I enjoy some sport or physical activity, hopefully in love and being loved. I'm still creating, and with any luck, I'd worry a little less about getting older.

Your collage artwork has become a significant focus. What draws you to this medium, and how does it differ from your previous work?
It was similar to when I started working with artboards, X-actos, and melted wax. I remember that with artboards, I'd squint to see what the layout looked like or look at it through the tissue paper... otherwise, I could see all cut lines or guidelines on the artboard. I never learned about grids, and when I finally

blue

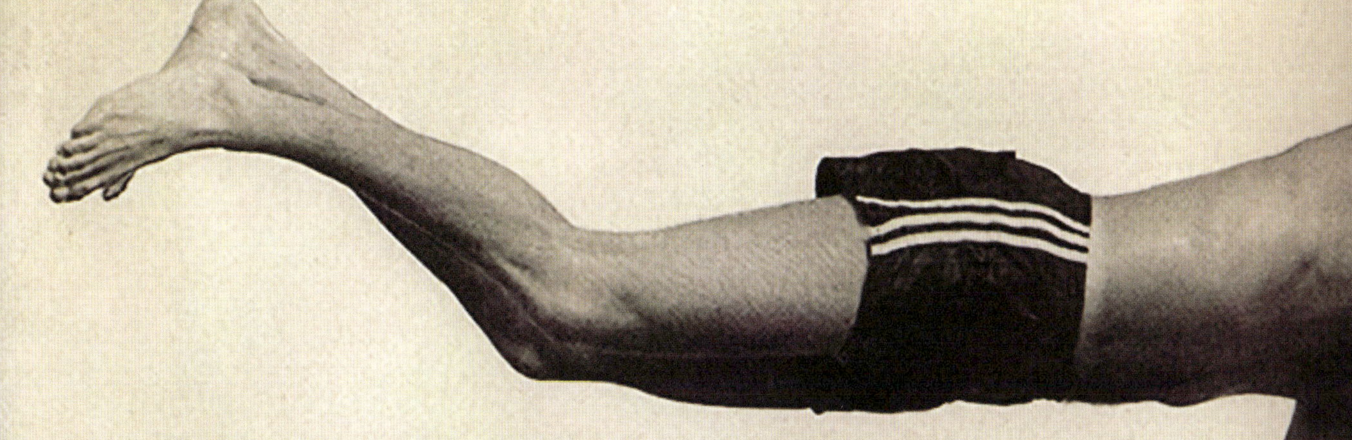

premiere issue

BEACH
CULT
URE
1990

Water

TOWER RECORDS
£ 1·99
790192

david
The First Interview
lynch

sinéad
o'connor

art+music surf + skate
style+attitude

the day
manson
met the beach boy

the birth of
the endless
summer

summer

VOL. 1 #3 AUG/SEPT $2.95

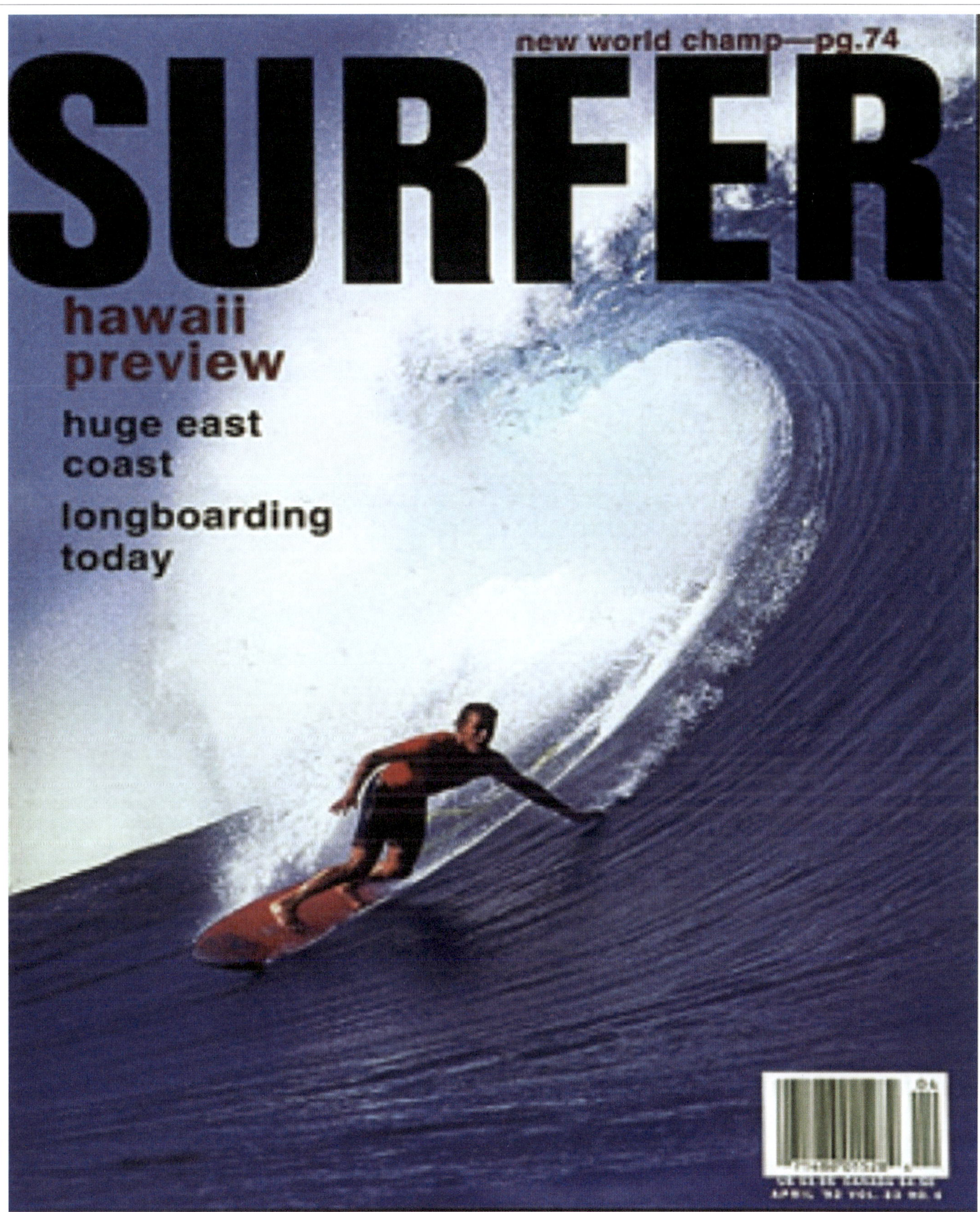

Surfer Magazine

did, I just didn't see a good use for them, though I understood their original intentions.

Over the years, it has allowed me to trust my eye and gut and basically just arrange things until they feel right. I've had a few exhibitions and a book about collage work, and some clients come to me specifically for the collage work, especially recently. But even before that, clients came to me for something different, something fresh, not just some jumbled type they saw somewhere.

By the way, there's no such thing as "grunge design" or "anti-design."

Can you describe how your collage technique influences or intersects with your client work, such as your recent project with The Macallan?
What they do is an art, no question about it. They want me to help get the message out about who they are through a visual experience, not just something software pushes out. I think the collage work speaks more to the emotional side of people viewing and experiencing it. Good graphic design can represent the client's signals, people, products, and heritage better than, say, an agency's cute headline, flush-left and all caps.

Looking at your work with The Macallan, how did you conceptualize the final pieces? What message or emotion were you aiming to convey?
Different collections or projects get their own unique interpretations. My bottle, then holidays, then color collection, then rebranding a new logo, and now 2025... later tastes, colors, heritage, and place were all interpreted. I was stuck in an early meeting about my new bottle when the head guy asked, rather casually, "Do you have a favorite number?" I said, "Well, I guess eight…" He said to another person at the meeting, "Okay, for your bottle, we'll make the alcohol level 40.8." (They are usually all 40%.)

And they did; it's on the bottle. After spending time with the actual whisky maker, a process they do by hand, eye, and taste, she tried to interpret who she felt I was from our time together in picking out flavors for that particular bottle. It made quite an impression that even with all the high-tech distillery machinery, it ultimately all comes down to the human touch. I like to think my work does something similar.

How do you ensure that the authenticity of your work is maintained while meeting a client's expectations and brand identity?
Good question. Sometimes, it's a matter of incorporating the collage into the media, but with their product or copy included. Of course, I always keep the "director's cut" versions, of which there are many, but often, they're not so different from what is used. Maybe partly because of the number and levels of clients I've had, not one work is so precious that I feel it's perfect or the only one. The goal is to get something I'm proud of out into the world while having it do what the client needs it to do. There are many levels of victories in what we do.

Your work often feels very personal. How do you balance your need for individual expression?
People sometimes ask, do you ever have time for personal

work? And I think, well, it's all personal. It's degrees; you can put more of yourself into some projects than others, but the key is to be sure you're at least in there. It's that collaboration that brings new life to new projects. It also shows how you do your best work and enjoy it the most. Every client and brief is different, and I trust my eye to help interpret their message visually, their heritage, and even their taste, sound, or vision of the product/client.

Do you find that your clients are becoming more receptive to unconventional approaches, and how do you navigate that dialogue?
Being able to explain the various elements and decisions you make is crucial. It is not just a color you like; once it is tied more to the brand's heritage or purpose or even physical location, that's a good thing for graphic designers. If you're just flowing information into software setup pages, those are the first jobs going to AI. They already are. People want to feel that a human is involved in the process now more than ever. I've always tried to keep the art in graphic design, while so many over the years seem determined to take it out.

What's on the horizon for you, David? Any upcoming projects that have you particularly excited?
I have a couple I can't mention yet, but they are with some brands people know. And some they don't. I've never had a ton of clients at once, but I do have a unique blend of brands and clients.

There's a big new project for The Macallan that will be dropping worldwide in 2025. I'm creating art for every room of a boutique hotel outside of Barcelona, Spain, including a special David Carson room—that'll be fun. I'm also working with skate and shoe companies. I'm working on a new building mural in Brazil, a new series of paintings, and, hopefully, some gallery shows in Europe. So, watch out for more Macallan work, a new book, and a few other surprises. And, as always, I'll check my email to see if any new jobs roll in. :)

Like a friend said when he first heard of The Macallan collaboration, "Wow, I didn't see that coming." :)

To the young creatives out there, what's your golden advice for developing a unique design style?
Trust your gut, listen to what your mind and eye tell you, and use your uniqueness in your work. When you think you've finished a piece, go back and see if you can make it even a bit better. Trust your way of seeing, your way of feeling. What is unique about you as a human being, and how can you put some of that uniqueness into your work? No one can copy that. Everyone can use and learn the same software, but no one is you. Run with that.

When all is said and done, what legacy is David Carson crafting?
Love what you do; trust yer gut. I get messages daily saying I had some effect on a designer's life and career choices. Usually, they're thanking me. :)

David Carson www.davidcarsondesign.com
See his Graphis Master Portfolio at graphis.com.

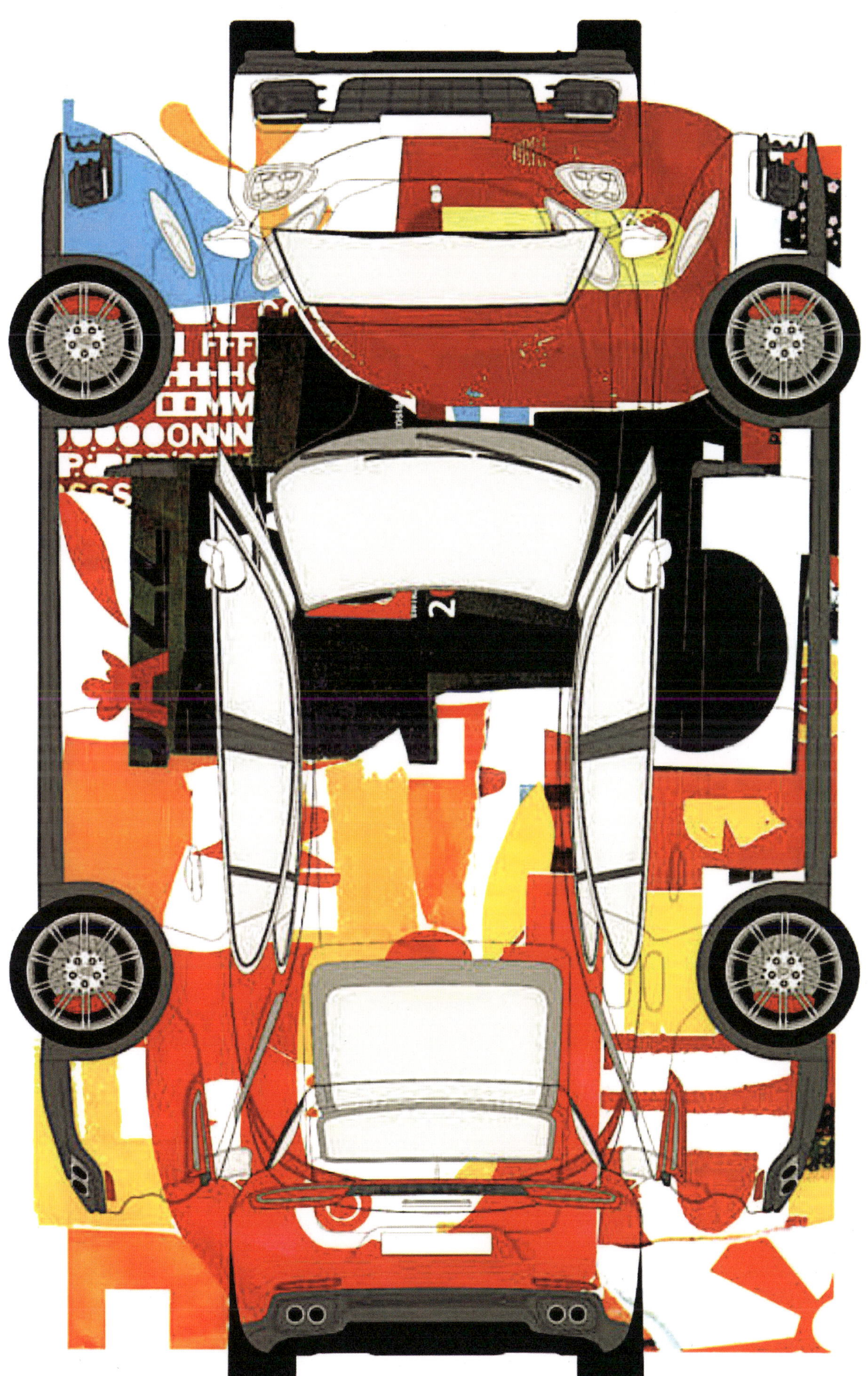

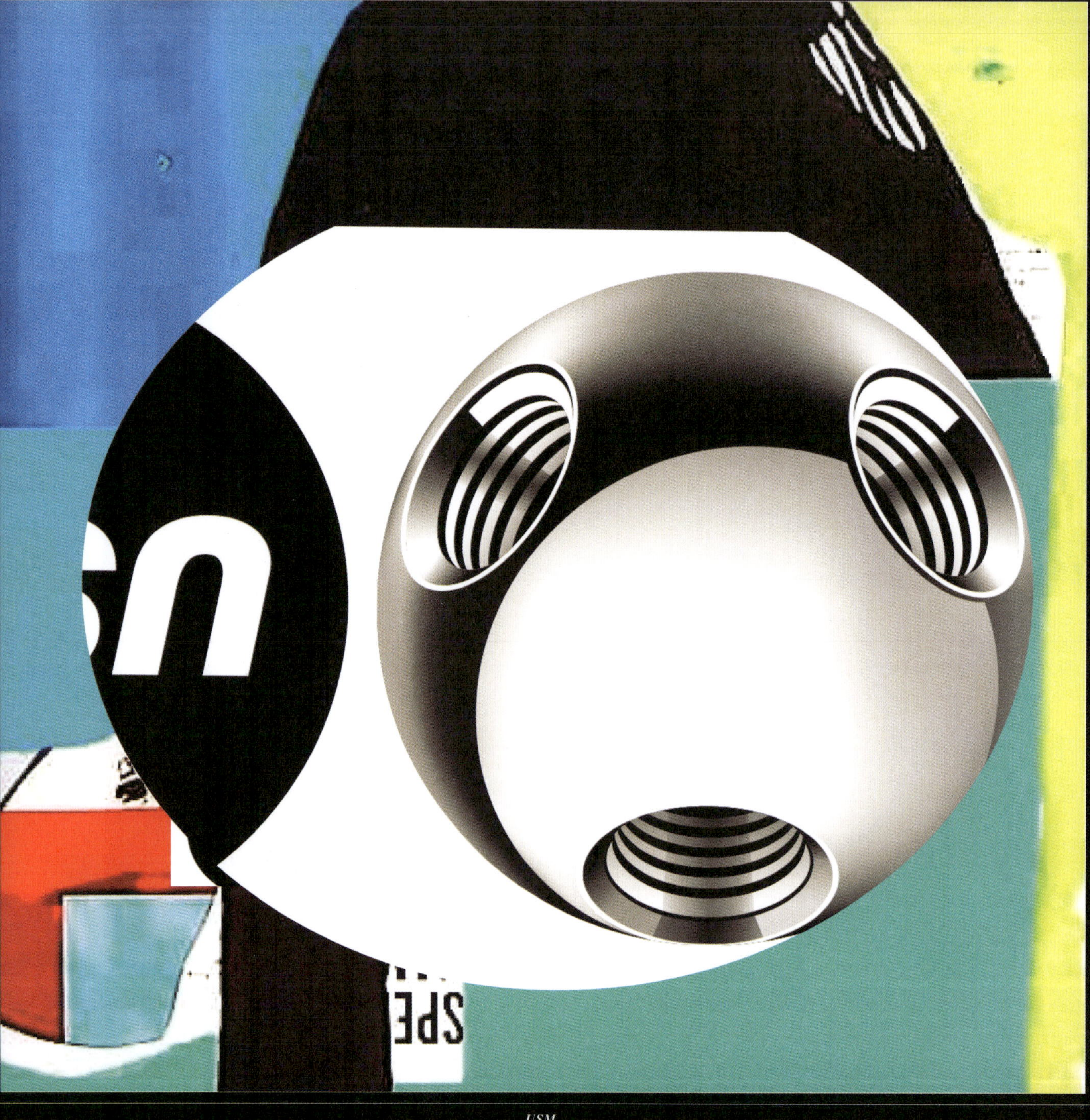
USM
USM

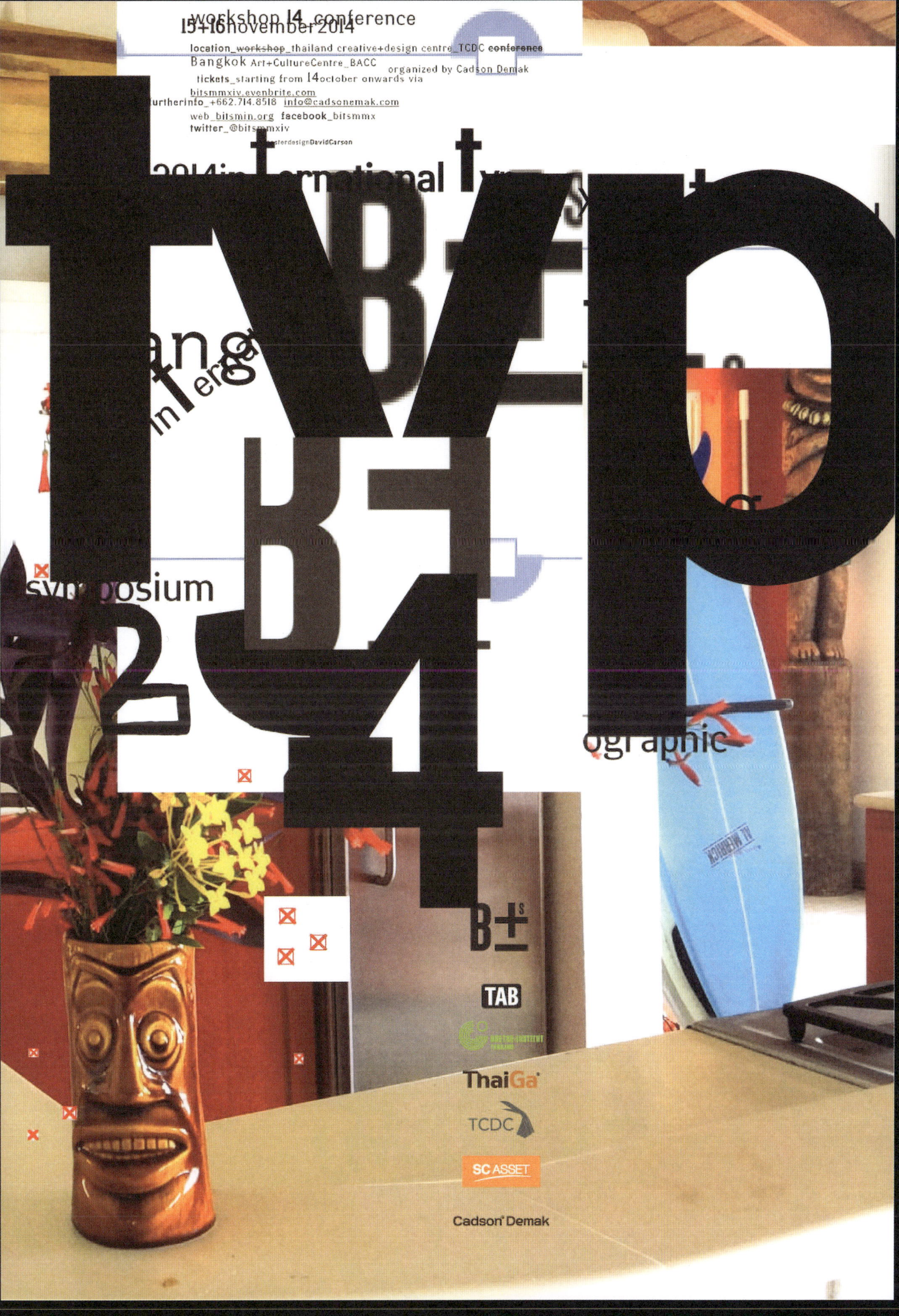

Bangkok Workshop Poster

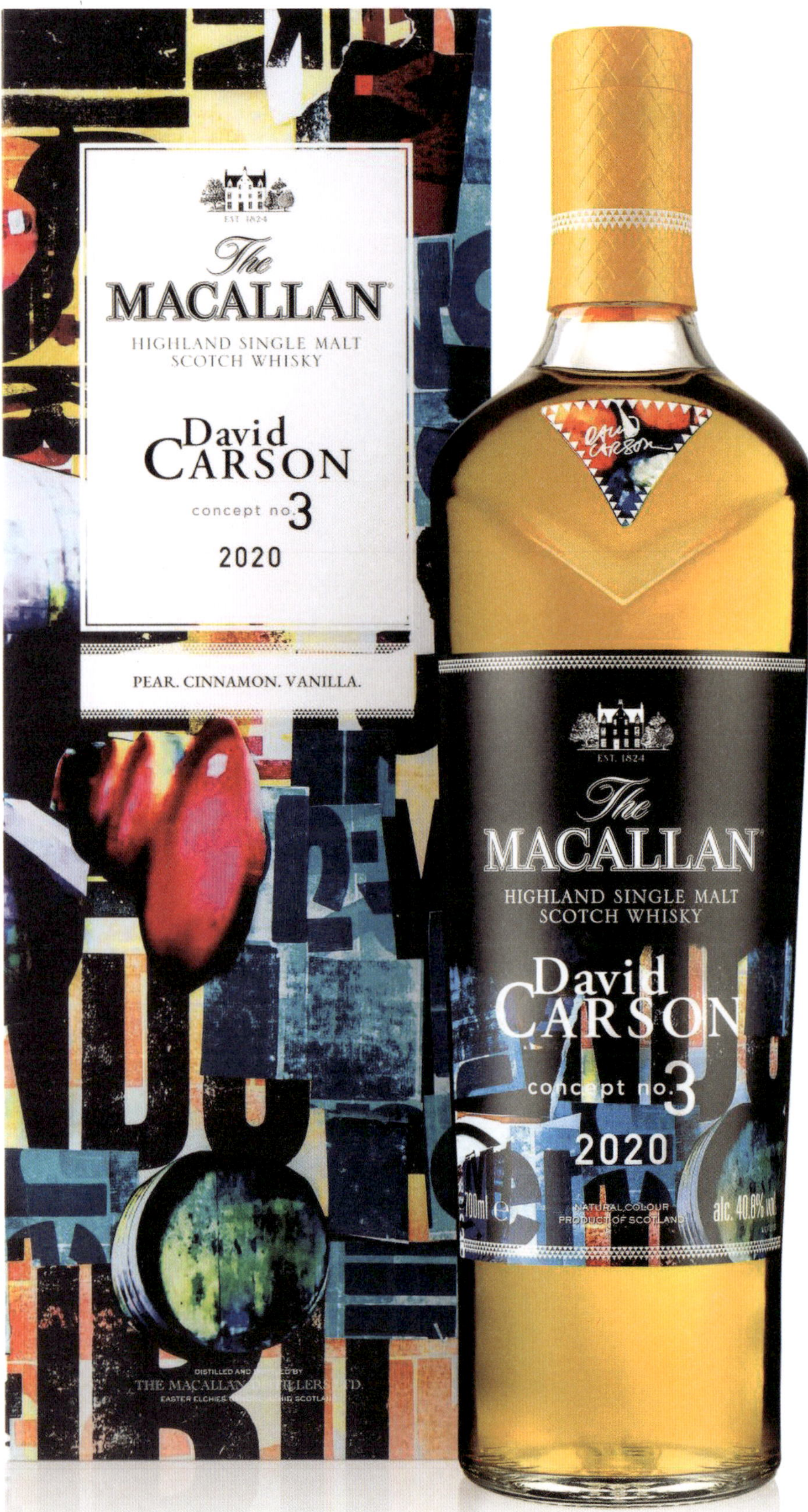
EST. 1824
The
MACALLAN
HIGHLAND SINGLE MALT
SCOTCH WHISKY
David
CARSON
concept no.3
2020
PEAR. CINNAMON. VANILLA.
DISTILLED AND BOTTLED BY
THE MACALLAN DISTILLERS LTD.
EASTER ELCHIES DISTILLERY, SCOTLAND
EST. 1824
The
MACALLAN
HIGHLAND SINGLE MALT
SCOTCH WHISKY
David
CARSON
concept no.3
2020
NATURAL COLOUR
PRODUCT OF SCOTLAND
alc. 40.8% vol.

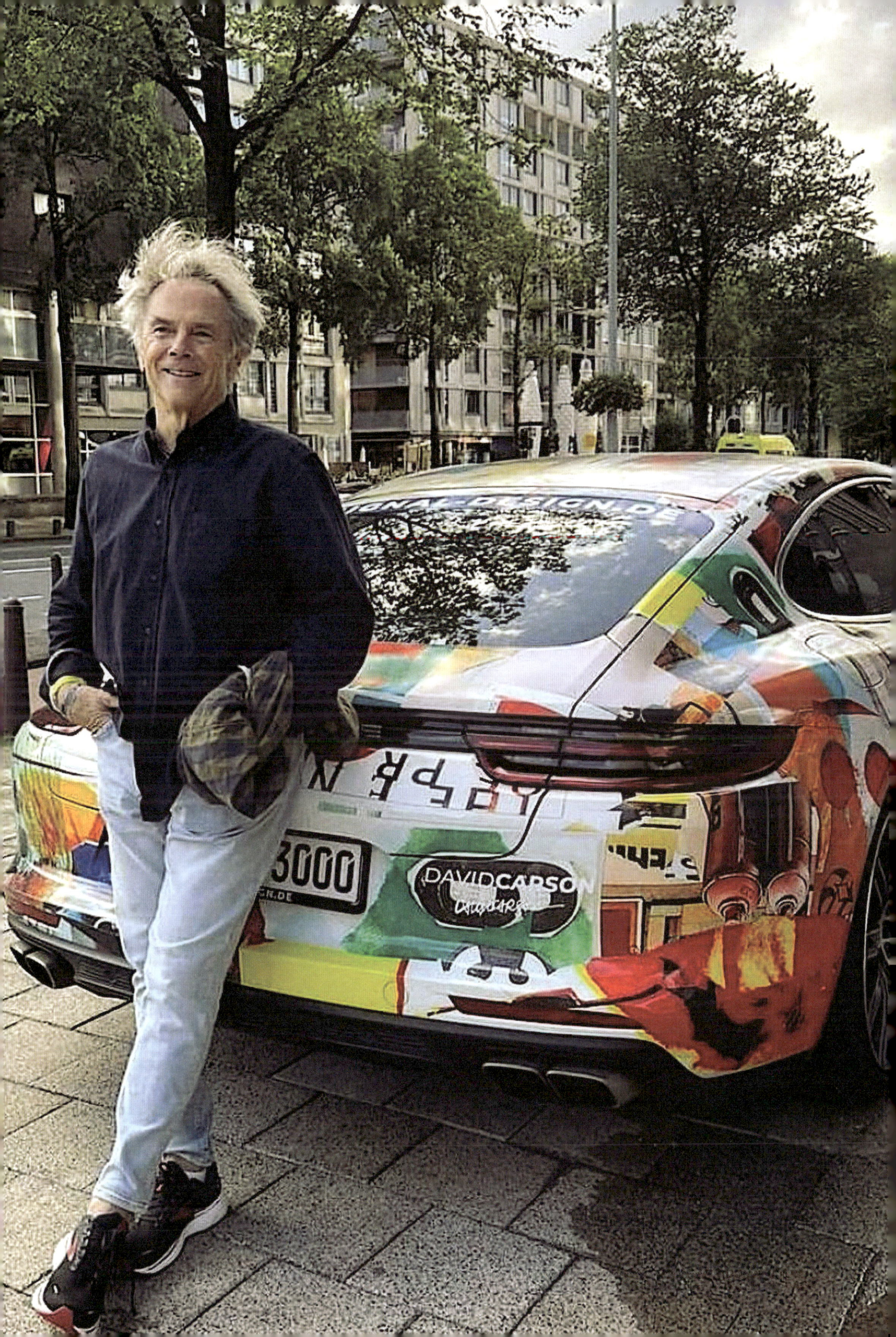

RON'S WORK IS NOTHING SHORT OF VIRTUOSITY WHEN HE TURNS TO HIS FORMIDABLE TALENTS IN THE WORLD OF MUSIC AND THE ARTS.

Dr. Erica Muhl, *Former President of Berklee College of Music & Former Dean of the Roski School of Art and Design & the Iovine and Young Academy at the University of Southern California*

I'VE WORKED WITH RON ON TWO GRAMMY AWARD-WINNING ALBUMS. HIS IMAGINATION IS BOUNDLESS. HE ELEVATES EVERY PROJECT HE TOUCHES WITH EXTRAORDINARY CONCEPTS.

Starr Parodi, *Grammy Award-winning Producer, Composer, & Recording Artist*

RON TAFT INTUITIVELY UNDERSTANDS THE EMOTIONAL IMPACT NEEDED FOR A CAMPAIGN. HIS DESIGNS SPEAK DIRECTLY TO THE HEART WITH BEAUTY AND ARTISTRY.

Amy Andersson, *Music Director & Conductor, Orchestra Moderne NYC*

JUST WHEN WE THINK HIS PORTFOLIO CAN'T POSSIBLY BE SUPERSEDED, RON REARRANGES REALITY WITH NEW, INSPIRED DESIGNS YET AGAIN, AS ONLY A TRUE MAESTRO CAN.

Matthew McCauley, *Music Producer, Arranger, & Composer*

RON'S WORK EMBRACES VISUAL SIMPLICITY THAT TRANSPORTS YOU THROUGH AN UNFOLDING STORY.

Angela Lester, *Principal, PwC US*

(Opposite page) 51st Emmy Awards Poster. Photography & Design: Ron Taft

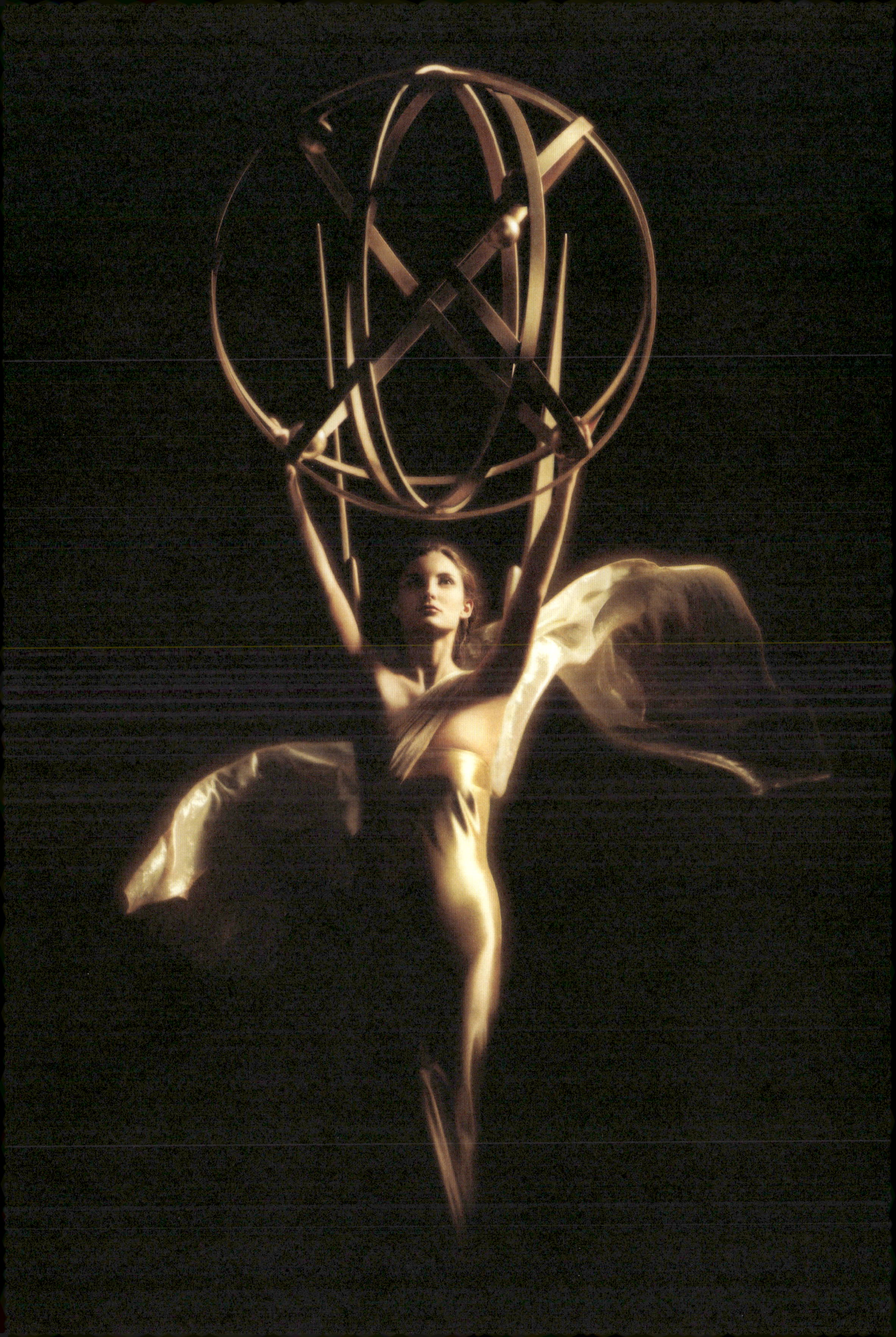

Ron Taft, as longtime aficionados of Graphis know, is one of the foremost graphic designers in the world. This is not new news. He's been doing it project after project, award after award, for five decades. After all this time, counterintuitively, the work always seems fresh. And remarkably, he never seems to waver. This brings us to the portfolio at hand: *Music, Arts & Entertainment*. Here, Ron uniquely captures the energy of entertainment. He brings to that energy an elegance, a cleverness, and a clarity of expression. It's a trifecta that raises the bar we all aspire to.

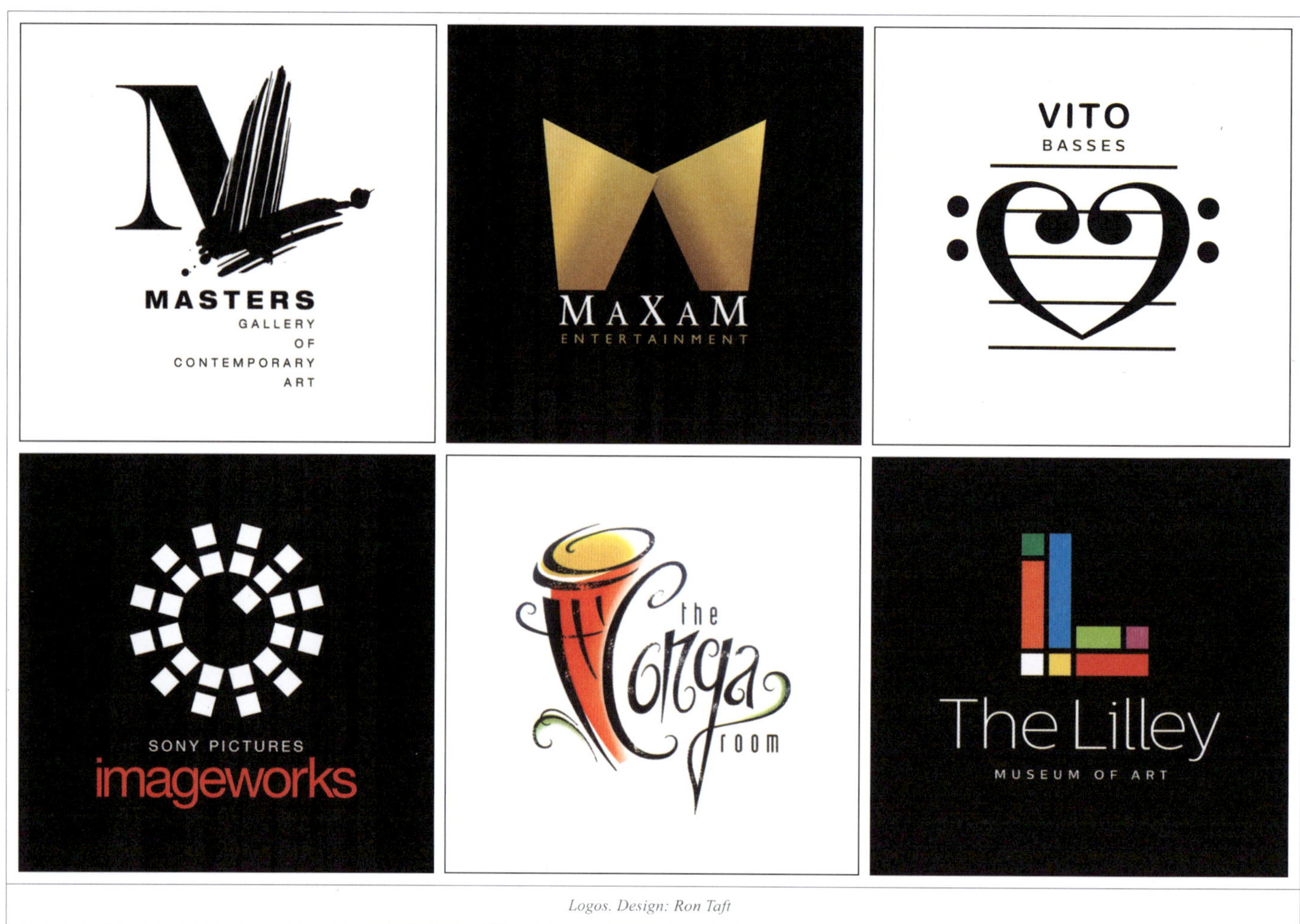

Logos. Design: Ron Taft

Q&A: Ron Taft

What do you consider to be the most significant influence on your expansive advertising and design career?
I'll have to travel back a tad to answer that question.

As a young boy, I had a penchant for both music and fine art, though music was my first love. My mother dabbled in art but also loved dancing and was quite the melophile. I had played guitar in bands throughout high school for all the reasons guys pick up the guitar. Then, 1965 came along, and America found itself at war in Vietnam. At the time, the lure of earning money by playing in bands was greater than my desire to finish high school, so I made a hasty decision and started playing in various bands around town. As luck would have it, I was primed to be drafted into the US Army, where, as I got closer to 18, the odds of being sent to Vietnam were high.

Now comes the more informed, strategic choice.

After much deliberation, I decided to enlist in the Army. Doing so allowed me to audition for duty in the 7th Army Band in Europe. This became my MOS (military occupational specialty), and I was stationed in Stuttgart, Germany. It was a fantastic tour, and I was proud to serve.

Music saved my life. While in Europe, I was able to study composition through a special correspondence course provided by the Berklee College of Music in Boston. By the time I was discharged, I was ready to begin my career as a musician. It was my good fortune to have the GI Bill help me through college.

Life is full of surprises, and I surprised myself when I decided to switch my college major to fine arts. I studied painting, sculpture, photography, and design. I wound up seeking a career in advertising, where I felt I could celebrate all facets of my creativity—including music—in a single, all-encompassing vocation. I discovered early on how the fundamental precepts of music were homogeneous with those of the visual and performing arts, which enabled me to adapt easily to their respective disciplines. The duality of music and design became an intrinsic element in all my creative work. I was hooked.

What areas of design do you enjoy the most or find particularly challenging?
As my experience and expertise grew, the world of branding became increasingly salient because it unified and codified

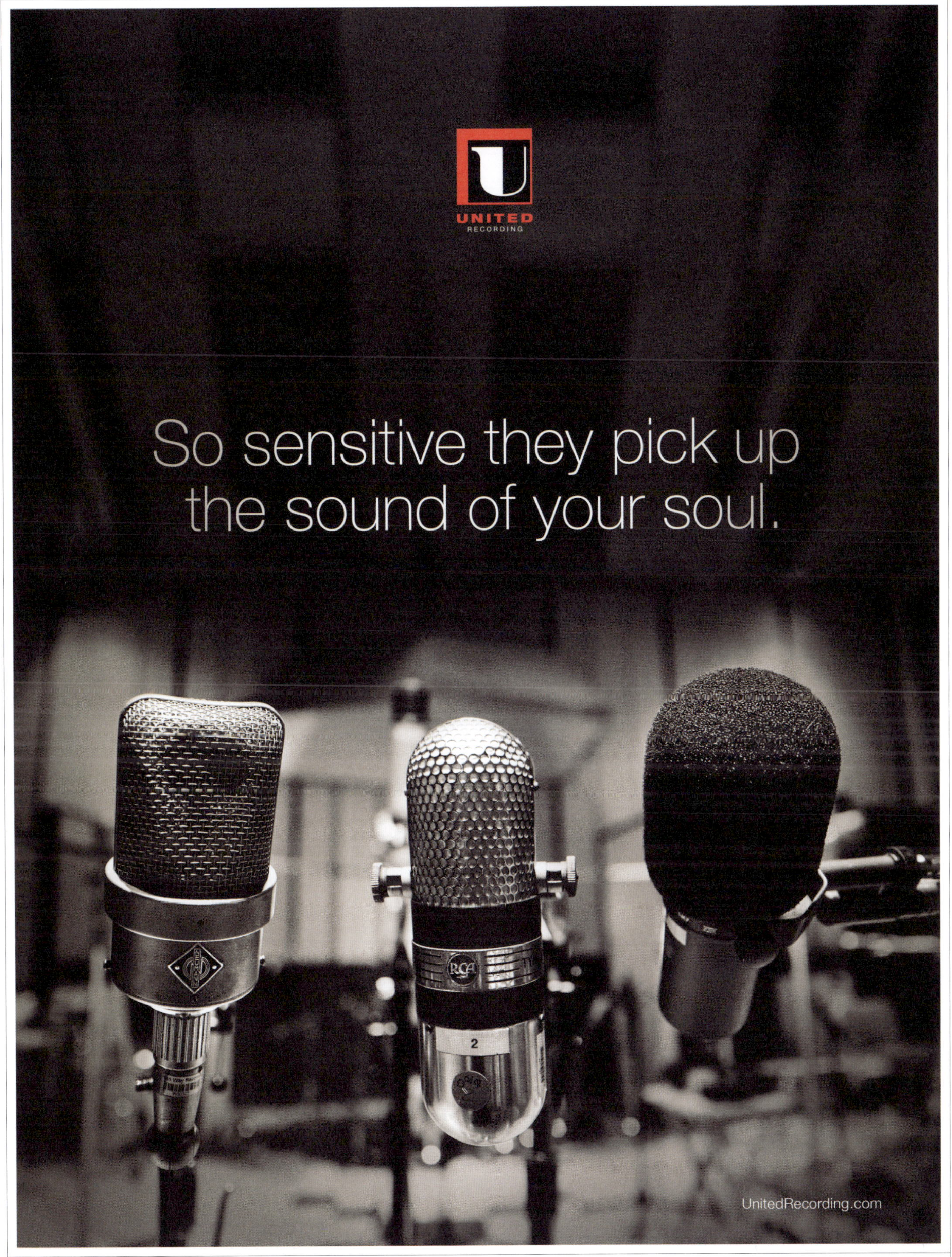

United Recording Mic Locker Ad. Copywriting, Art Direction, & Design: Ron Taft

a brand's messaging into a simple, singular expression: its unique, emotional heartbeat—just as the counterpoint of instruments in an orchestral composition can be woven into a distinct, memorable, musical moment.

And speaking of themes, I've worked on many different types of advertising and branding over the years, including automotive, consumer electronics, and fashion, as well as many luxury brand products and corporate initiatives. Film, television, and performing arts projects became a recurring theme—often in an orbit of one kind or another around music.

My passion for music served as a magnet for attracting music-related branding assignments and NPO participation. I

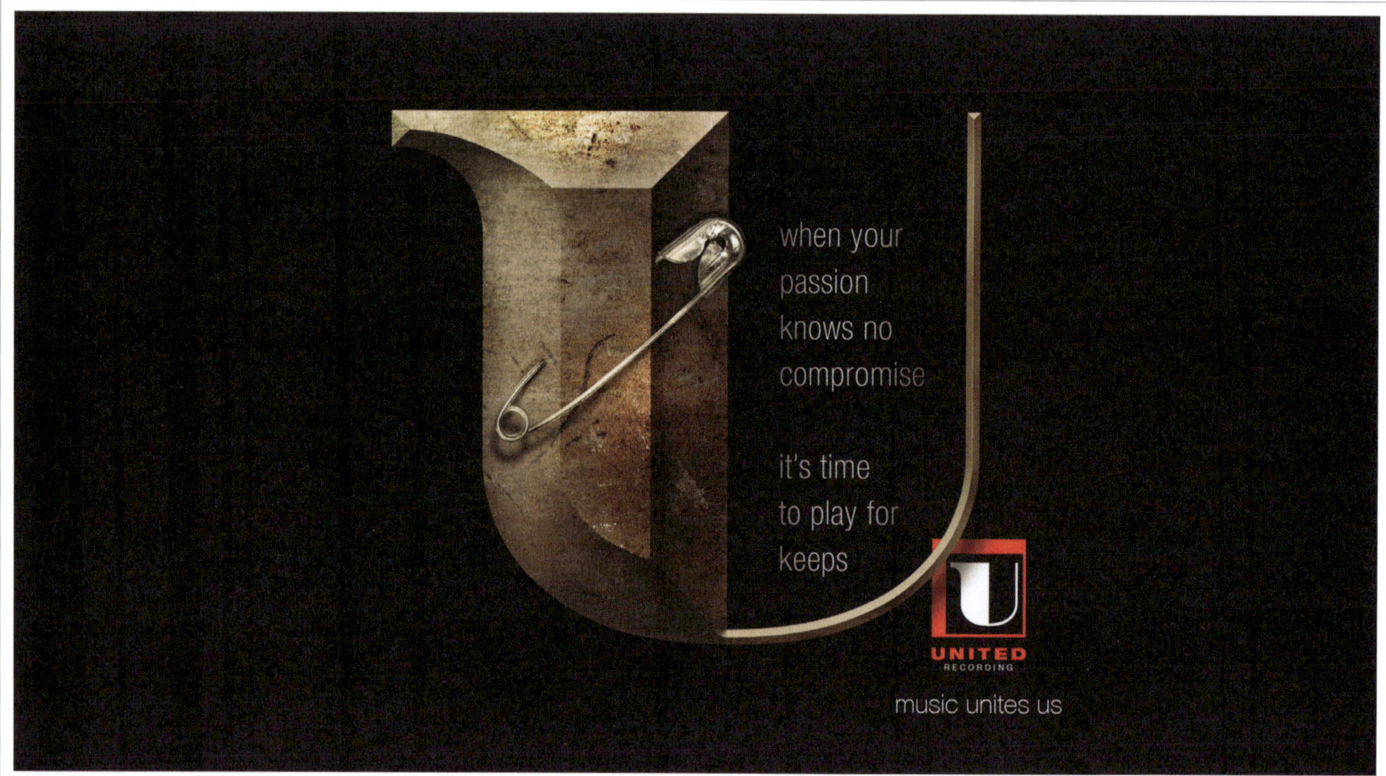

United Recording "U" Campaign – Punk. New logo & brand identity campaign for United Recording where the "U" celebrates various music genres. Copywriting, Design, & Illustration: Ron Taft

have served on the boards of both Mr. Holland's Opus Foundation and the Quincy Jones Musiq Consortium and directed promotional initiatives for NARAS and NAMM.

I have also developed communication strategies and event promotion for the Berklee College of Music, spearheaded organizational development and cultural enhancement initiatives for Guitar Center (which included interior design for 90,000 square feet of their corporate offices), and have taken on numerous award-winning brand innovation and media arts assignments for studios and individual artists.

To me, music and the performing arts have always celebrated the highest aspirations of the human spirit.

What is your process for concept development?

I always look for the inherent drama in an idea. Whenever possible, my goal is to execute it in an iconic form. Most importantly, I strive to surround myself with brilliant thinkers who are often music people. One of my partners, Matthew McCauley, is an extraordinary composer. We met many years ago on a project that took us to London to produce a major music package for a new cable TV launch. Matthew had written the music and conducted the London Symphony Orchestra for the on-air package. We have remained friends and collaborators ever since and actually worked on a very exciting project for NASA where Matthew's science and mathematical prowess contributed immensely to the project's success. (Something about math and music sharing space in the same brain, right?)

Another partner, Frank Nuovo, a genius product designer/engineer and an equally gifted drummer, has been an invaluable collaborator over the years. There's that special music connection again—left brain, right brain.

Point being: The process of collaboration is a great thing. To me, musicians (at least the good ones) develop a unique feel for collaboration. It is born out of improvisation—where you listen and creatively build upon an established groove. So, whenever I have an idea, whether music-related or not, I love to bounce it off the people I trust. It's a creative feedback loop I value deeply.

Cliff Einstein is a preeminent copywriter, creative force,

and longtime partner (and, though not a musician, definitely a bilateral brainer). Music is in Cliff's genes. His son is a Berklee College of Music graduate and has become one of the most sought-after commercial directors in advertising. That music connection seems to find its way into every aspect of my personal and professional life in some way or another.

Someone once said, "Music picks up where words leave off," intimating that not every emotion can be translated into words. But sometimes words can bring music to your ears. I love how Netflix cleverly branded TUDUM as their website.

Which clients or projects gave you exceptional satisfaction as they relate to the influences in your background?

Rob Goodchild, former studio manager for United Recording, brought me in on an assignment to rebrand the studio and celebrate its expansive, rich heritage. Rob has always been a champion of good branding practices but chose to leave United Recording when it fell under the purview and in-house creative of its corporate entity.

Right out of the gate, I saw an opportunity to marry the company's name with a tagline that spoke to the bigger idea behind the recording of music, and that was that MUSIC UNITES US—a perfect pairing of name and shared purpose. It was a strategy that led to many inspired ads and promotions that resonated with both producers and artists. Rob was an executive who knew how to relate to his clients, and the work speaks for itself. United's branding spoke from the soul of musicians and recording artists while leveraging the legacy and technical prowess of a reimagined recording facility.

It's hard to find executives who don't buckle under corporate pressure today. Great campaigns must be effectively and consistently championed by people who understand the long game, or the vision can fade. There's always that pesky battle that looms between artist and enterprise. But these agendas are not mutually exclusive, and it's magic when they coexist.

Amy Andersson, music director of Orchestra Moderne NYC, created a concert performance series in which she conducts a live orchestra for her award-winning documentary

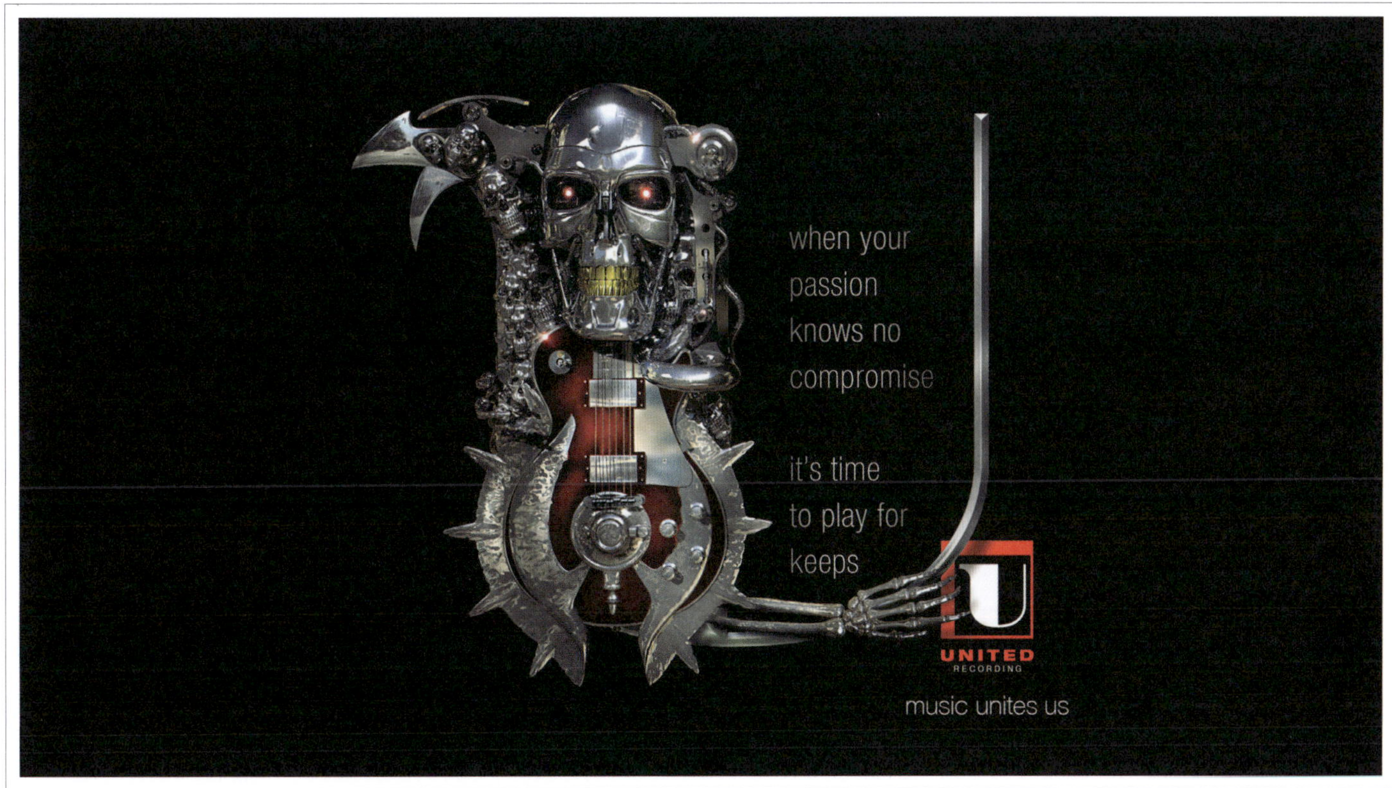

United Recording "U" Campaign – Heavy Metal. Copywriting & Design: Ron Taft. Illustration: John Dismukes

Women Warriors: The Voices of Change, which she also produced and directed.

Amy's timely and compelling film highlights the lives of more than 65 human rights activists. It debuted at Lincoln Center to rave reviews. Lauded for its stunning orchestral soundtrack composed by a team of eight renowned female composers, it had won over 20 international awards—but not the coveted Grammy for music.

Amy needed a compelling, iconic idea for her upcoming 2022 Grammy campaign that would capture the essence and power of her film score but, most importantly, an idea that would attract academy voters. Grammy campaigns are very competitive, and studios spend vast amounts of money on consideration campaigns. Hence, it's hard for a newcomer to the Grammy world to rise above the noise level and get attention. All the more reason you need a visual idea and tagline that really pulls the voters in.

There's a lot of added pressure when you are asked to design something for someone who has put their heart and soul into something for years, and you are the person who needs to deliver the idea that puts the Grammy on the shelf. Having a client's unconditional confidence and trust, as I did with Amy, is a wonderful thing. The only thing better—and you know what's coming here—was seeing Amy bring home her first Grammy.

But I have to say that one of my most exhilarating and rewarding experiences—by far—was working with Garry Shandling on *The Larry Sanders Show*. Garry and I hit it off early on when I became the go-to creative director on his campaigns and promotions.

Garry had seen some of the award-winning entertainment advertising I'd done as creative director at Columbia TriStar Television (CTT). He told Brad Grey to set up an appointment with the president of CTT and, at the meeting, asked if they would be willing to loan me out to work on *The Larry Sanders Show*'s first-year Emmy consideration campaign. The studio head said, "Yes, of course—as long as you let us syndicate *The Larry Sanders Show* when the time comes." Then and there, the deal was made. After I left CTT, Garry continued insisting that I be brought in to be his creative director wherever he went.

Garry was a former adman, and he and Judd Apatow were always champions of out-of-the-box thinking. One of Garry's things was to always trust your audience. Let them discover the message. "Lose the elbow in the ribs." The key to our campaign was to carry over the Larry Sanders character's neurotic obsessions to the ad campaign. Every year, the show received numerous awards, and after 56 nominations, Larry (Garry) finally realized his dream with three Emmys. Our Emmy consideration campaign broke new ground and was one of the most celebrated campaigns in the business.

I deeply miss Garry.

Years earlier, I was executive creative director at a global branding agency when David Copperfield contacted our New York office. He wanted to discuss the possibility of our agency working with him to develop new concepts and marketing strategies for future shows. I was ECD in our Los Angeles office then, and that particular new business opportunity was determined to be handled exclusively from New York, where David lived.

When David and his agents visited the New York office, David noticed a particular campaign I had done out of LA, and (sound familiar?) he insisted that I be brought in to work with him directly. And here's the caveat: no agent, manager, or account director—just one-on-one, no middle-management go-betweens or filtering committees. David flew me out to meet with him at his amazing rooftop palace, and it was one of the most pleasurable, incredibly productive meetings I have ever had. One meeting of the minds, and we were off executing ideas.

From then on, I understood the advantage of having direct contact with the ultimate decision-maker at a company, the one who can actually say, "Yes," cutting through so many superfluous processes. That's not to say that typical agency protocol is not effective or appropriate in its own way; it's just that direct communication feels right to me. The model was set for me to start my own brand marketing and communications company, which I greatly enjoy today.

Ron Taft www.rontaft.com
See his Graphis Master Portfolio at graphis.com.

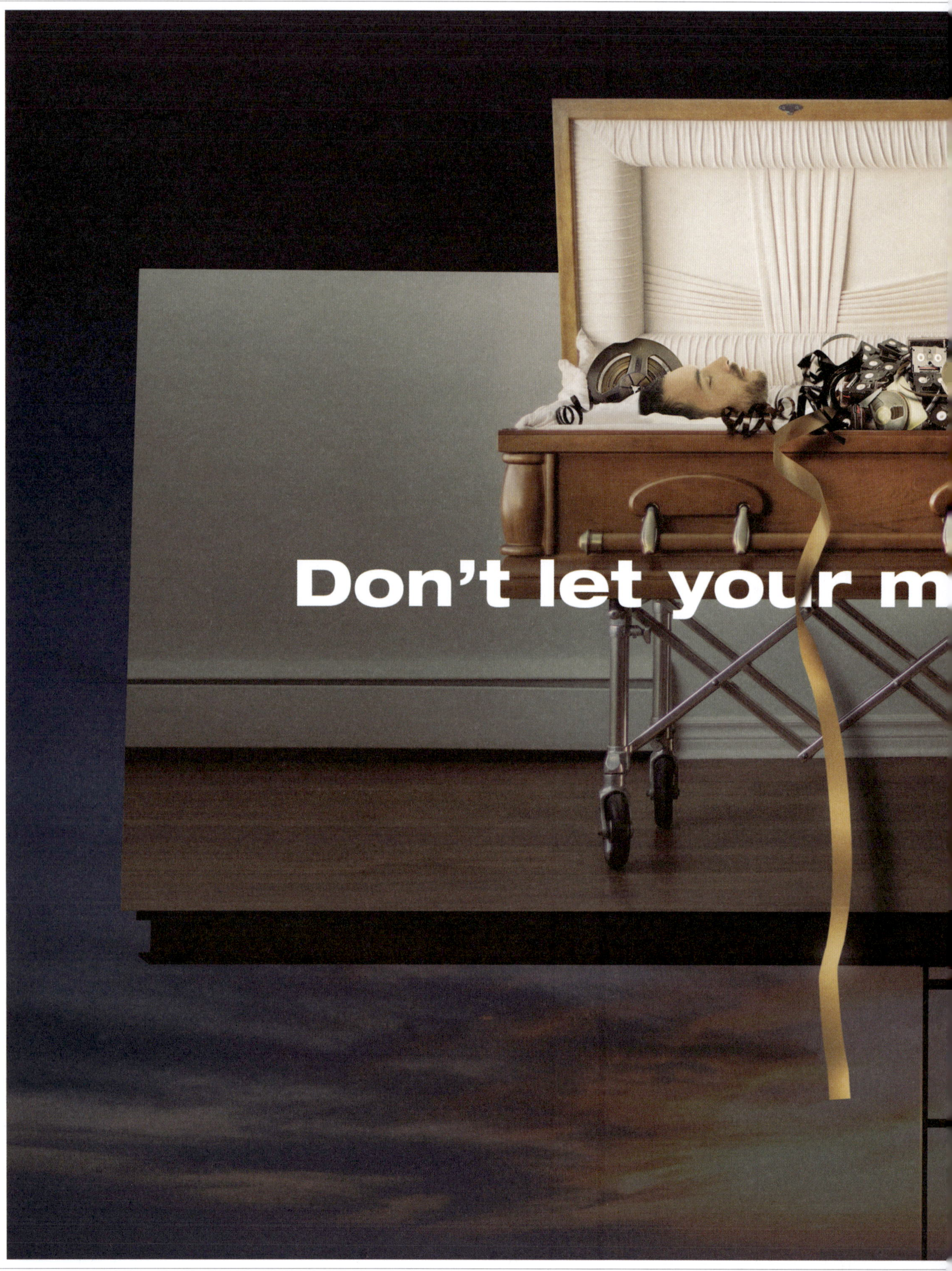

Don't let your m

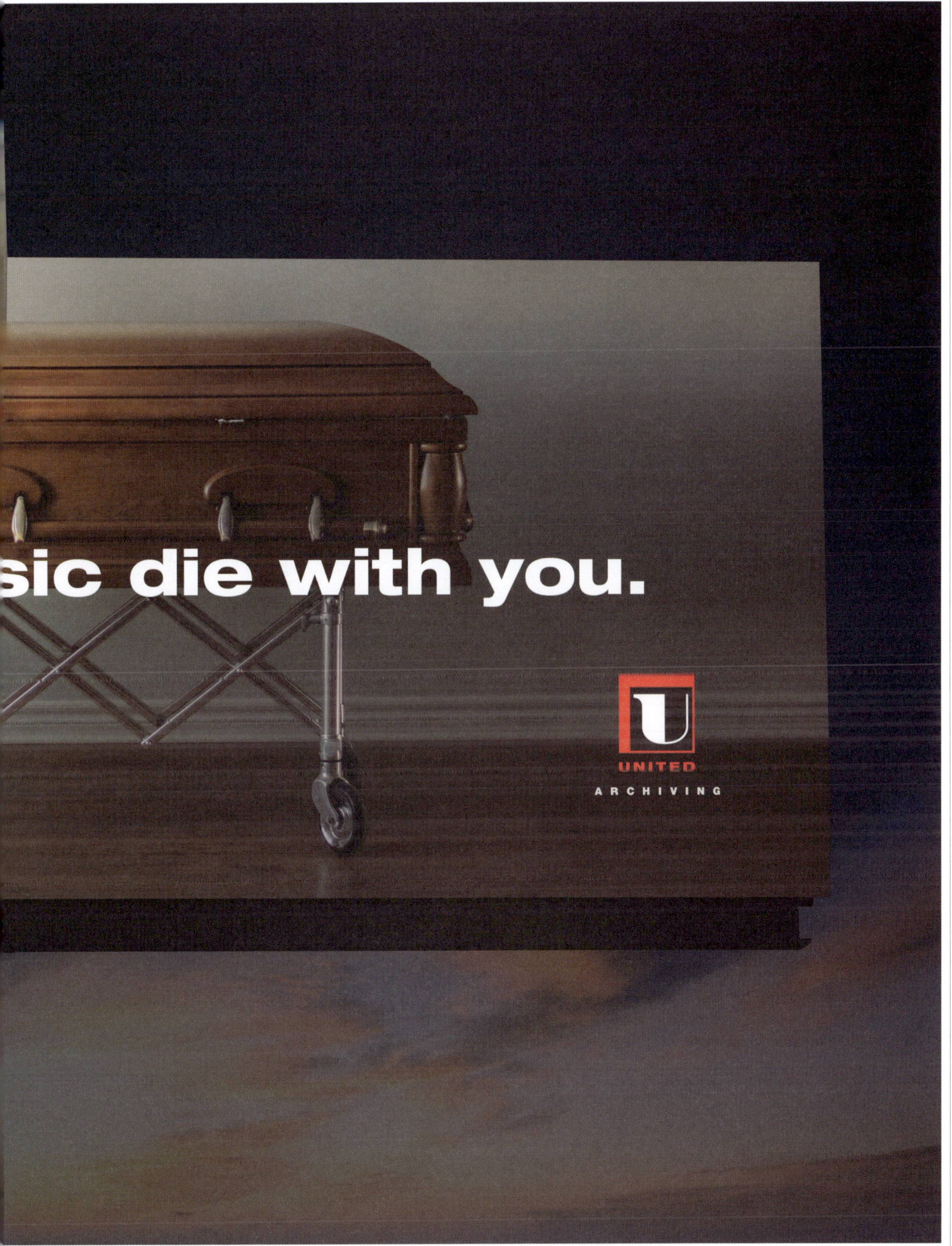

United Archiving Billboard. Copywriting, Design, & Photo Compositing: Ron Taft

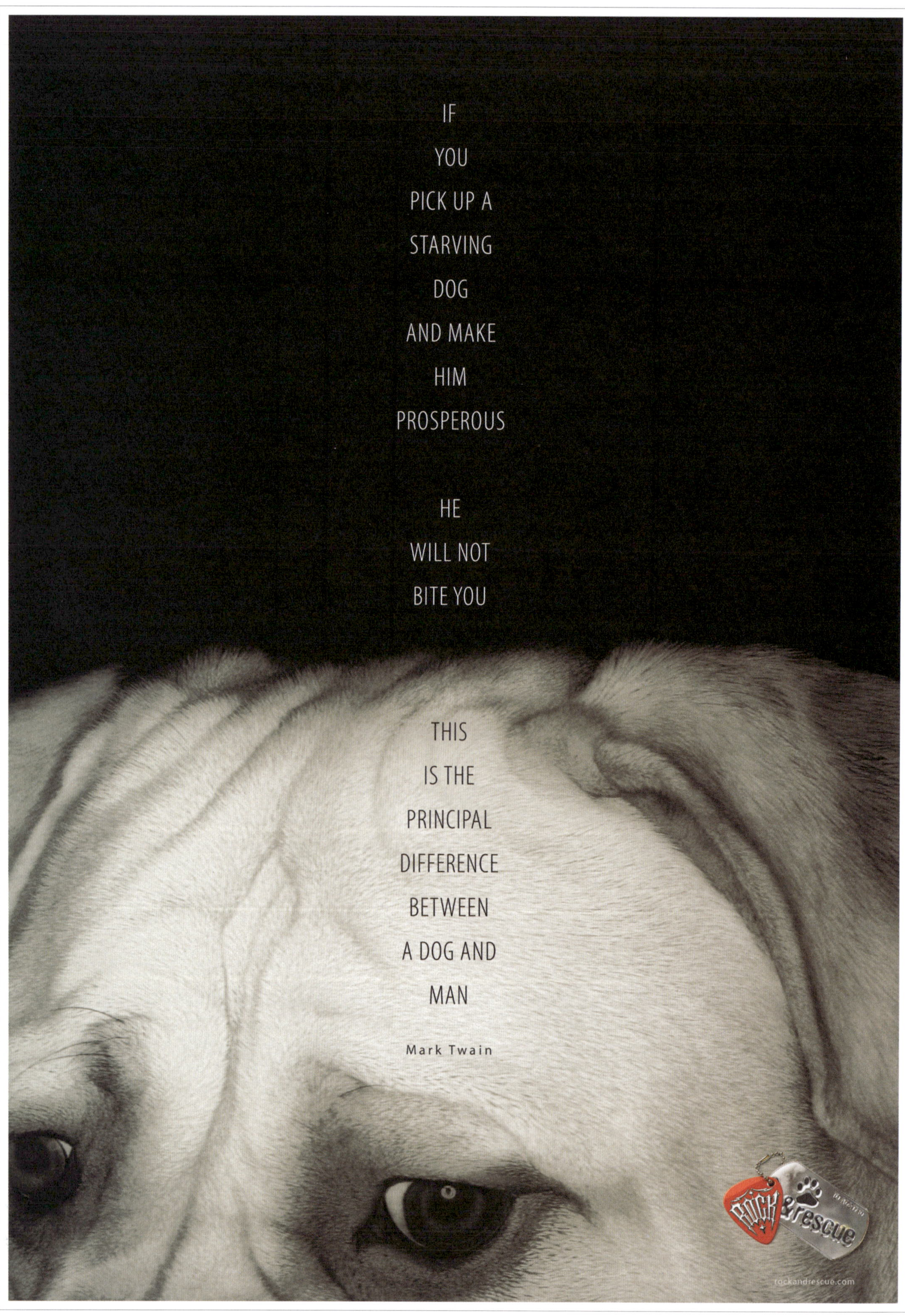

Rock & Rescue Bullmastiff Poster. Design: Ron Taft. Photography: Deborah Samuel

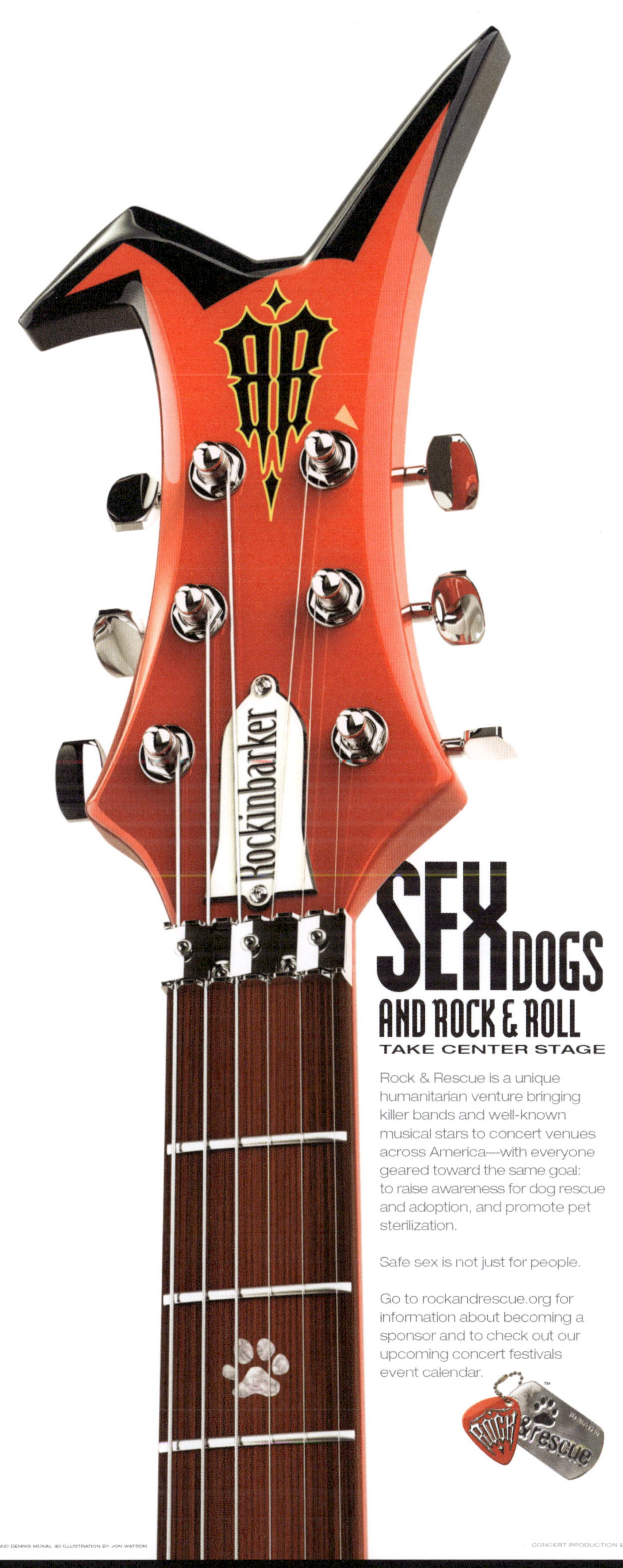

Rockinbarker
SEX DOGS
AND ROCK & ROLL
TAKE CENTER STAGE
Rock & Rescue is a unique humanitarian venture bringing killer bands and well-known musical stars to concert venues across America—with everyone geared toward the same goal: to raise awareness for dog rescue and adoption, and promote pet sterilization.

Safe sex is not just for people.

Go to rockandrescue.org for information about becoming a sponsor and to check out our upcoming concert festivals event calendar.

ROCK & rescue
DESIGN BY RON TAFT. GUITAR DESIGN BY RON TAFT AND DENNIS MUKAI. 3D ILLUSTRATION BY JON WATSON
CONCERT PRODUCTION BY

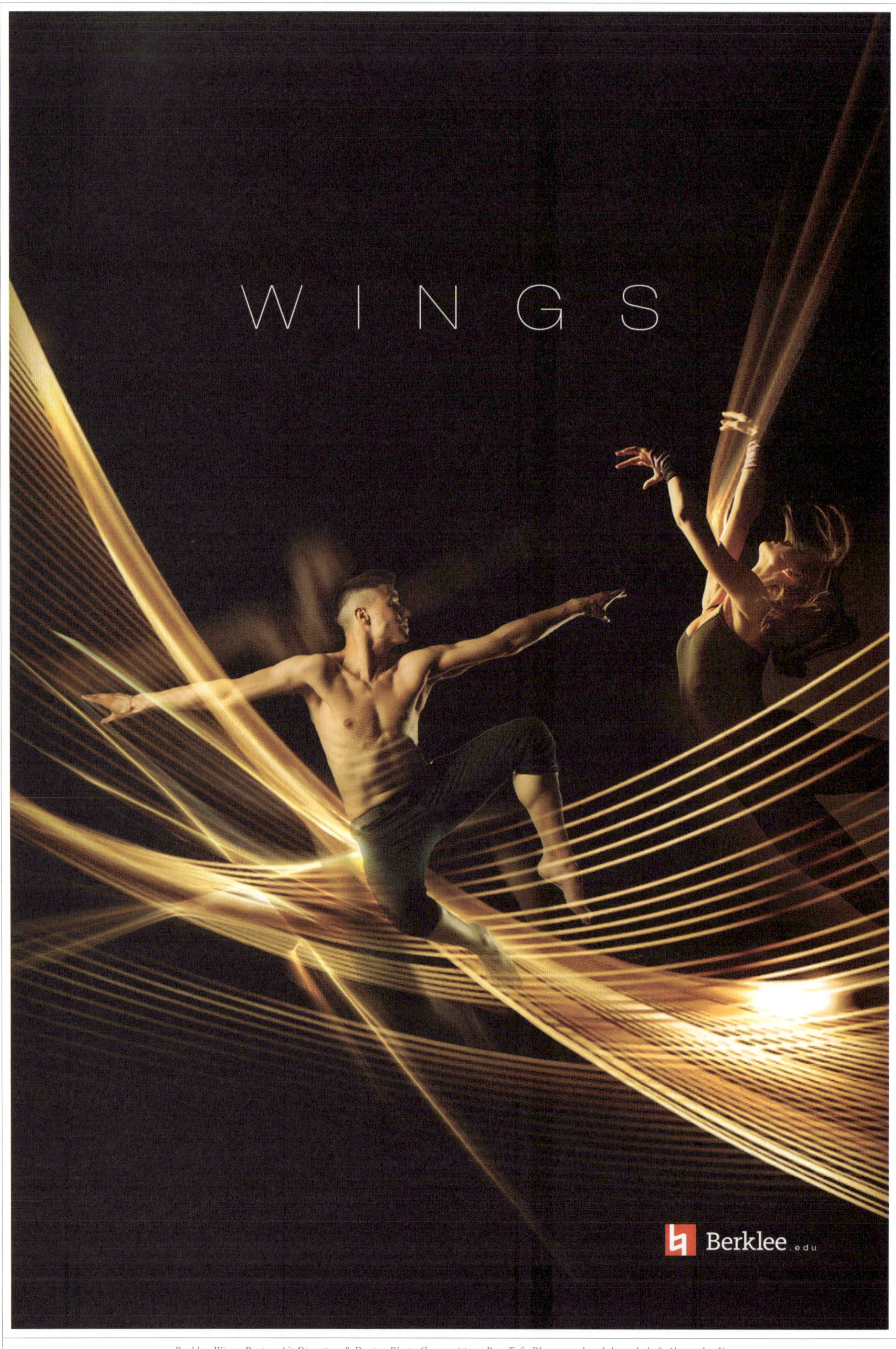

Berklee Wings Poster. Art Direction & Design Photo Compositing: Ron Taft. Photography: Julenochek & Alexander Y

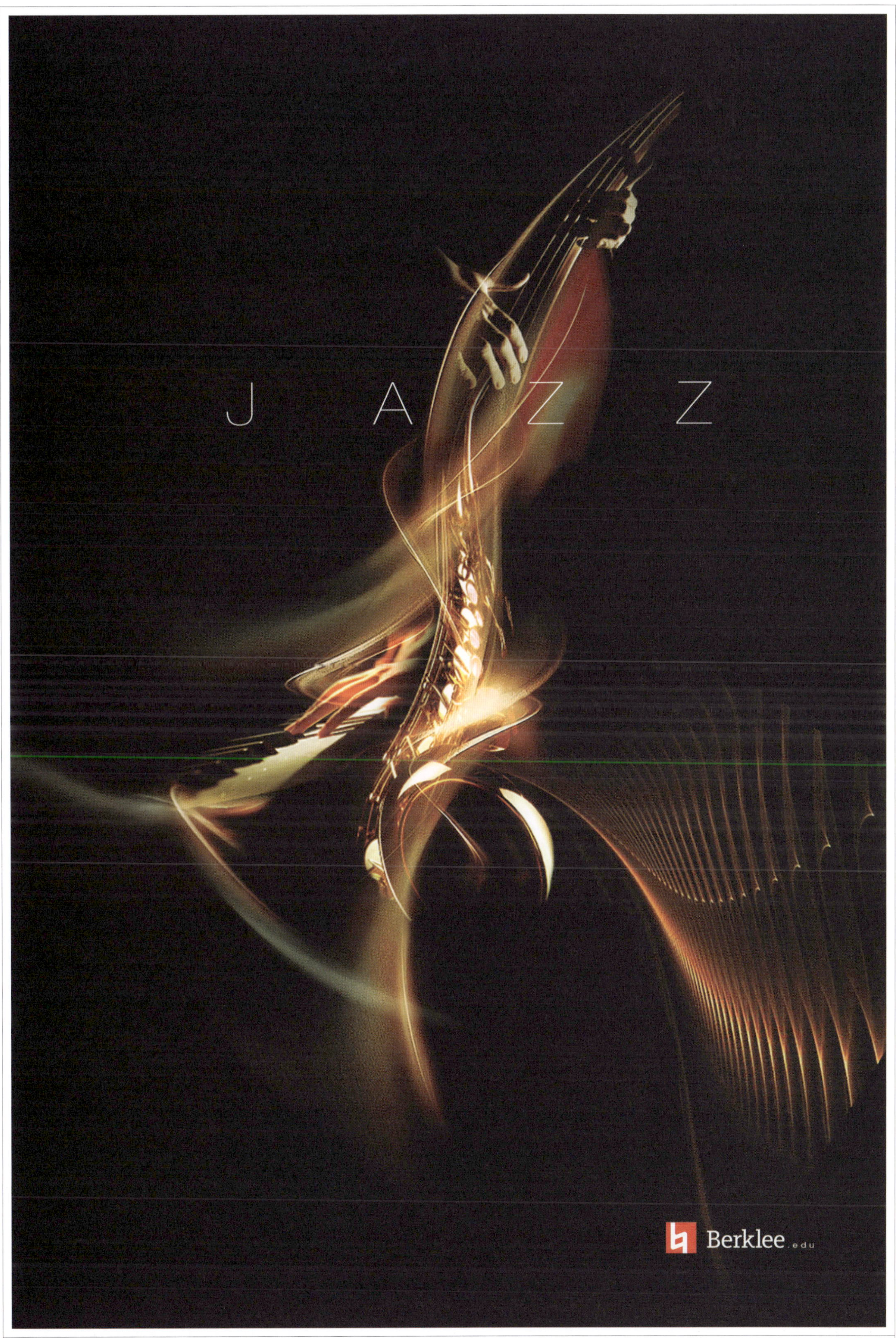

Berklee Jazz Poster. Art Direction, Design, & Photo Compositing: Ron Taft

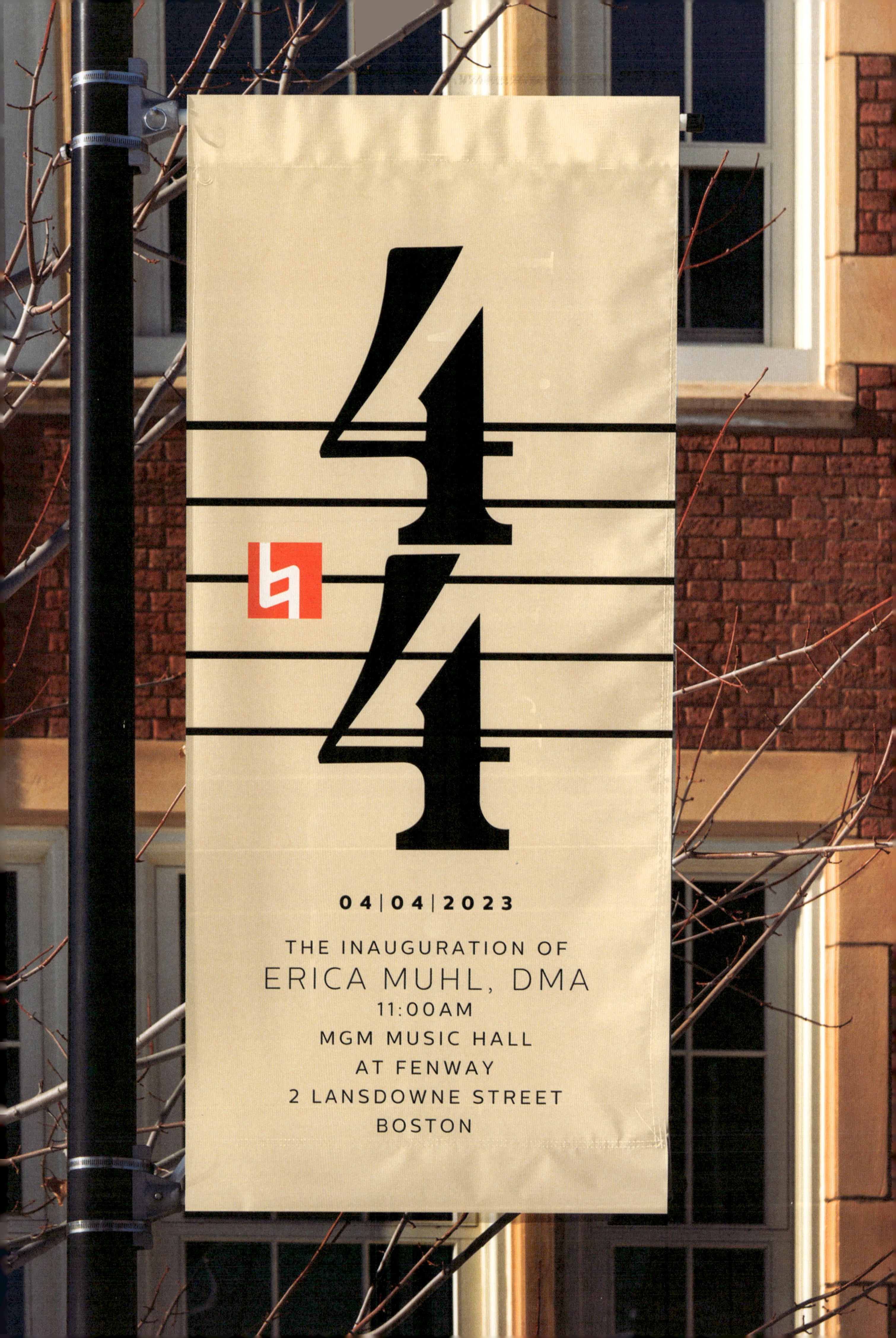

04 | 04 | 2023
THE INAUGURATION OF
ERICA MUHL, DMA
11:00AM
MGM MUSIC HALL
AT FENWAY
2 LANSDOWNE STREET
BOSTON

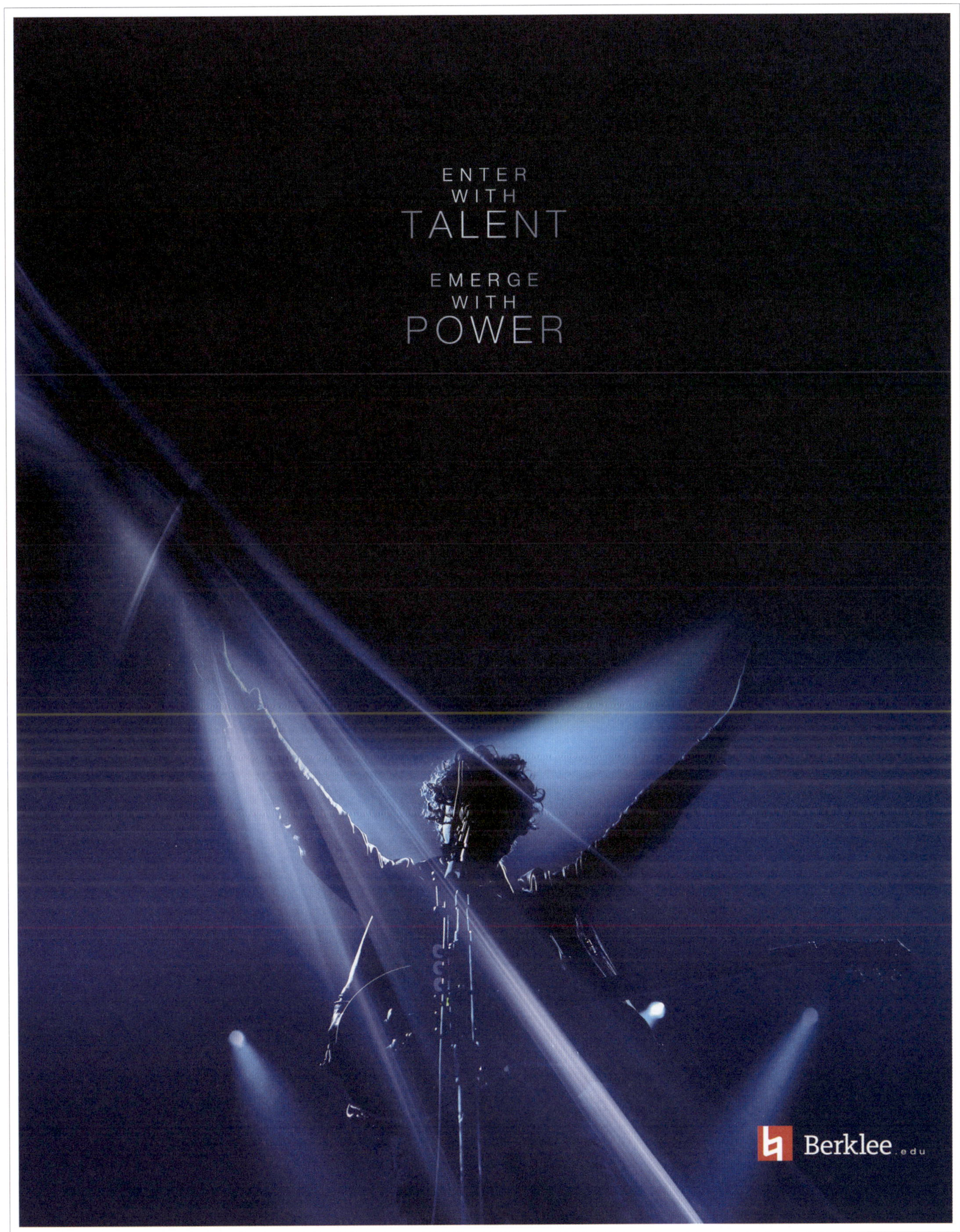

(Opposite page) Berklee Campus Banner. The musical time signature of 4/4 happened to beautifully coincide with the date of the inauguration. (Or was it the other way around?). Concept & Design: Ron Taft
(Above) Berklee Power Poster. Copywriting, Art Direction, & Design: Ron Taft. Photography: Kondr Konst

RON TAFT IS A MULTI-TALENT IN MUSIC
AND DESIGN. MOST OF HIS WORK IS FINE ART
WITH GREAT IDEAS. **B. Martin Pedersen,** *Designer & Creative Director, Graphis Inc.*

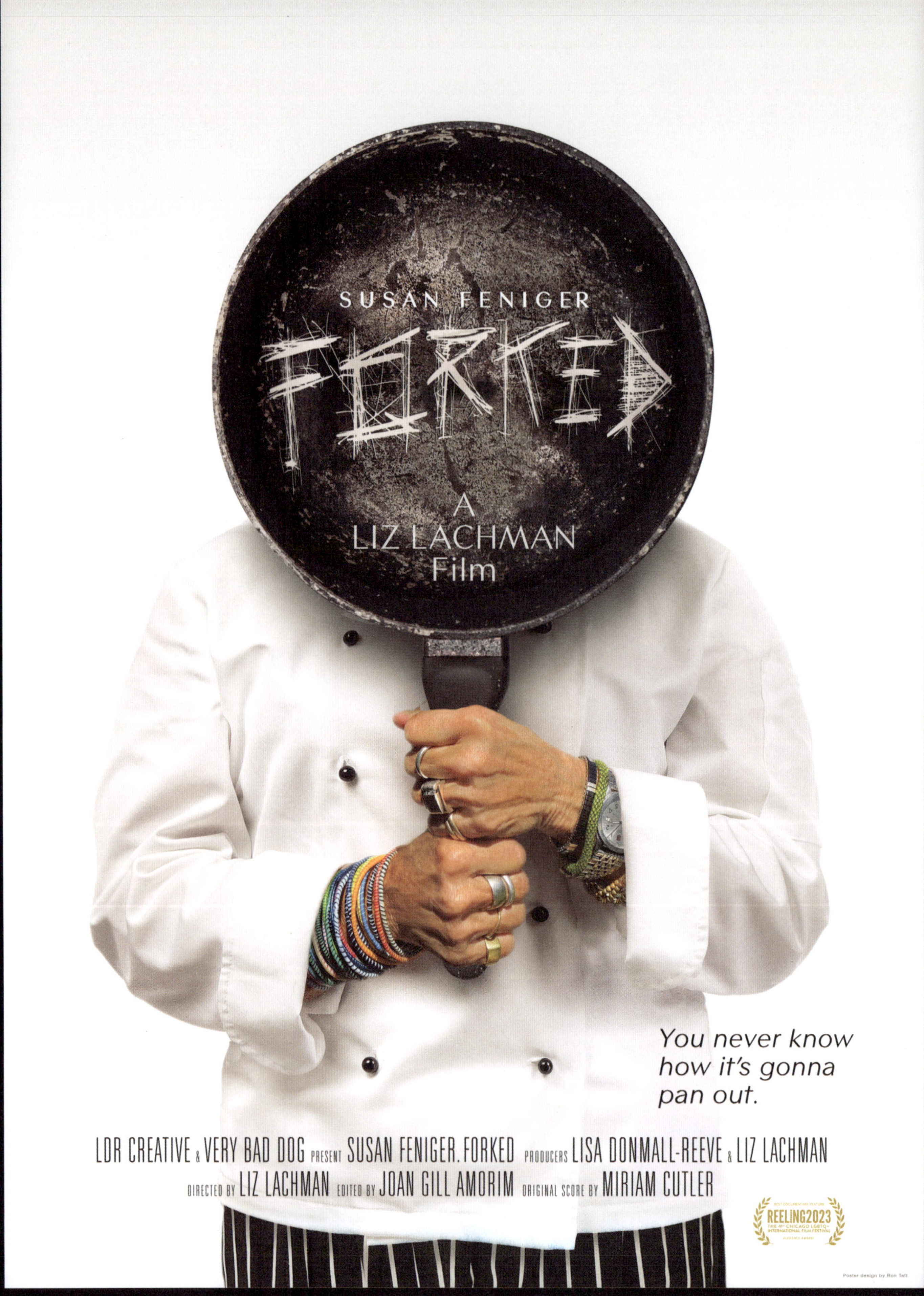

SUSAN FENIGER

FORKED

A
LIZ LACHMAN
Film

You never know
how it's gonna
pan out.

LDR CREATIVE & VERY BAD DOG PRESENT SUSAN FENIGER. FORKED PRODUCERS LISA DONMALL-REEVE & LIZ LACHMAN
DIRECTED BY LIZ LACHMAN EDITED BY JOAN GILL AMORIM ORIGINAL SCORE BY MIRIAM CUTLER

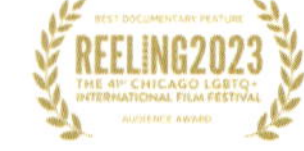

Poster design by Ron Taft

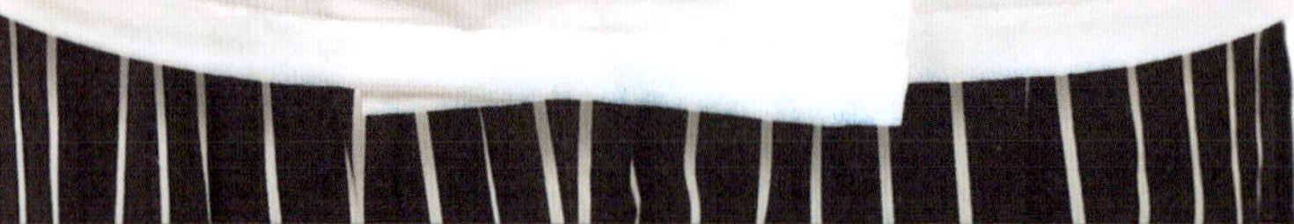

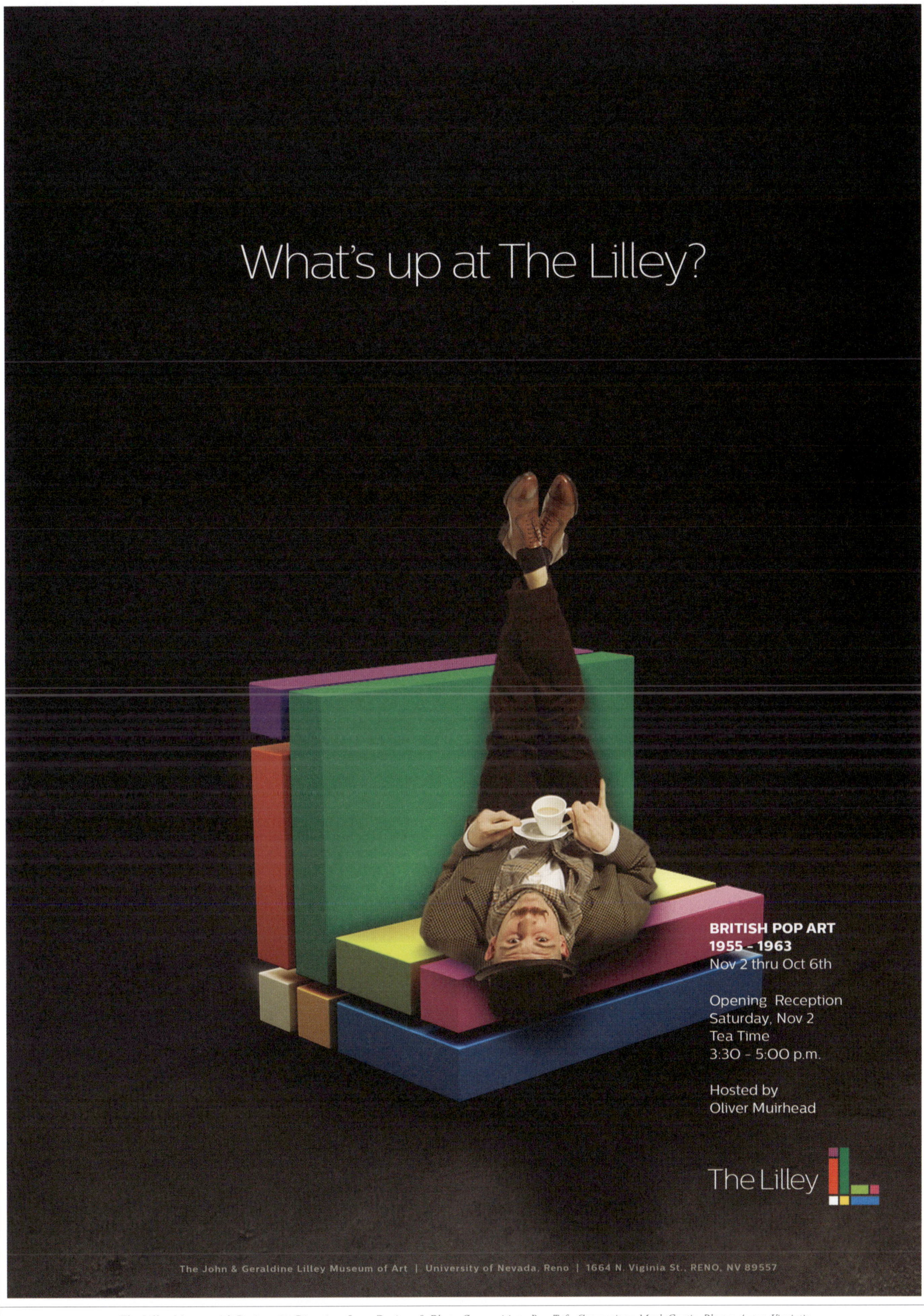

What's up at The Lilley?

BRITISH POP ART
1955 - 1963
Nov 2 thru Oct 6th

Opening Reception
Saturday, Nov 2
Tea Time
3:30 - 5:00 p.m.

Hosted by
Oliver Muirhead

The Lilley

The John & Geraldine Lilley Museum of Art | University of Nevada, Reno | 1664 N. Viginia St., RENO, NV 89557

A
ADVERTISING
44 GOODBY, SILVERSTEIN & PARTNERS / USA

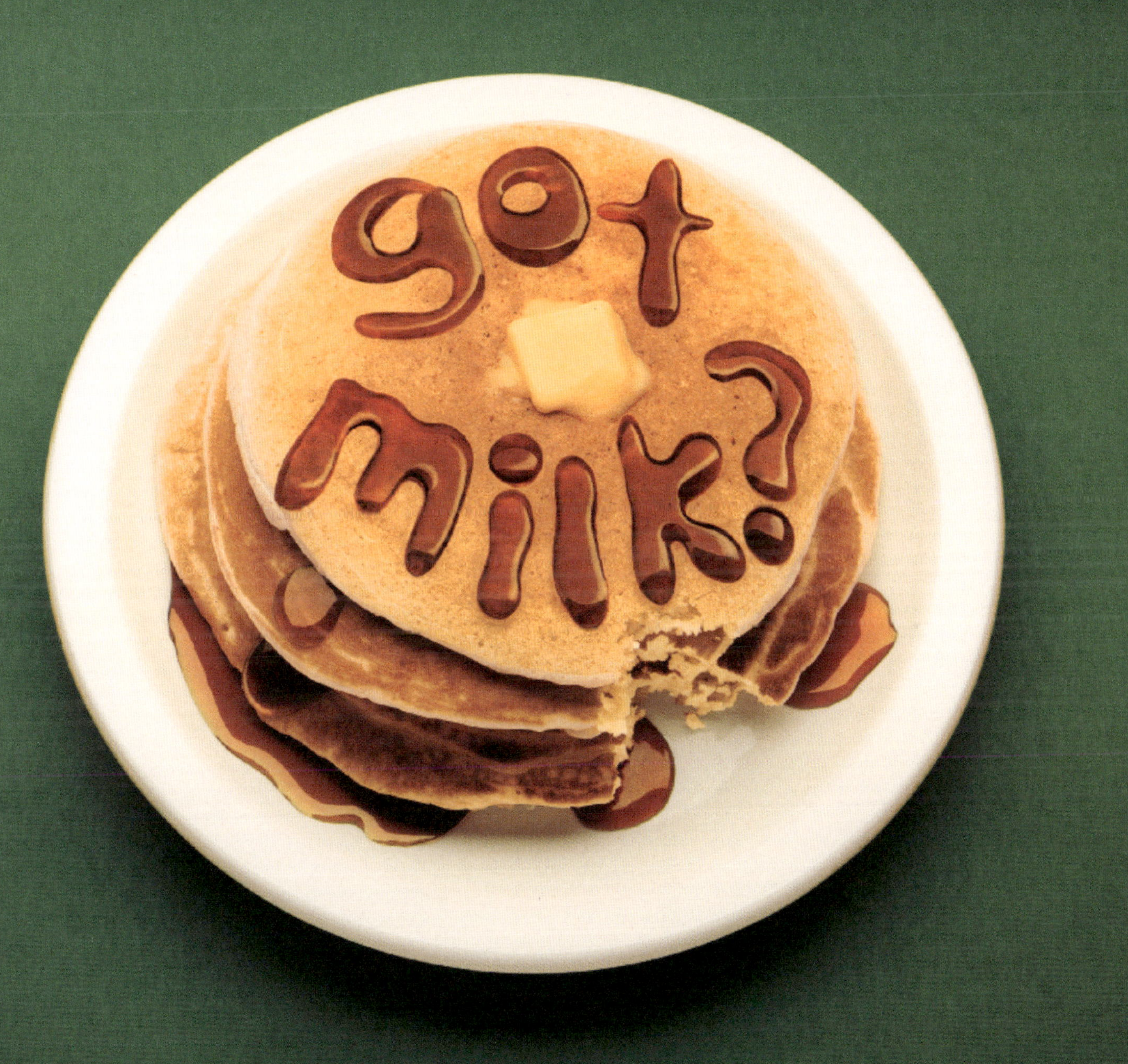

got milk?

RICH HAS A UNIQUE ABILITY TO PUSH THE EDGE AND BE A DISRUPTER IN A WAY THAT IS BOTH VERY TASTEFUL AND FULL OF SOUND JUDGMENT.

Mike Sinyard, *Founder & Former CEO, Specialized Bicycle Components*

WITHOUT A DOUBT, RICH SILVERSTEIN HAS CHANGED THE FACE OF ADVERTISING. OFTEN IMITATED BUT NEVER EQUALED, HE HAS MADE AN UNFORGETTABLE IMPRESSION ON THE INDUSTRY.

Ann Lewnes, *Former EVP & CMO, Adobe*

RICH'S LOVE OF DESIGN AND ART DIRECTION HAS BROUGHT CLASS TO AN INDUSTRY THAT TOO OFTEN GOES FOR THE LOWEST COMMON DENOMINATOR.

Gerry Graf, *Co-founder & CCO, SlapGlobal*

PRETTY MUCH EVERYONE AT W+K HAS ALWAYS ADMIRED, ADORED, AND SOMETIMES BEEN JEALOUS OF THE ONE AND ONLY JEFF GOODBY.

Susan Hoffman, *CCO, Wieden+Kennedy*

JEFF HAS BEEN THE CREATIVE ENGINE BEHIND OUR MOST IMPACTFUL CAMPAIGNS FOR NEARLY TWO DECADES, BRILLIANTLY LEVERAGING THE POWER OF ADVERTISING TO TELL OUR STORY.

Brian Roberts, *Chairman & CEO, Comcast*

JEFF SHOWED US THAT BRILLIANT CREATIVE AND BRAND BUILDING ARE NOT MUTUALLY EXCLUSIVE, THAT HUMOR AND HUMILITY SELL, AND PRODUCT CLAIMS SHOULD BE OFFERED TO CONSUMERS, NOT CRAMMED DOWN THEIR THROATS.

Jeff Manning, *Former ED, California Milk Processor Board*

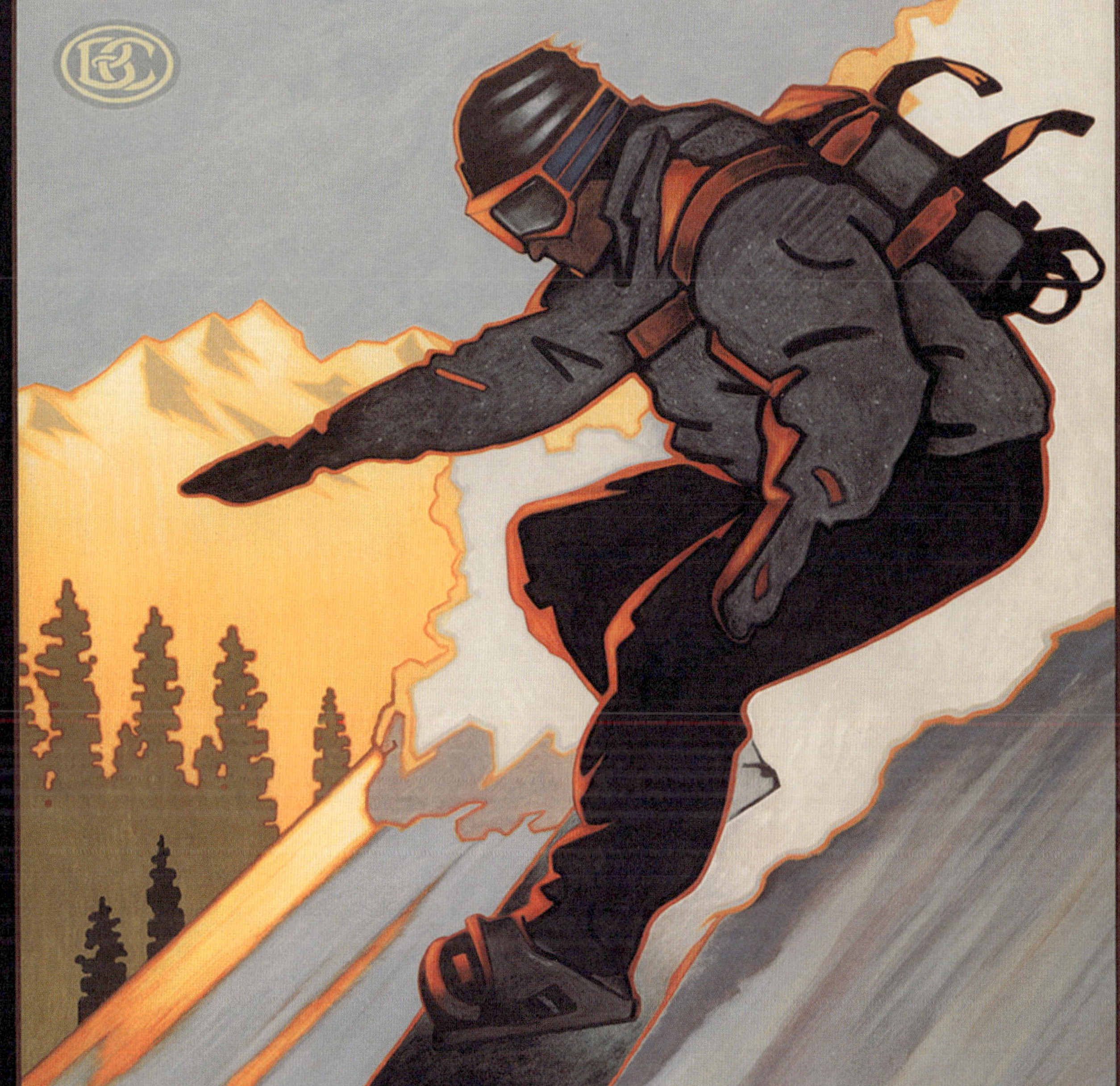

(Page 43) Got Milk / (Above) Beaver Creek

Introduction by Margaret Johnson *Chief Creative Officer & Partner, GS&P*

Working for Jeff Goodby and Rich Silverstein is like riding shotgun with the Terminator—relentless, unstoppable, and exhausting in the best soul-crushing way. Jeff's all about digging up the surprise in everything, pulling diamonds out of the mud. Rich? He's a lightning bolt and sees the solution before you've finished explaining the brief. But here's the kicker: These guys *never* repeat themselves. They reinvent. They push. Mentors, legends—and, yeah, they'll knock you down just to make you come back stronger.

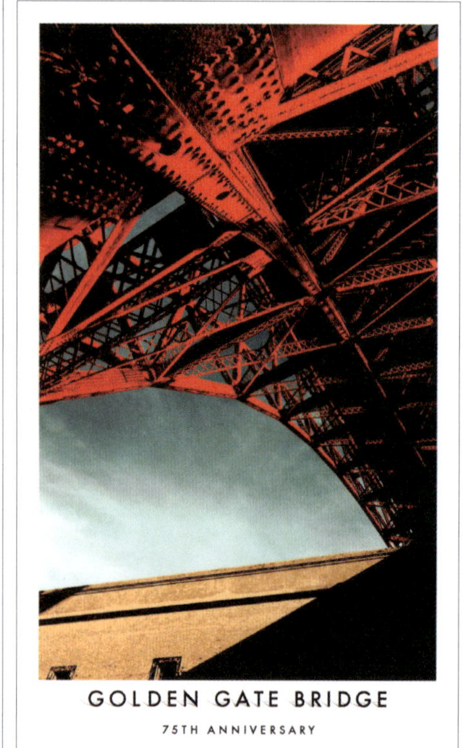

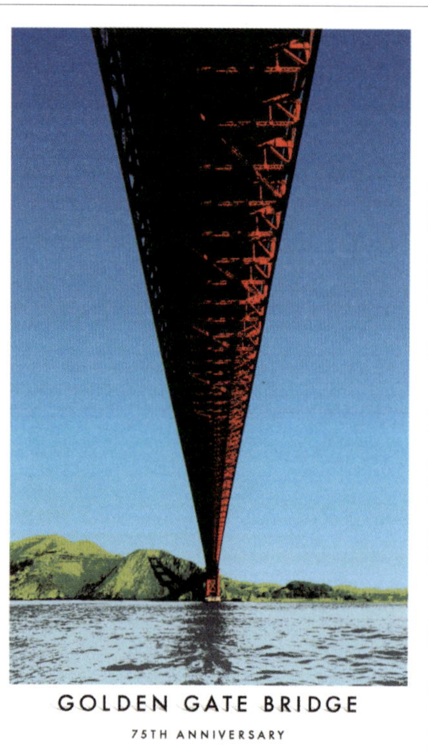

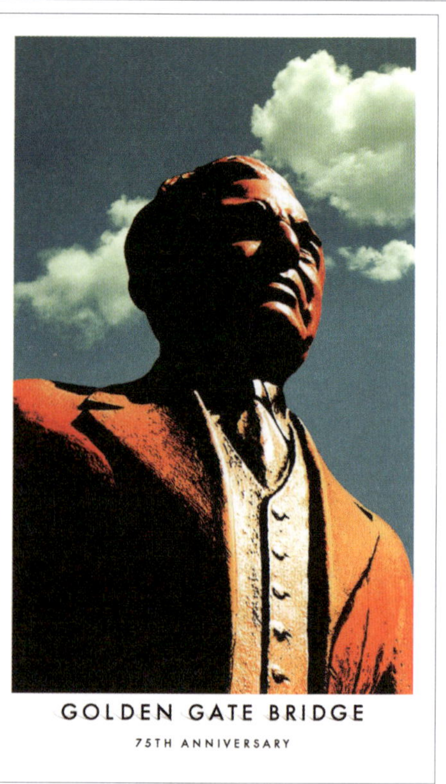

Golden Gate Bridge 75th Anniversary

TRENDS CAN GET YOU IN TROUBLE. I WOULD SAY ANY IDEA THAT IS RELEVANT AND TIMELESS IS WHAT WE LOOK FOR.

Rich Silverstein, *Co-Chairman, Founder, & Partner*

I ENCOURAGE PEOPLE TO EMBRACE A SPIRIT OF VANDALISM. BE NAUGHTY. SMASH PUMPKINS. DO THINGS YOU JUST CAN'T WAIT FOR THE WORLD TO SEE.

Jeff Goodby, *Co-Chairman, Founder, & Partner*

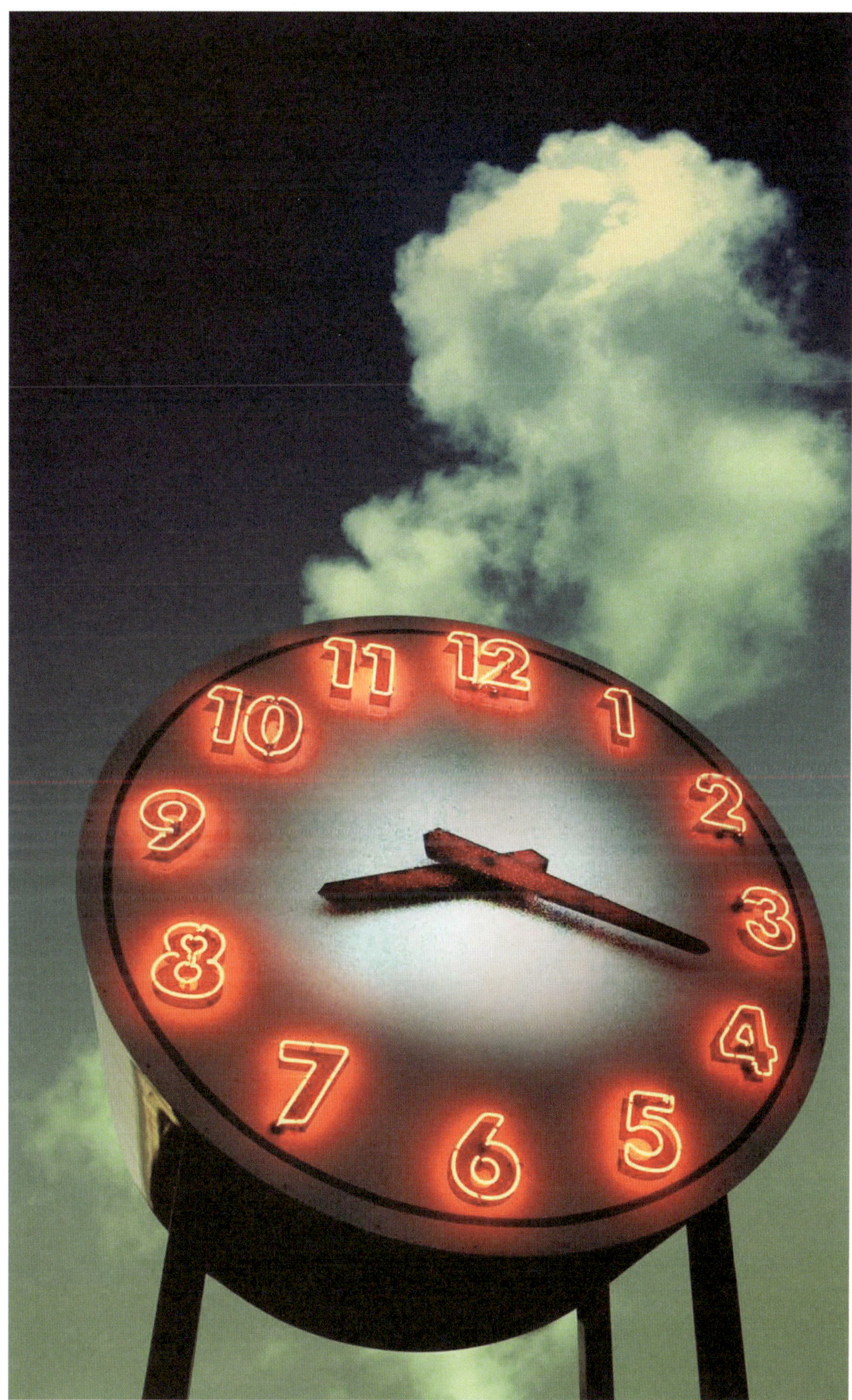

GOLDEN GATE BRIDGE

75TH ANNIVERSARY

Golden Gate Bridge 75th Anniversary

What has inspired or motivated you in your career?
Rich Silverstein, Co-Chairman, Founder, & Partner: Growing up, there were no cell phones, internet, or search engines. Apple was a music label. Silicon Valley grew fruit. Artisans actually handset type. Retouching was done with a brush and knife, not Photoshop. And you cut film by hand. There was no 24-hour news, and there were three TV stations, not counting PBS, which no one actually watched. It was too dull.

So let's start at 2937 Meadowcrest Drive, Yorktown Heights, New York. Northern Westchester, Middle America. In that house behind me, all the insecurities that any kid had? That's me. And then came *TIME* magazine. Oh my God, it was a window into the world. One section, the art section, just spoke to me. I don't even know why, but visually, I continuously pored over it.

How do you two see your roles evolving alongside the next generation of leaders at GS&P?
R.S.: Jeff and I will continue working on accounts, but we have also inspired a new level of creative directors to take a more hands-on approach to our clients. Jeff and I love to teach and become editors of great work. Our doors are always open at any level to hear ideas and help shape the work.
Jeff Goodby, Co-Chairman, Founder, & Partner: In the book *Built to Last*, they say the first responsibility of a great business is to reproduce what's great about it without getting stuck in a rut. I think Rich and I are doing that in a couple of ways. I have instituted a formal mentorship program in which I meet with four different people each week for a month. We also act as trusting sorcerers rather than insistent kings. We are lucky to have Leslie and Margaret but also a whole battery of terrific people around them. Stand back and let the big dogs eat.

What is your work philosophy?
R.S.: When you're a graphic designer, the evil is advertising. And somehow, I've found myself in advertising. But [Jeff and I] have always tried to bring the aesthetic of graphic design and editorial together.

What balance do you strike between tradition and innovation at GS&P, especially with new technologies like AI?
R.S.: We embrace and demand powerful storytelling ideas that can come from any form of media. The medium is the message! So traditional and innovative ideas are just different ways to play in a creative sandbox. We were working in AI for BMW and the Dali Museum before it was called AI.
J.G.: Our tradition IS innovation. I tell people: If your brother or sister or best friend or some guy from college could have thought of it, don't do it. We love things that have never been done before. That might be AI right now, but we want to do the next thing after that.

Who is or was your greatest mentor?
R.S.: After high school, I went to Parsons School of Design, but I actually didn't think art school was all that important. Really, what I did is I found this mentoring idea, finding someone who I could look up to, and Dick Hess, who was a Renaissance man, was a designer and illustrator who said, "To be in this business of design, you should be willing to do anything—shovel gravel at the designer's house." So I took

him up on that, and I got an internship with Dick. That was my introduction. To this day, he has been a great influence on me. And I would say to anyone who is in this business and who is young—find mentors or, you know, work at any job to start.

Are there any emerging trends that GS&P should be leading as the industry evolves?
R.S.: Trends can get you in trouble. I would say any idea that is relevant and timeless is what we look for.
J.G.: I agree with Rich. There was a time in the '80s when we decided that the funniest things in the world always involved sex, food, and death. That kind of timelessness started around a campfire, and every great trend comes out of telling such stories.

What is it about design that you are most passionate about?
R.S.: I think the aesthetic of storytelling in print is really good and valuable.

In what ways do you both see GS&P's core values being preserved and expanded by the next generation?
R.S.: Always treat the consumer respectfully, never talk down, and encourage them to participate in the message and 40-year-old timeless beliefs.
J.G.: I encourage people to embrace a spirit of vandalism. Be naughty. Smash pumpkins. Do things you just can't wait for the world to see.

What is the most difficult challenge you've overcome to reach your current position?
R.S.: High school was pretty hard for me. I wasn't a very good student. I know I've talked about this before. I didn't know I was dyslexic. The one thing that got me through it was lacrosse. It's an American Indian game. It's brutal. It can be beautiful. My social studies teacher, Jim Turnbull, was also my coach. I've always looked to mentors, and that's where it started.

What do the two of you consider essential for GS&P's continued success and creative excellence?
R.S.: Never settle and always improve.
J.G.: Hiring people that are better than we are.

Who have some of your greatest past influences been?
R.S.: For me, the father of graphic design is Milton Glaser. There is no one better. Here's a guy who attends art school and learns how to paint. Like, really paint. And then gives that up and finds a way to deconstruct that into beautiful graphic design. I mean, that Dylan poster is still good today; it's amazing. It's not just design; it's wit. It had a language; it had an idea behind it. It's not just fluff; it's not just pretty. It's the intelligence of graphic design that has moved me forever. I only hope that Jeff and I have a little bit of that in us.

It's not just about the still image. There's this guy named Saul Bass. He was a great designer, but he was so ahead of his time; he would take images and start moving them. And they became great title sequences for movies. So, you look at his work right now; it's still great. And it's because the idea has been put to music and has wit, energy, sound, and drama. It's all out of two dimensions, animated.

One thing I haven't talked about is photography. Between Diane Arbus and Irving Penn, I mean, I was like, "Yes." Irving

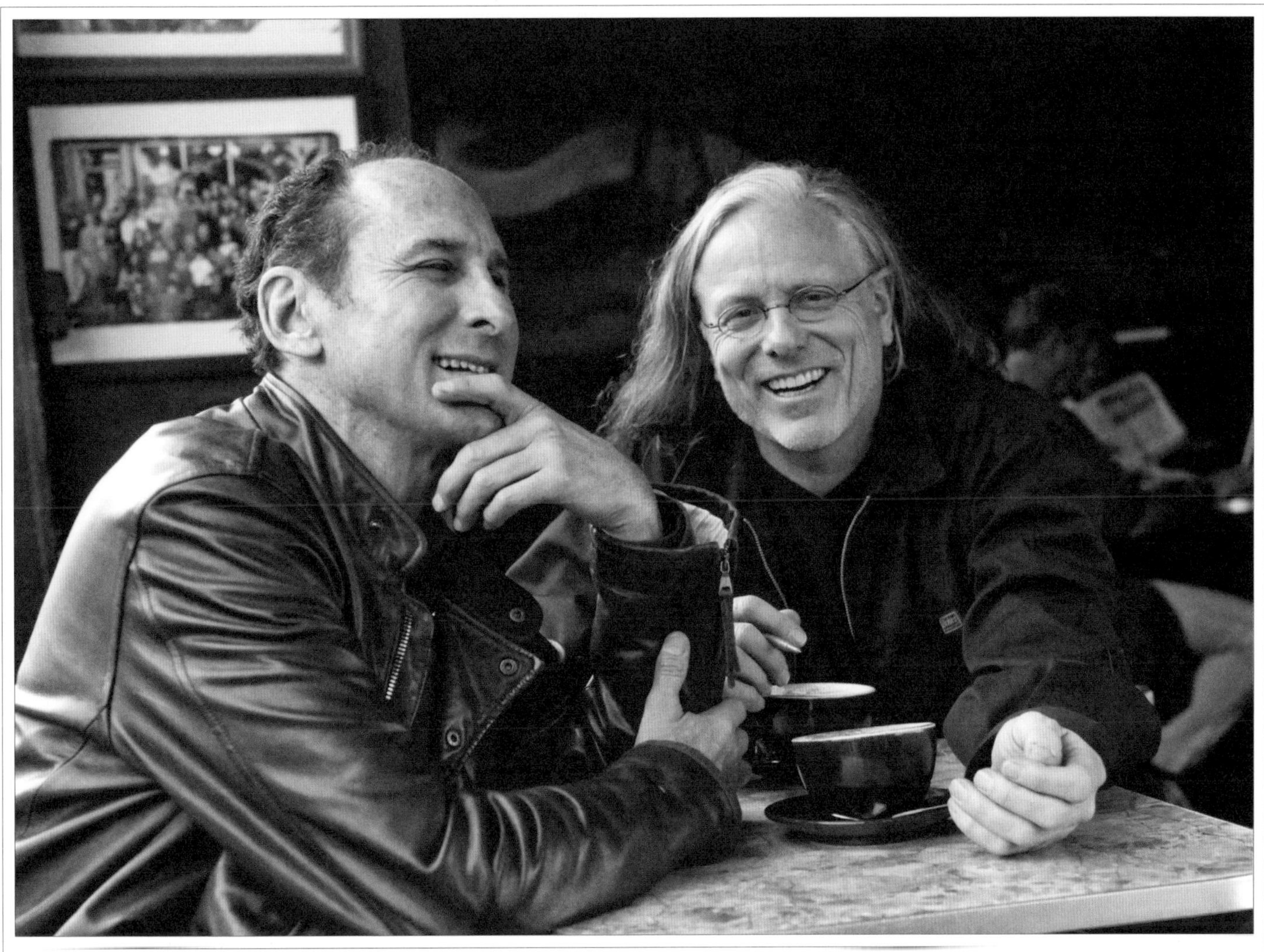

Rich & Jeff

didn't mind being in the commercial and art world together. And I've always admired that. It's not only the aesthetic but also the craft of his printing. It's all in the details. If you saw Irving's prints, you want to touch them. They're alive. And it's details like that that have stayed with me forever.

In what ways do you think the agency's ethos will continue to influence the broader industry?

R.S.: Surprise and delight, or how in the hell do they keep doing great work?
J.G.: If you're lucky enough to be successful, there's a tendency to keep doing those things that got you there. We consciously fight this. I hope people will notice that we don't have an agency style.

What do you consider your greatest professional achievement so far?

R.S.: After working at *Rolling Stone*, I got a job at Hal Riney. Hal was known as, you know, pretty much a genius of advertising and then a son of a bitch. And he said, "You're going to be working with this guy, Jeff Goodby." (I didn't know who Jeff was.) "And you're going to work on Billy Ball."

Jeff loved baseball, and I liked its aesthetic. I didn't know much about baseball. It worked. We discovered that we both don't have to know much about the product; at least one does. But without Hal, there would be no Goodby, Silverstein & Partners.

If you could pass on one key piece of wisdom to the new leaders, what would it be?

R.S.: Be humble, be smart, be kind, and respect the client.
J.G.: Be brutally honest with yourself. How good is your work, really?

What advice do you have for students starting out today?

R.S.: I would say to everyone: Have mentors, have people you look up to, study things, don't try to do everything yourself, and there's always something to learn. Because I'm still learning.

Where do you find inspiration?

R.S.: In art school, I was introduced to Bauhaus, and there wasn't any aesthetic in the Bauhaus that was wrong. It was so exciting. It didn't matter if it was graphic design, photography, fashion, jewelry, or architecture. Even today, if I see Bauhaus design, I actually get goosebumps.

I also remember being introduced to Helvetica in art school, and that is another thing that changed my life. I mean, the Swiss design—I didn't know anything about it. And still, even today, type is so important to me.

GS&P www.goodbysilverstein.com
See their Graphis Master Portfolio at graphis.com.

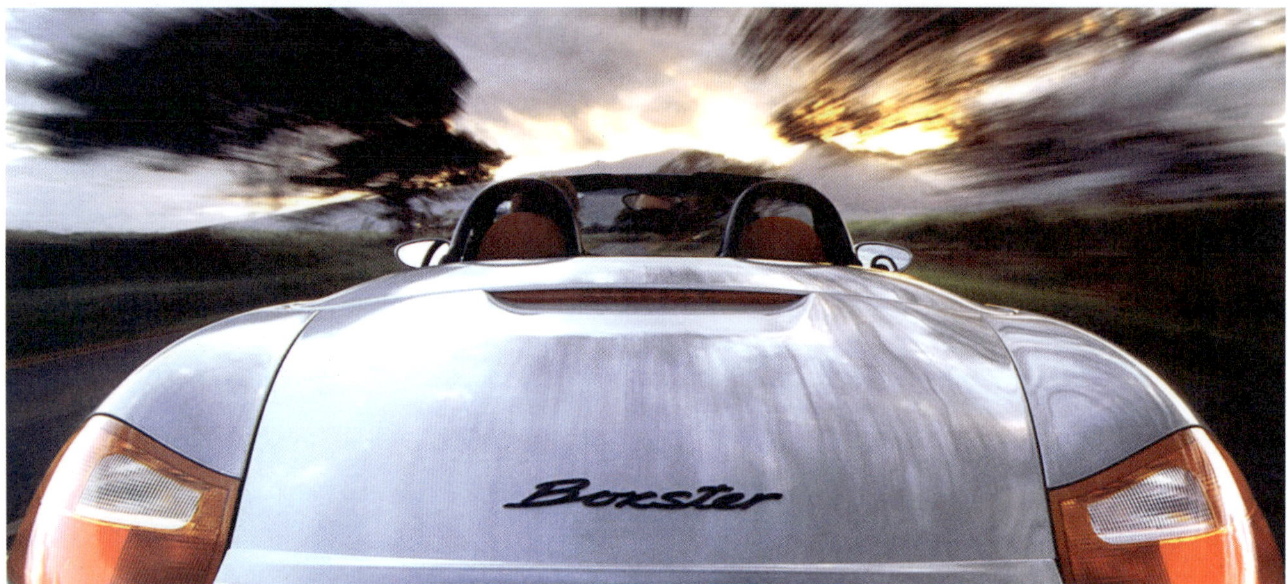

1956 meets 2001.

It's classic, yet futuristic. It's a cross between a 550 Spyder and the space shuttle. It's the first

mid-engine Porsche roadster in over 40 years. And it's in the Here and Now. The Boxster.

Starting at $41,000. Contact us at 1-800-PORSCHE or www.porsche.com and come to believe:

Porsche. There is no substitute.™

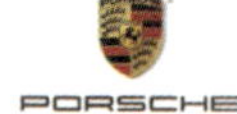

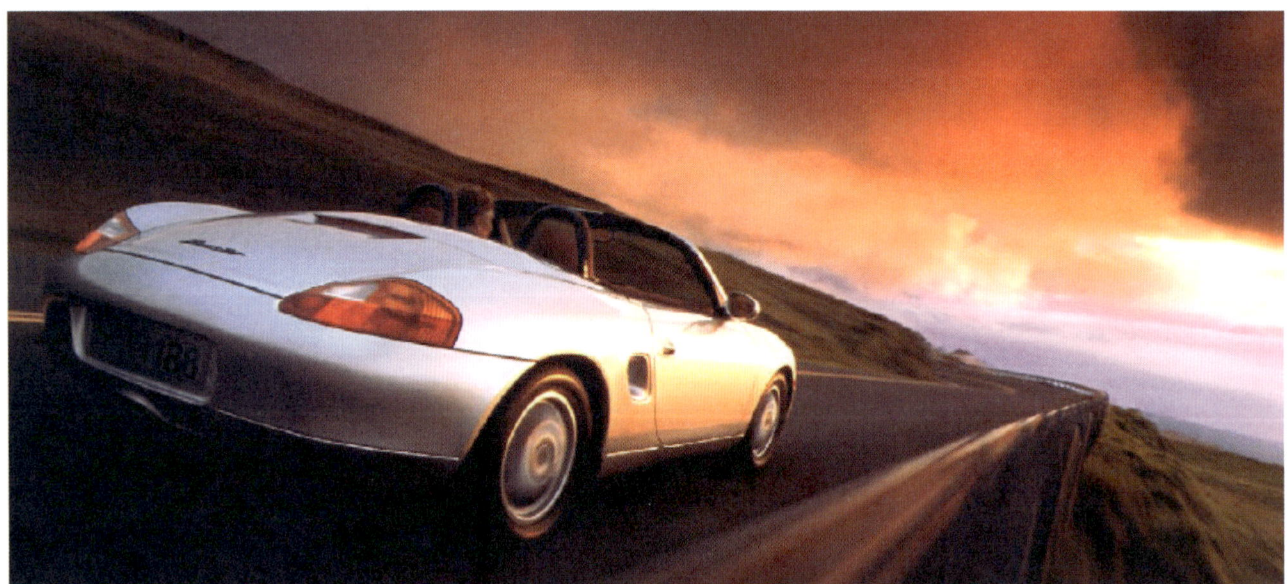

Bring a map.

The top disappears in seconds. Thanks to the mid-mounted flat six, so do you.

But not to worry, you can always use the two trunks for survival gear. The Boxster.

Starting at $41,000. Contact us at 1-800-Porsche or www.porsche.com and realize:

Porsche. There is no substitute.™

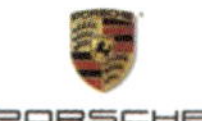

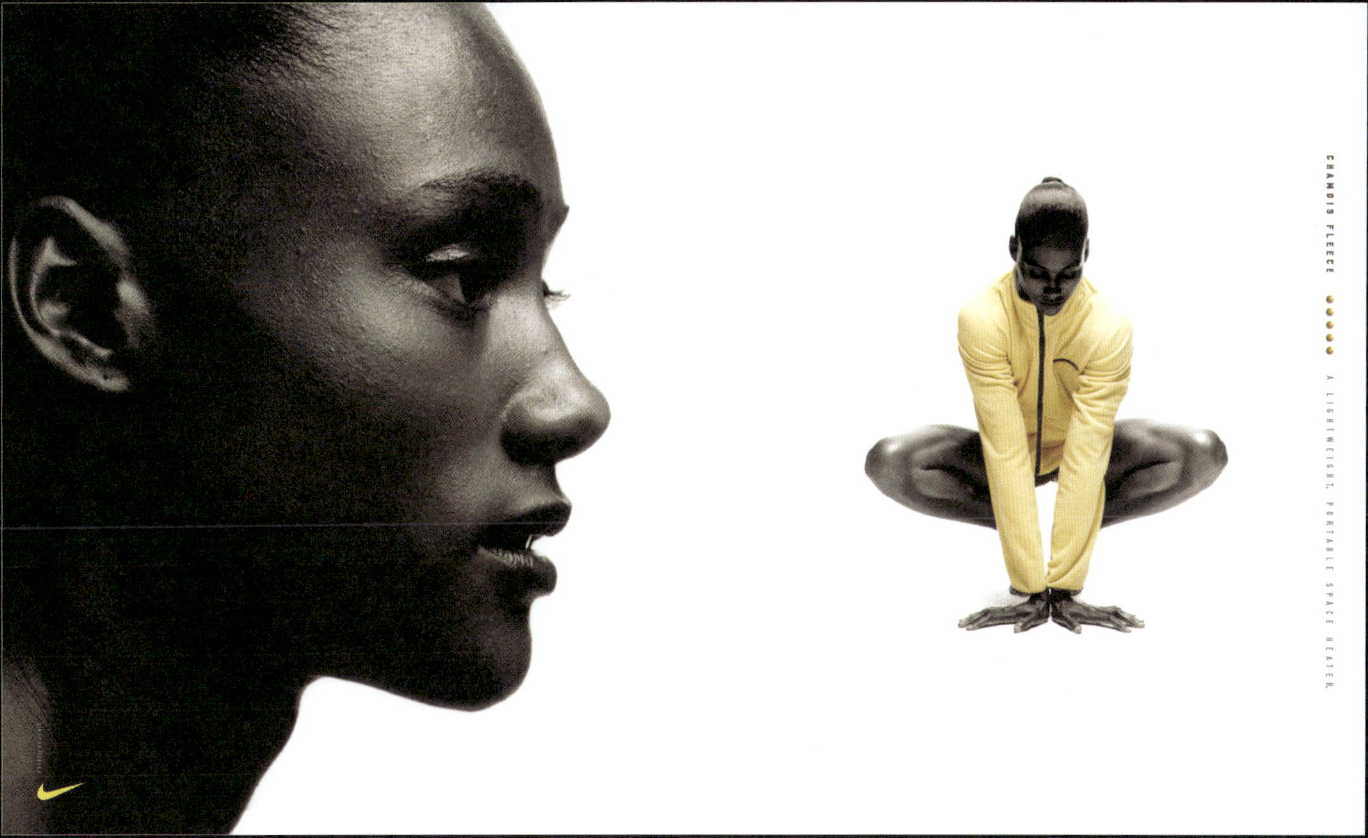

CHAMOIS FLEECE
A LIGHTWEIGHT, PORTABLE SPACE HEATER.

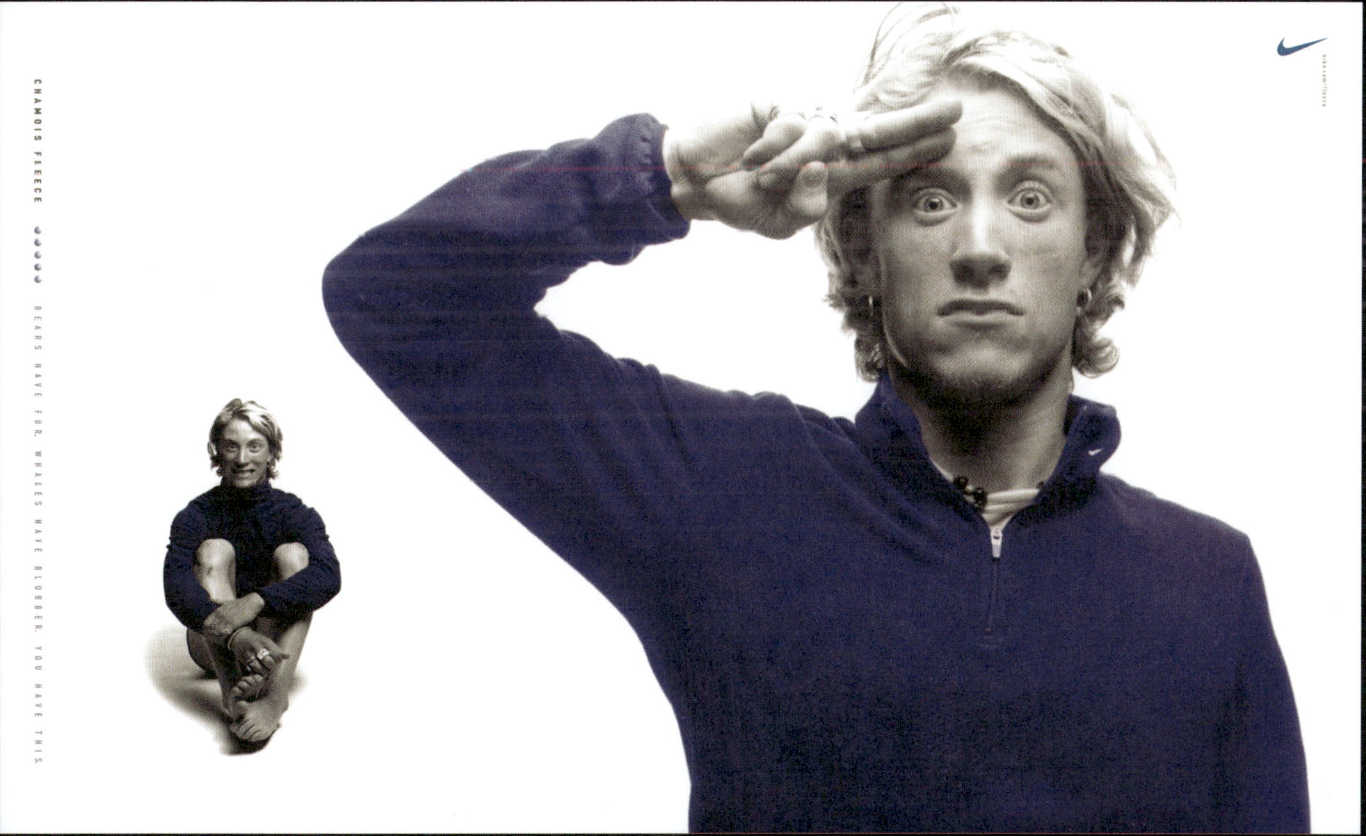

CHAMOIS FLEECE
BEARS HAVE FUR. WHALES HAVE BLUBBER. YOU HAVE THIS.
nikewomen/fitness
Nike

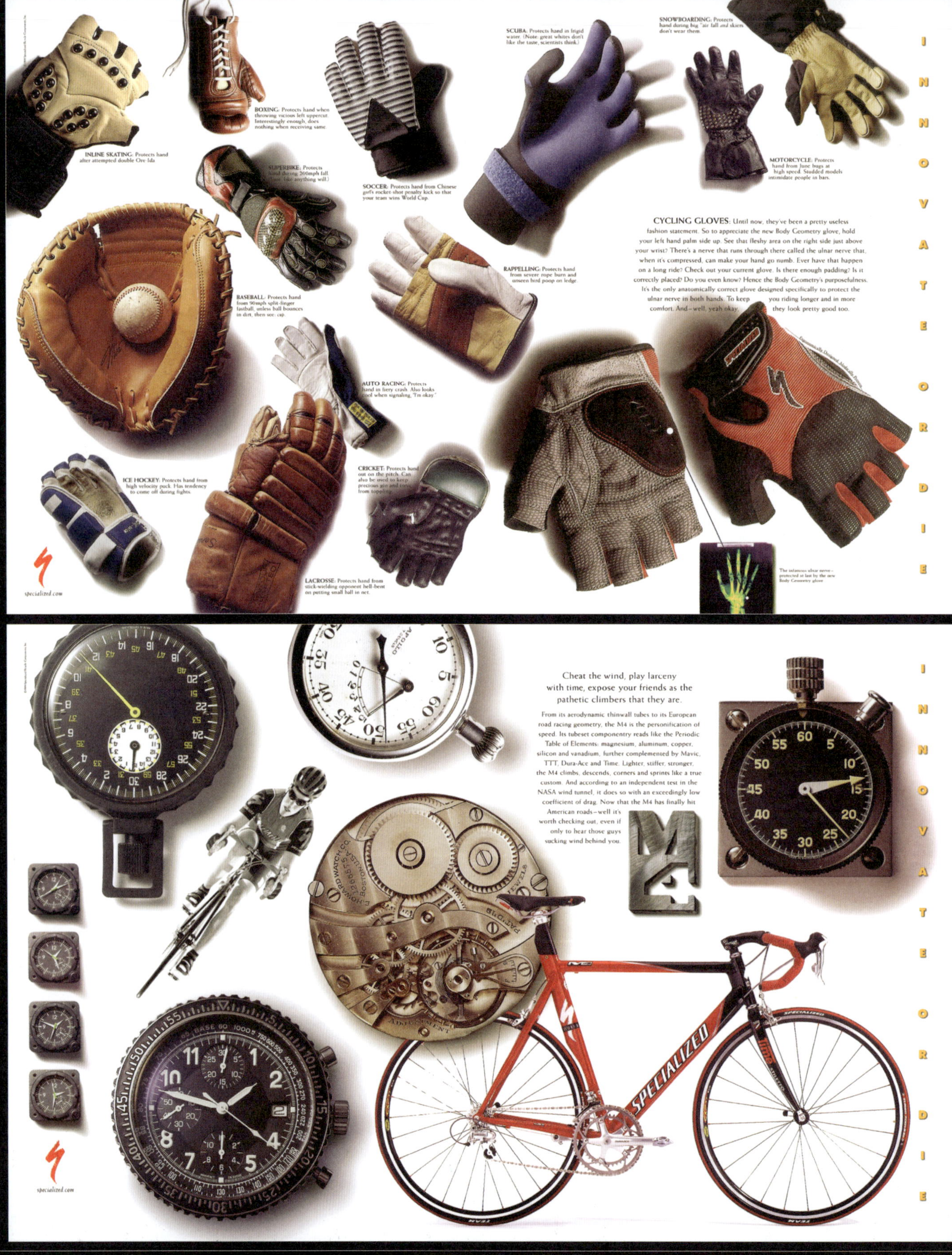

Specialized

THE 6TH UNWRITTEN LAW OF DRIVING

WHERE THERE'S A HILL THERE'S A MOTOR HOME.

DUAL OVERHEAD CAMS
MORE AIR MORE FUEL MORE BANG
MORE POWER

EXHAUST
AIR

The new Isuzu Trooper has been thoughtfully redesigned to include a powerful 190 horse, dual overhead cam, 24-valve V6 engine,* which can eat up a stretch of highway pretty quick. Even that steep part. You know, the one that every slow moving vehicle in the world knows you're going to be on so they go there just to irritate you? Well, dust 'em with that new Trooper of yours.

ISUZU
Practically/Amazing

*LS model. Always wear a seat belt. And please, treat the environment with respect. © American Isuzu Motors, Inc., 1992

THE 58TH UNWRITTEN LAW OF DRIVING

THE ROAD IS PAVED WITH IDIOTS.

UNLIKE MOST 4WD VEHICLES, DUAL AIR BAGS COME STANDARD.

HIGH GROUND CLEARANCE FOR A BETTER OVERALL VIEW

THE ONLY 4WD WITH STANDARD 4-WHEEL VENTI-LATED DISC ABS BRAKES

IMPACT ABSORBING STRUCTURE DESIGNED TO PROTECT THE CABIN.

HEAD LAMP WIPERS CLEARLY A BENEFIT, ESPECIALLY IN MUD.

They're out there, those runners of stop signs, those no-signal lane changers. And while we can do little to stop them, we've gone to great lengths to make them less of a threat. Presenting the new Trooper Limited. For more information please call (800) 726-2700.

ISUZU
Practically/Amazing

Always wear a seat belt. And please, treat the environment with respect. © 1992 American Isuzu Motors Inc.

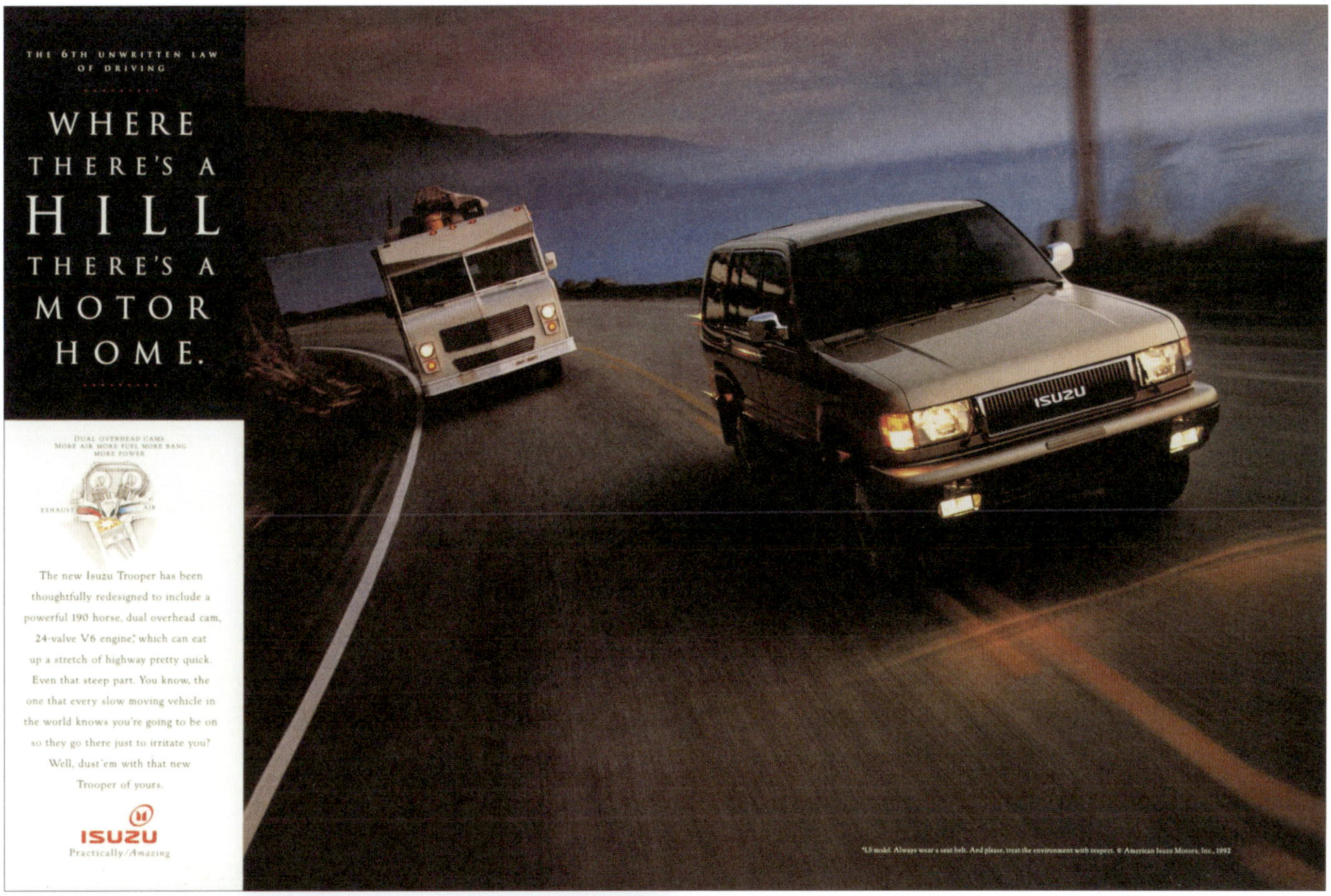

Isuzu

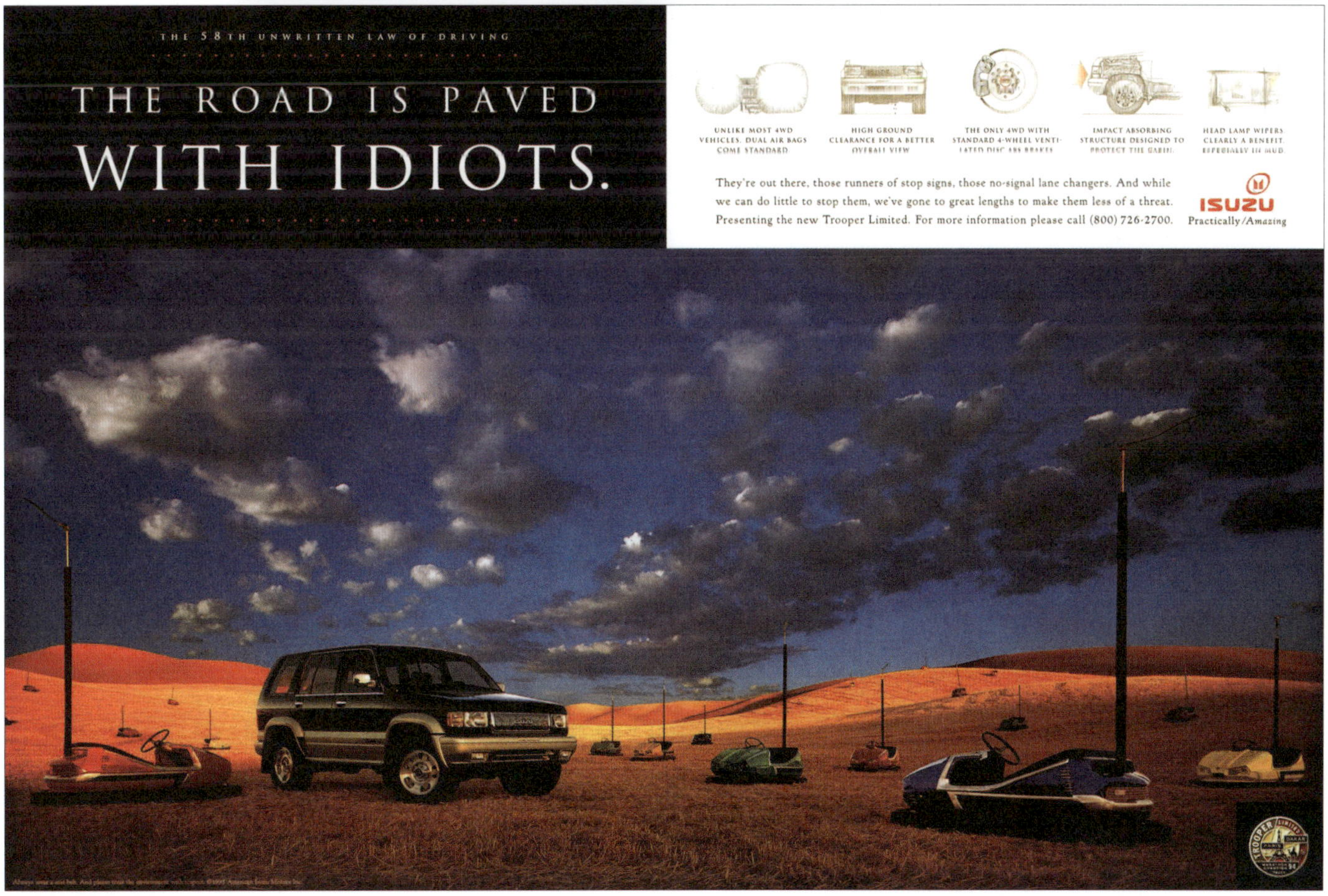

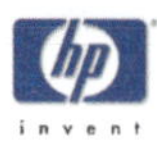

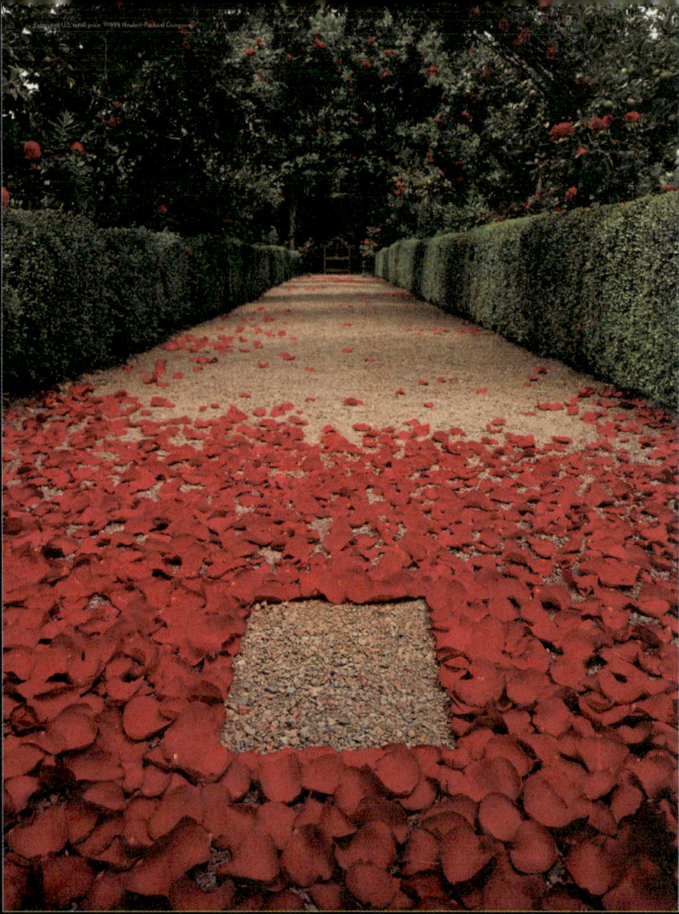

True to the original.

Capture life's vibrant colors.

Discover the nuances of light and shadow.

Printouts most like your original photos.

The new HP DeskJet 970C.

Just $399. www.hp.com/go/original.

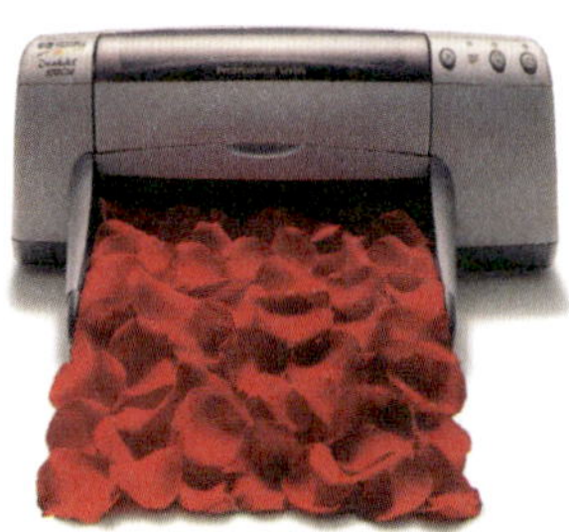

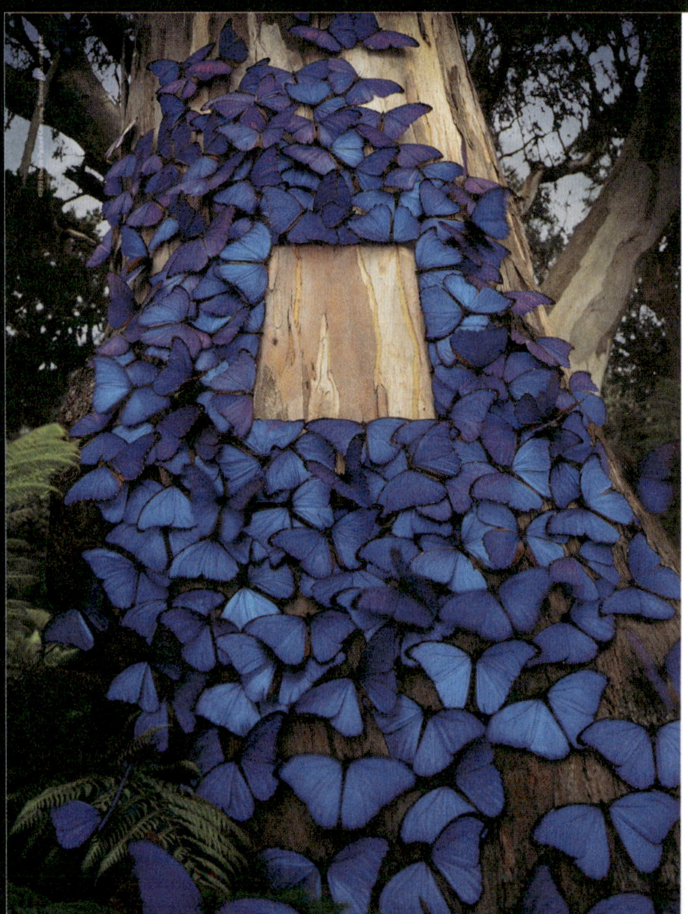

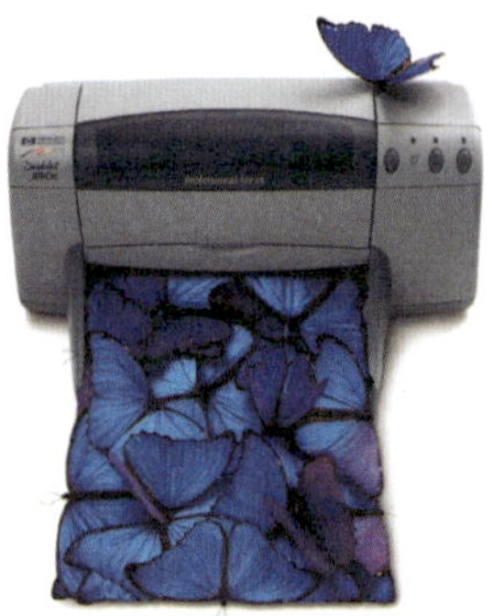

True to the original.

Discover life's vibrant colors. Capture delicate detail
and rich shadow. Printouts most like your original photos.
Without sacrificing razor-sharp text and graphics.
The new HP DeskJet 970C. Up to 10 ppm color. Just $399.
Achieve superior results with HP supplies.
www.hp.com/go/original.

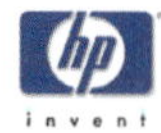

Arriving At The Proper State Of Mind Requires Just The Right Vehicle.

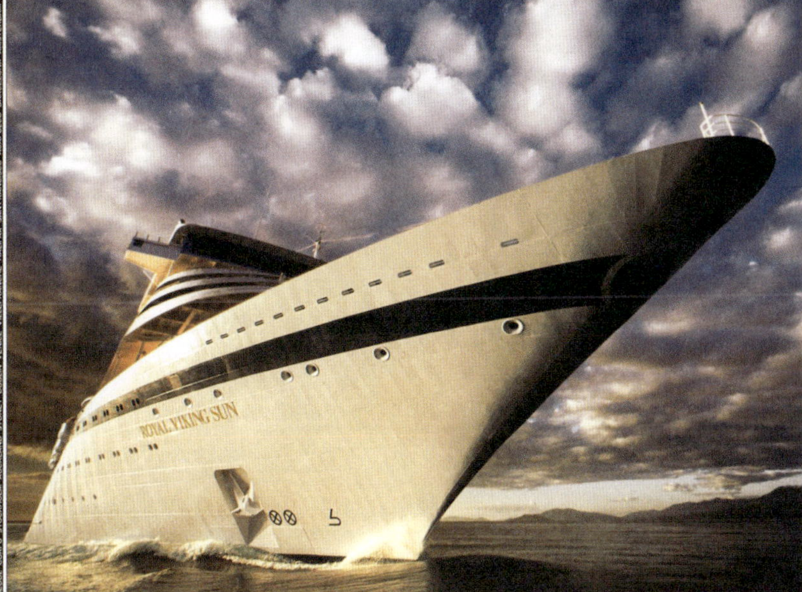

Pictured below: The Royal Viking Sun, Reality's Number One Cruise Vessel, her hold full of pleasant dreams, somewhere off the coast of Bali.

THERE ARE NO MAPS TO STEER YOU EAST OR WEST. Yet it is possible to get there, and perhaps the best way is by ship.

But not just any ship. It should be one filled with the elegance and little touches that make a vessel worthy of being designated five-star-plus. We have not just one, but an entire fleet of such remarkable crafts.

Each of our ships is equipped with candlelit dining rooms that offer unhurried single seating. Aboard every one, you'll find kitchens where 33 European-trained chefs will prepare fine delicacies. In the staterooms, fresh flowers appear magically each morning. Surrounding each vessel are the most spacious, most strollable decks.

At every turn, you'll witness the alert, gracious service that inspired the readers of *Travel-Holiday* magazine to vote us the Most Courteous Cruise Line for three years running.

So in the end, it is not a question of whether you can arrive at the proper state of mind by way of our ships. It is merely a question of how soon you will choose to do so. Your travel agent will help you decide, or call us at (800) 426-0821. We look forward to your call and to seeing you on board.

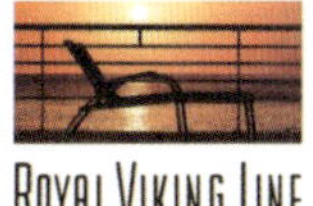

An afghan from Norway, a deck chair resting on authentic Burmese teak. These are the kind of tools you'll need — and will be provided.

ROYAL VIKING LINE
THE WORLD'S FINEST

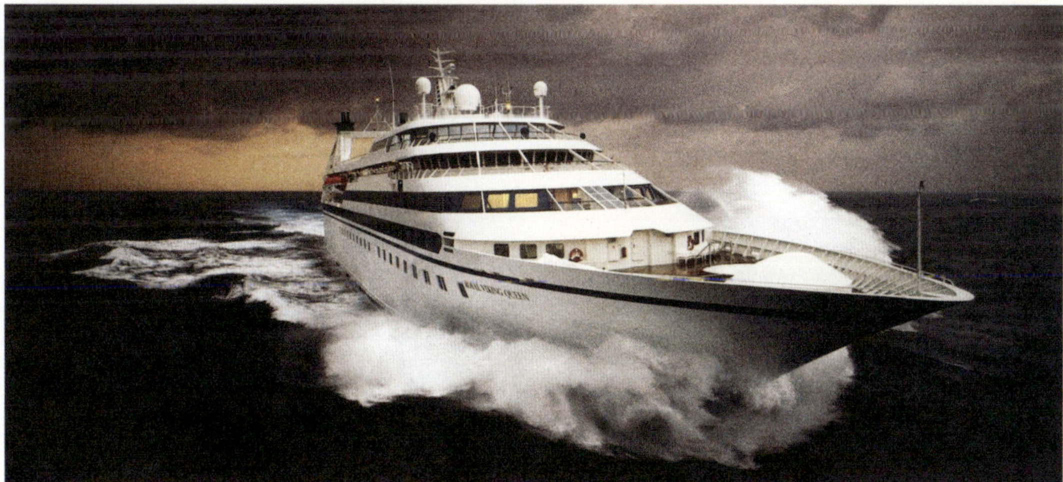

Civilization Is Advancing At A Stately 18 Knots.

Long before reaching your destination, you will experience a sense of having arrived. Such is life aboard our newest ship, the intimate *Royal Viking Queen*, and her larger, more stately companion, the elegant *Royal Viking Sun*.

Here, all that has made sailing Royal Viking Line so wondrous over the years is heightened as never before. Consider mingling with learned experts in World Affairs. Or collecting secrets of aquatic life from the Cousteau Society.

Elsewhere, guest chefs the likes of the renowned Paul Bocuse will provide exquisite nourishment for areas found somewhat south of the mind.

We do not wish to prod, but if this appeals to your sense of adventure, there is no better time to experience it all than now, as we depart for 165 charmed ports including the storied waters of Europe. Your travel agent has particulars, or call 1 (800) 457-8599. We look forward to seeing you on board.

ROYAL VIKING LINE
THE WORLD'S FINEST

© 1993 Royal Viking Line

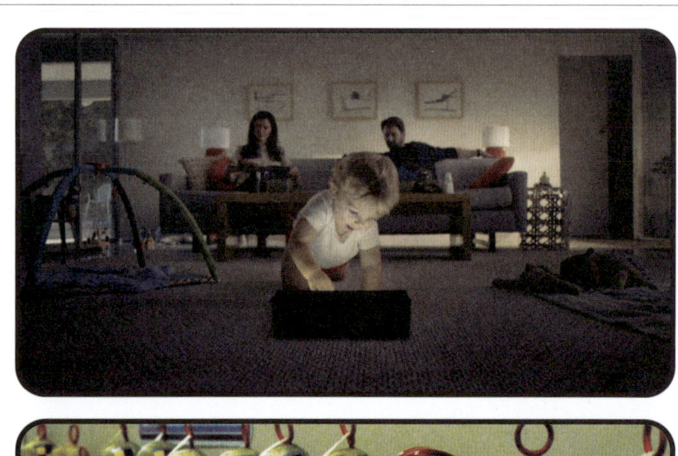
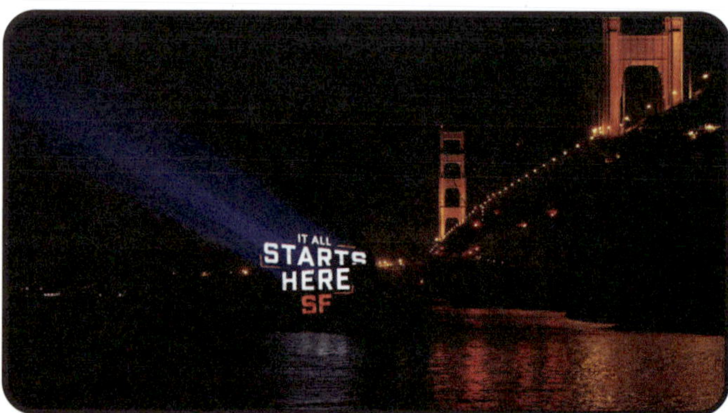

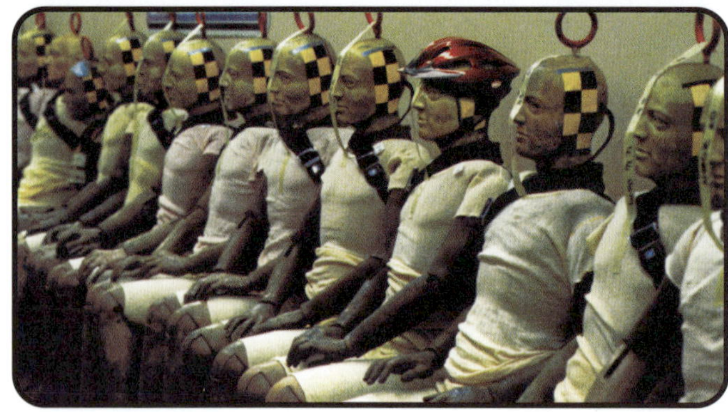
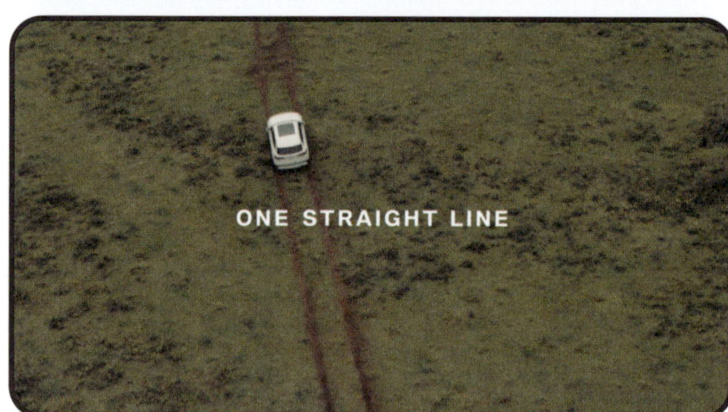

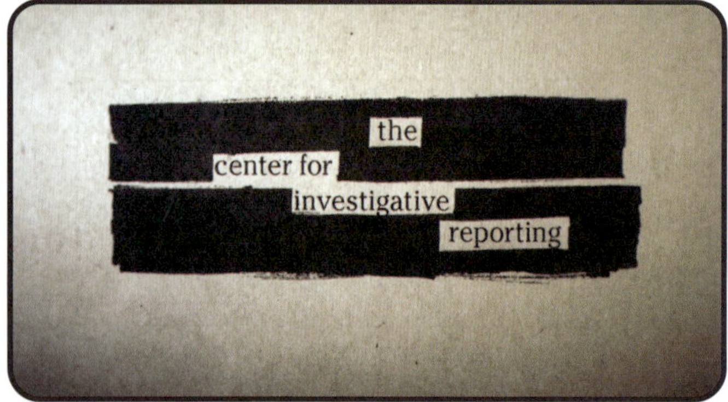

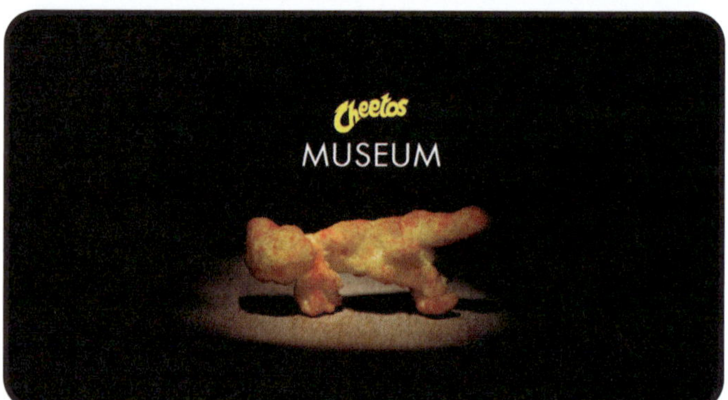

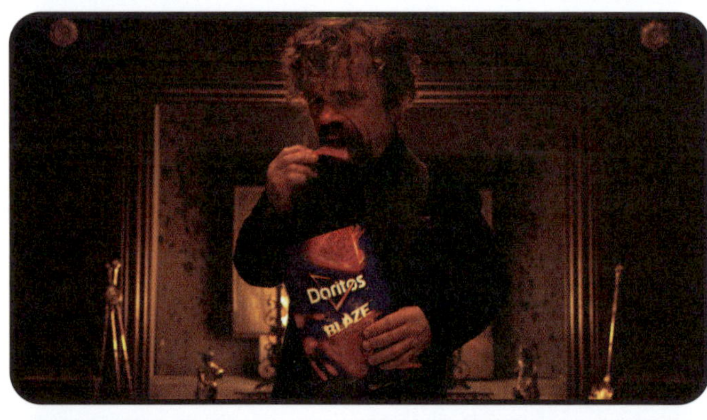

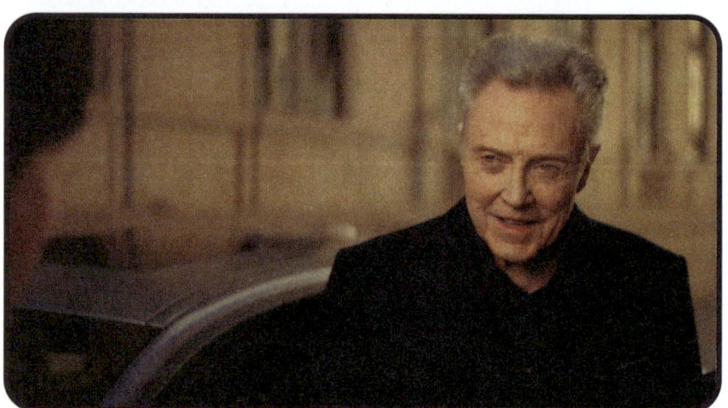

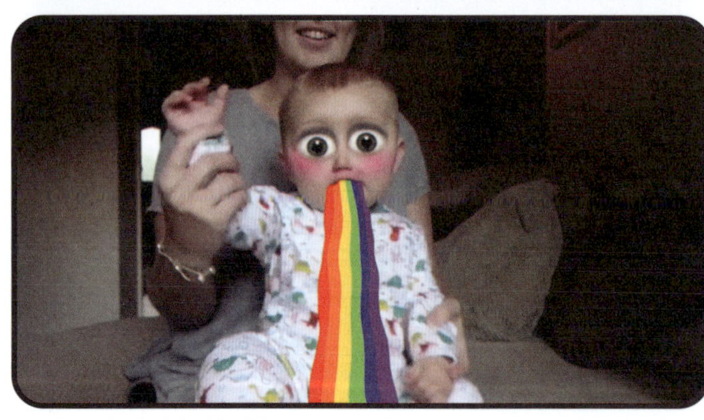
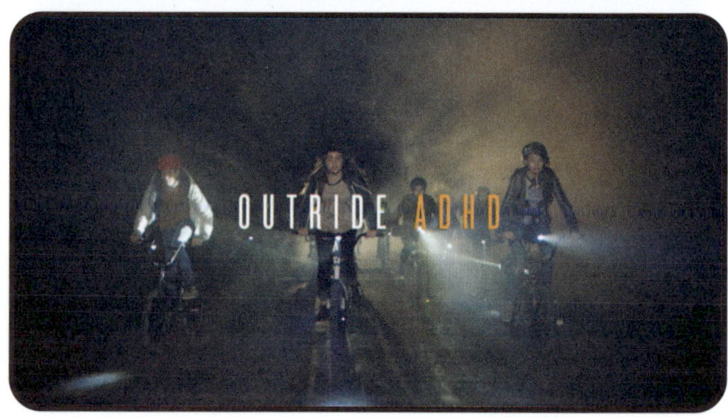

(Left to right) Adobe, Advanced SF, Bell Helmets, BMW, Center for Investigative Reporting, Cheetos, Doritos, BMW, Hewlett-Packard, Specialized

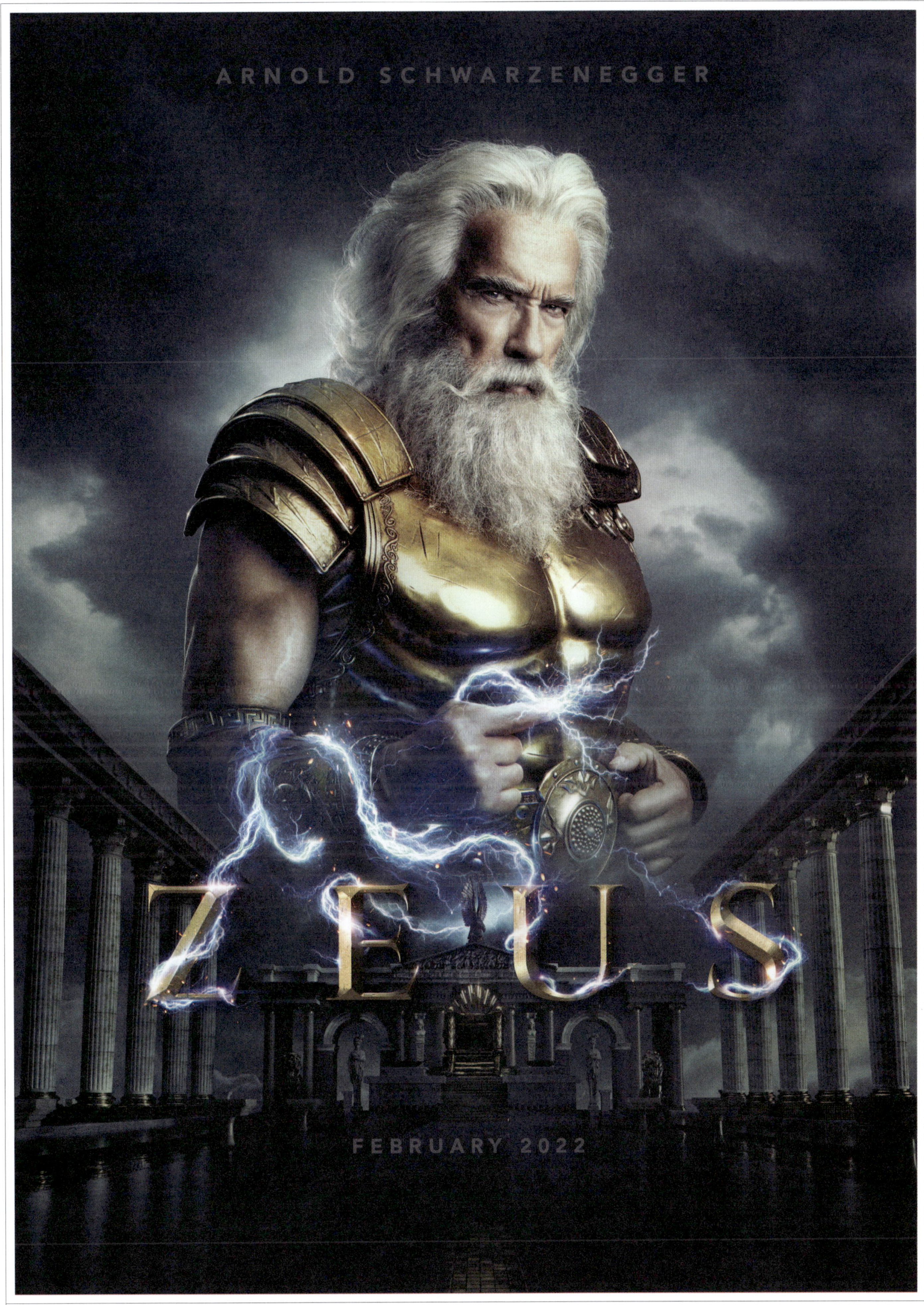

BMW Zeus Poster

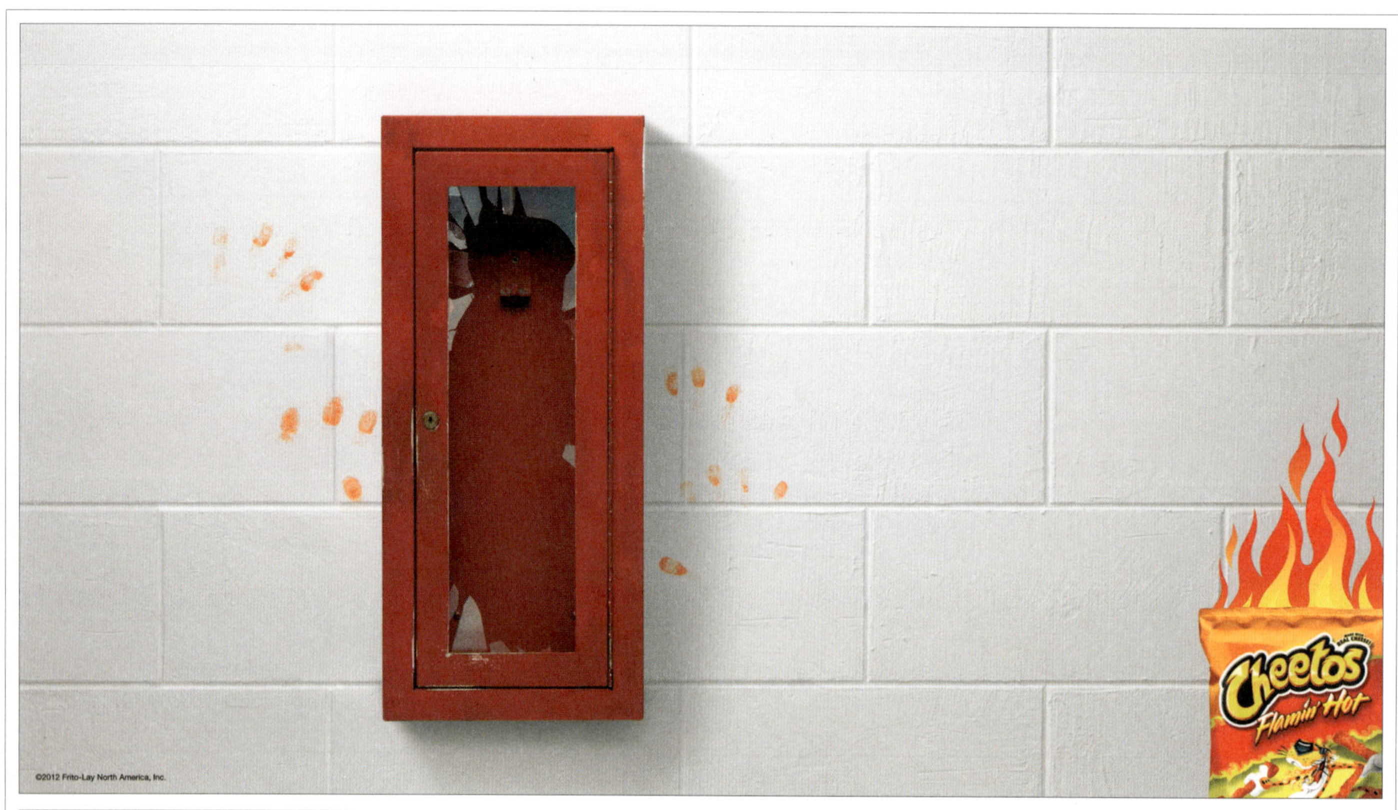

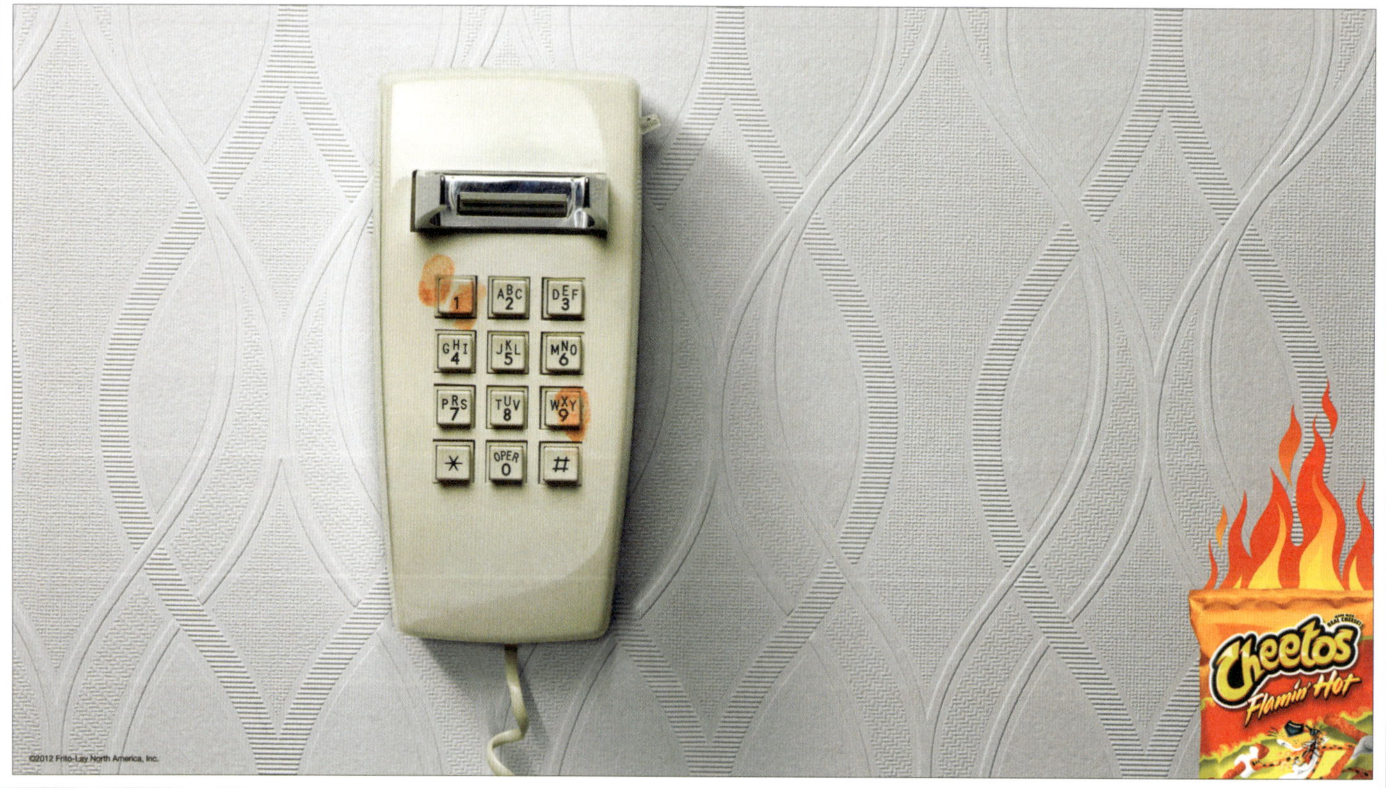

Cheetos

JEFF GOODBY AND RICH SILVERSTEIN PROVIDE
CLIENTS WITH GREAT IDEAS, AND EACH
AD CAMPAIGN THEY DELIVER IS BRANDED.

B. Martin Pedersen, *Designer & Creative Director, Graphis Inc.*

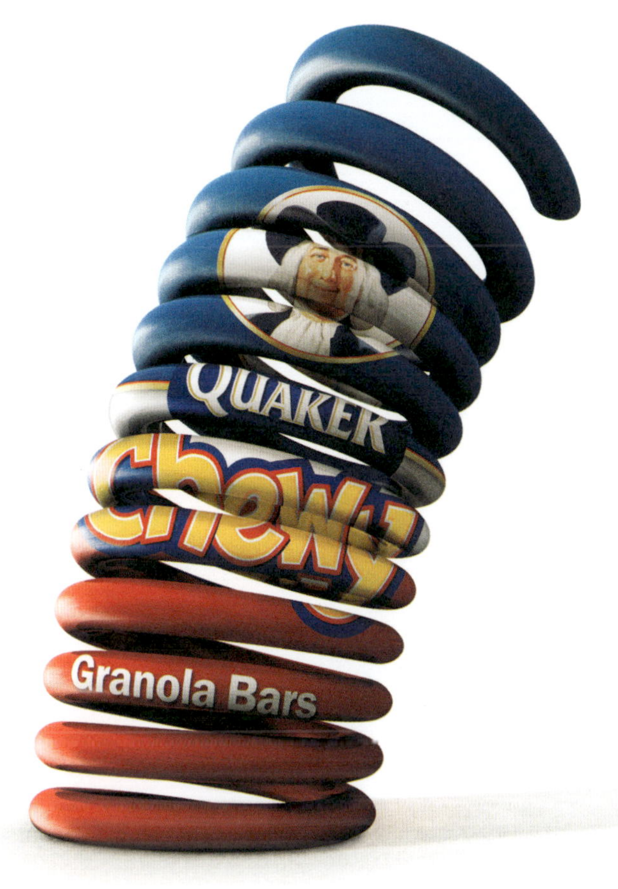

Put a little spring in your step.
With Quaker Chewy® bars made from whole grain Quaker oats.

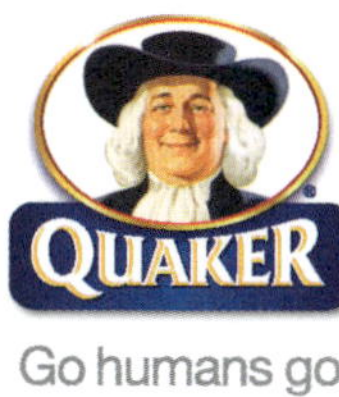

Go humans go

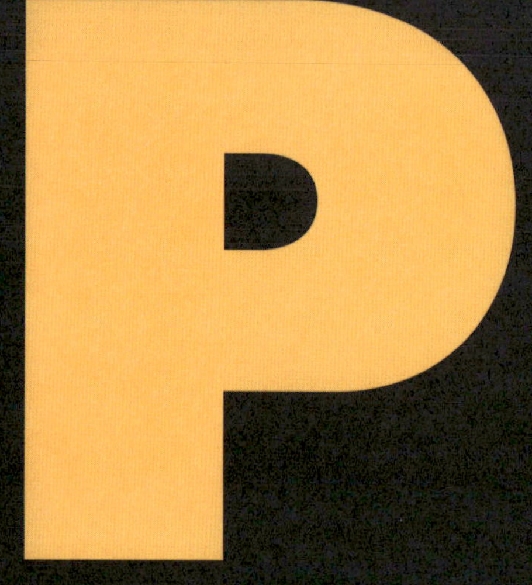

P

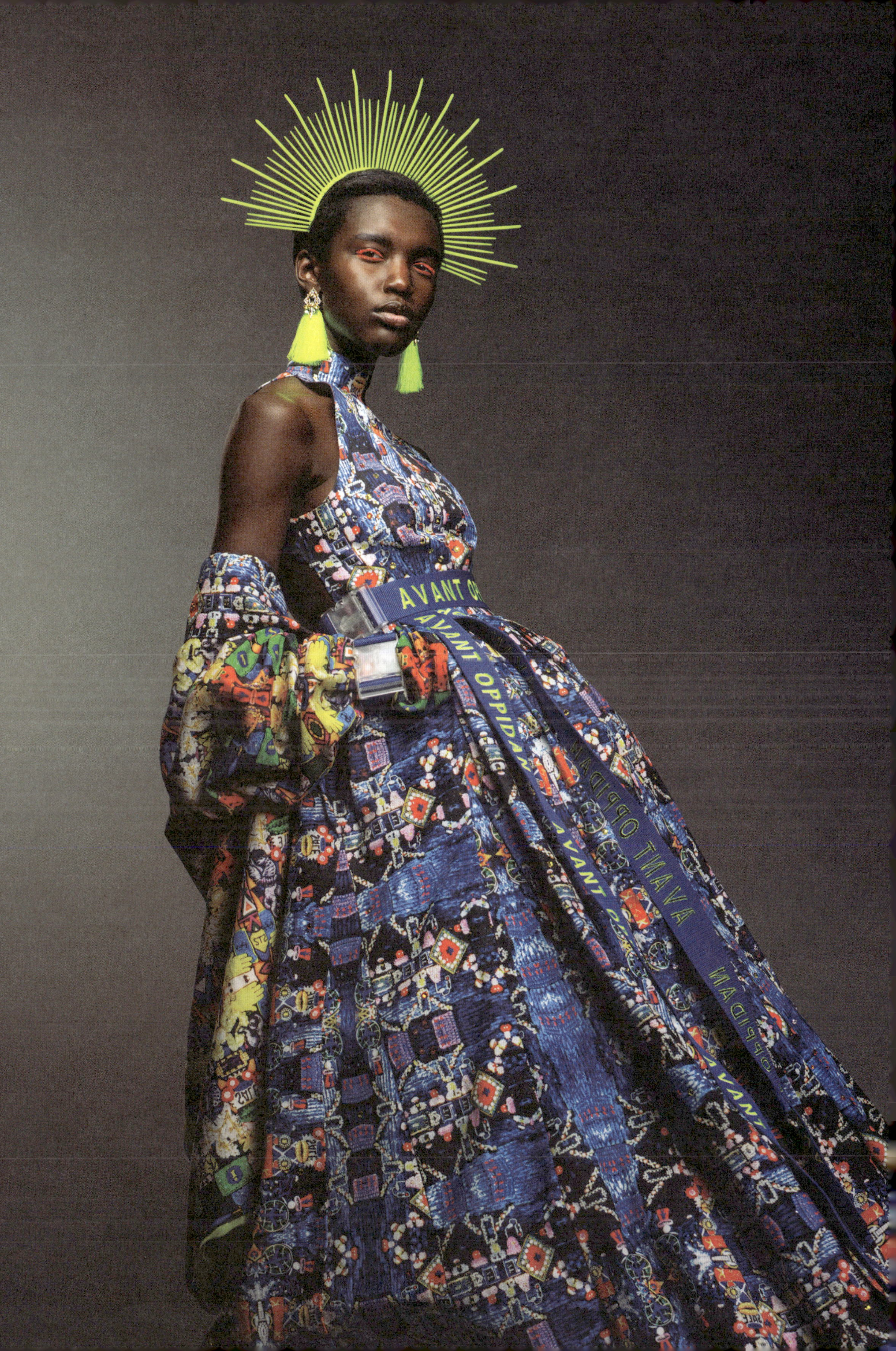
AVANT OPPIDAN
AVANT OPPIDAN
AVANT OPPIDAN

COLIN'S WILD CREATIVITY ELEVATES EVERY SUBJECT, BRINGING FAR MORE TO EACH SHOOT THAN JUST GREAT LIGHTING AND STYLE.

Victoria Will, *Photographer & Director, Victoria Will Photography*

COLIN IS MY FAVORITE HUMAN WITH A CAMERA. HIS ART IS AS SHARP AS HIS RAP GAME. HE'S AN INSPIRATION. AND HIS HEART? PURE GOLD.

Aman Shakya, *Head of Creative, DIGU*

COLIN IS ONE OF THE KINDEST PEOPLE I'VE HAD THE OPPORTUNITY TO WORK WITH. HIS AMBITION IS CONTAGIOUS AND MOTIVATING!

Michael Abrego, *Owner, AgX Brooklyn*

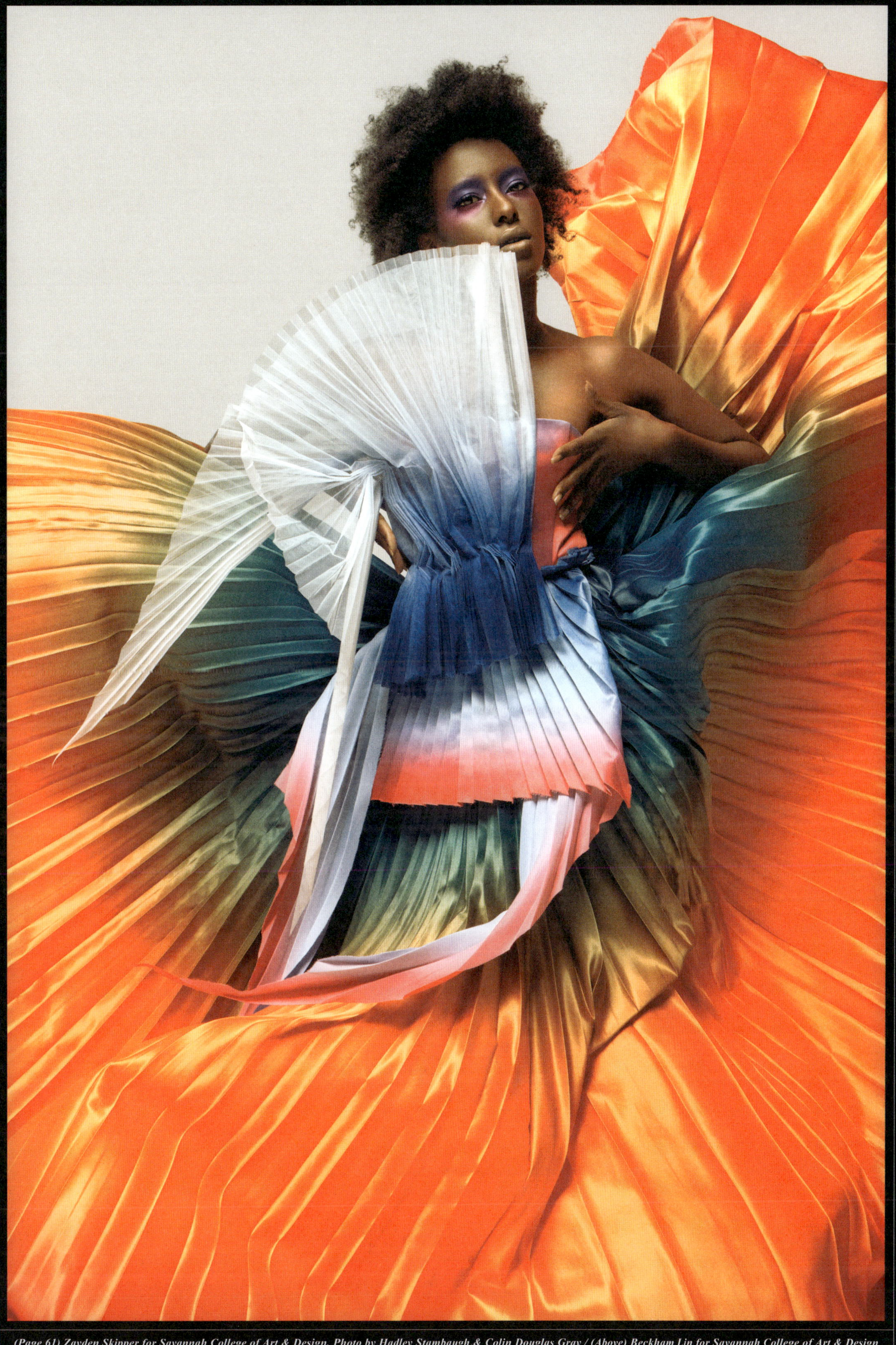

(Page 61) Zayden Skipper for Savannah College of Art & Design. Photo by Hadley Stambaugh & Colin Douglas Gray / (Above) Beckham Lin for Savannah College of Art & Design

Introduction by **Hadley Stambaugh** *CD of Photography & Photographer, Savannah College of Art & Design*

Colin Douglas Gray is a true master of his craft, effortlessly blending artistic vision with technical expertise to create stunning photographs that resonate on a deep, emotional level. Based in Atlanta, Georgia, his work is as diverse as it is compelling, from capturing the charisma of A-list actors and pop stars to documenting raw humanity. I've enjoyed working with Colin for several years on various projects, including books, fashion events, and creative endeavors. As a colleague and a dear friend, I can personally attest to his unparalleled talent and dedication to the heart of an image. Working alongside Colin on any project is an experience. He has the ability to make difficult tasks feel effortless, for you to always feel heard, and for the day to be filled with laughter. Colin's ability to connect with his subjects and capture their true essence is remarkable. His work is not just photography—it's an art form that resonates deeply, leaving a lasting impression on anyone who experiences it. Colin's creativity, professionalism, and genuine warmth make him an absolute joy to work with, and I cannot wait to see what brilliance shines from him in the future.

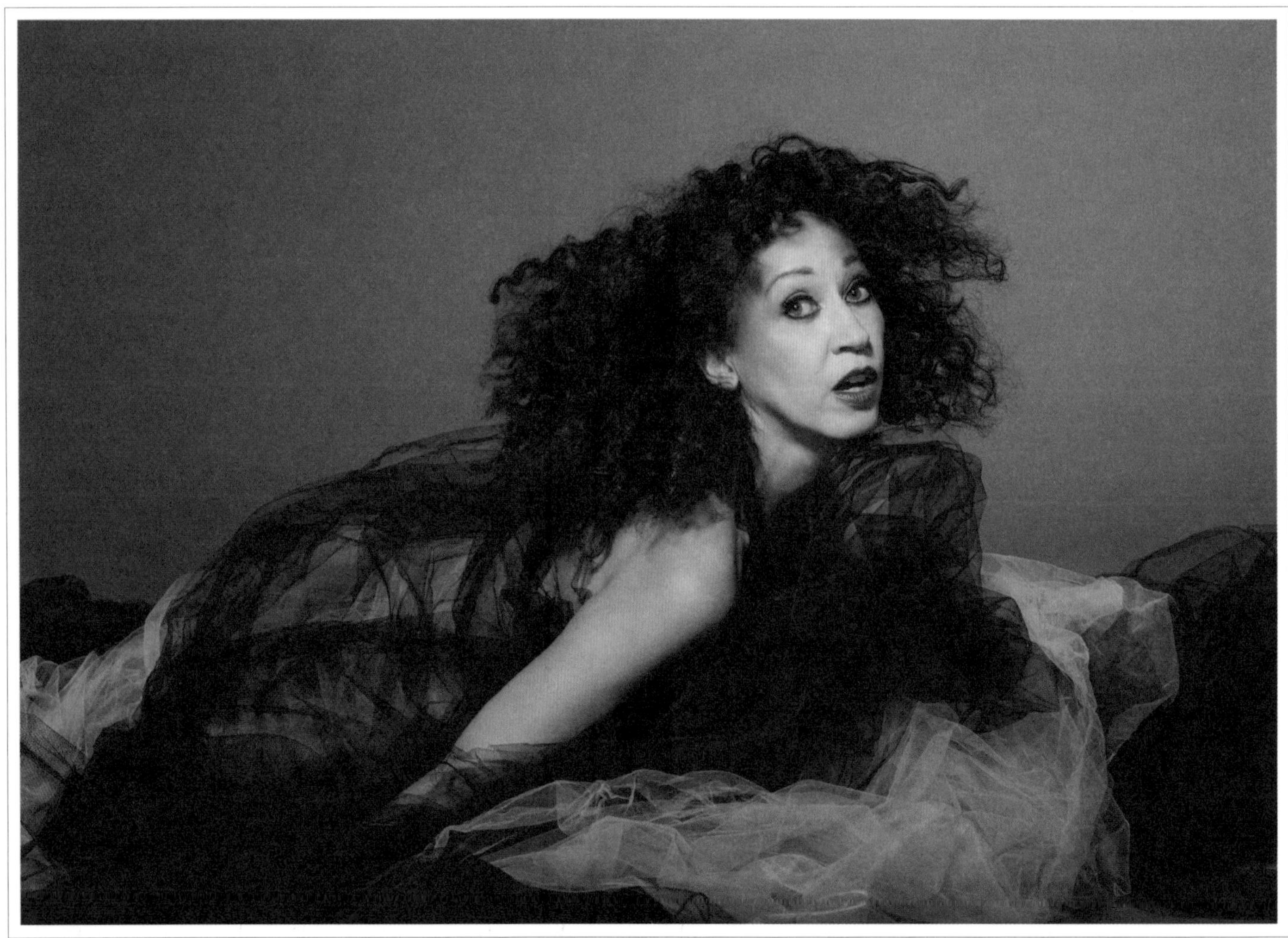

Pat Cleveland directed by André Leon Talley

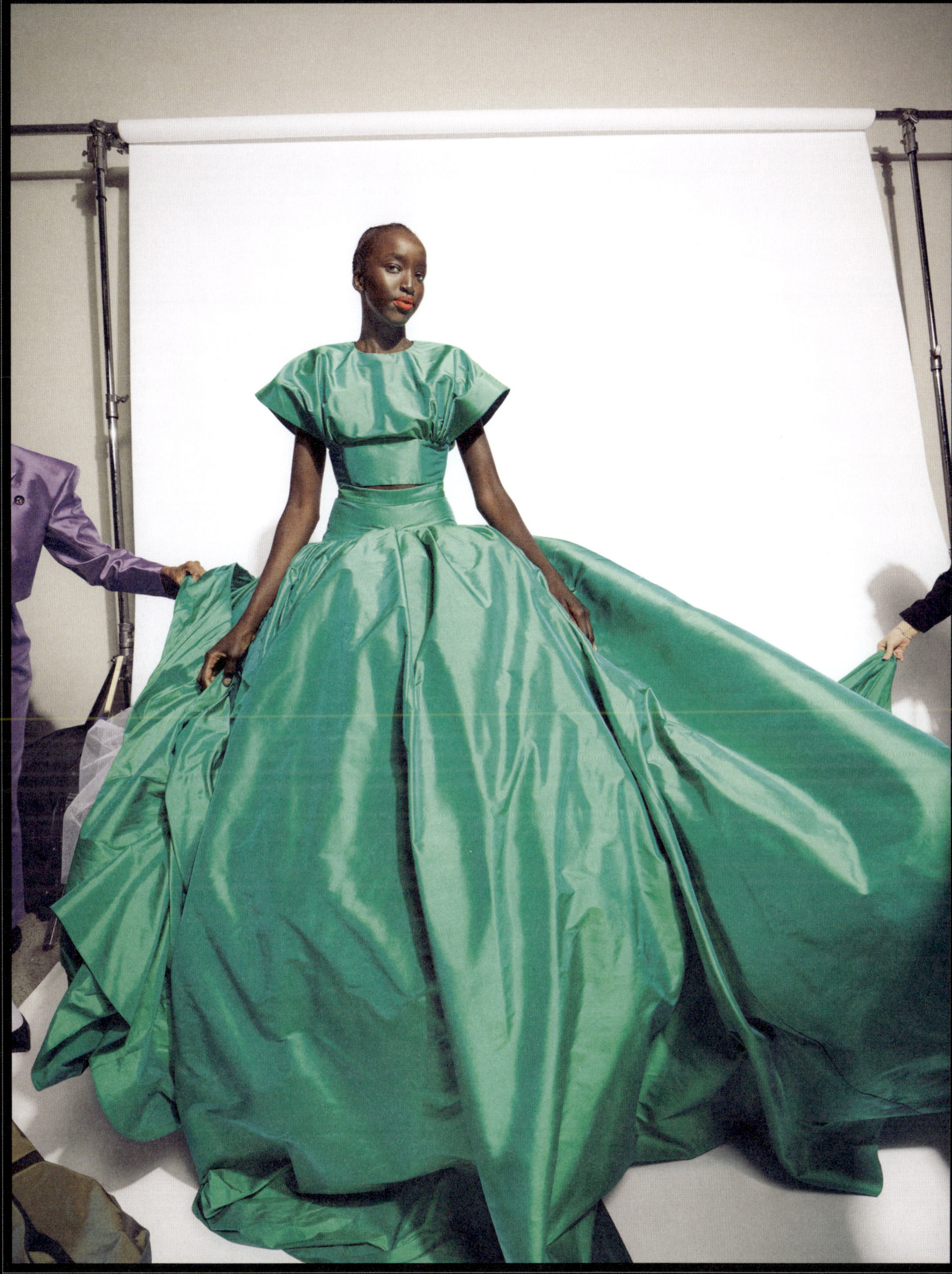

What has inspired or motivated you in your career?
My inspiration comes from constantly keeping my eyes open and scanning the world for something beautiful, intriguing, or captivating. I find these qualities in so many things… a person's face, a work of art, a grand landscape, a costume, or some other garment. I've never stopped being motivated to progress my skills and craft to best capture what inspires me.

What is your work philosophy?
As an artist, I always strive to create iconic images. I want to produce pictures that could easily be magazine covers, book covers, or posters. When photographing people, I always aim to take the best picture that my subjects have ever seen of themselves. This is next to impossible with models or celebrities who have been photographed thousands of times, but I know that I've succeeded a couple of times. When photographing someone who hates having their picture taken, it's always a great feeling when I show them what I've got and get the reaction of, "Wow, that's actually really good! Thank you."

Who is or was your greatest mentor?
Throughout my life, I've been very fortunate to have several mentors or teachers to help me further develop my craft or process. As a kid, my first favorite artist was my cousin John Fellows. He inspired me to get better at drawing. In high school, I had some excellent art teachers, starting with Julia Hoffmann, who nurtured my love of many different types of art and gave me the resources I needed to learn new things. When I first started doing photography in college, I learned a lot from going out and shooting nighttime landscapes with my friend Adam Kuehl. My professor, Catherine Cardarelli, pushed me to get better at shooting portraits, which changed the trajectory of my life. When I first moved to New York, I assisted Victoria Will and learned how to shoot celebrities. A few years later, I met André Leon Talley, who believed in me and opened many doors in the fashion world. I wouldn't be where I am today without all of them.

What about photography are you most passionate about?
All my favorite photos I've shot are of people, whether portraiture or fashion.

What is your favorite type of photography to shoot?
I love shooting portraits and fashion or a combination of the two. The personal work that I'm most passionate about is photographing cosplayers at different conventions, especially the New York Comic Con.

What is the most difficult challenge you've overcome to reach your current position?
In my younger years, I was much quieter and more introverted. I had to study and learn good communication techniques and train myself to be more extroverted when necessary. It's probably not apparent to most people, but I'm still constantly critiquing myself in that regard.

Who have some of your greatest past influences been?
Richard Avedon was the photographer whose work most connected with me as I learned photography and developed my style.

Who among your contemporaries today do you most admire?
Most of my friends are also artists, and they're the people I admire most. I've always loved a little friendly competition and know that it pushes me to improve. However, I try not to spend too much time paying attention to the work coming out of the photography industry because I also know that comparison is the thief of joy and that it's easy to get caught up in thinking that you're not doing enough. I would say that out of the more prominent photographers, the one I admire most is Jonathan Mannion, who has been creating iconic images of hip-hop artists for decades.

What would be your dream assignment?
I've got a few dream assignments…
- Be the on-set stills and key art photographer on an upcoming Star Wars film!
- Go on tour with Lil Wayne and shoot his next album cover.
- Shoot a *Vogue* cover with Zazie Beetz, Natalie Portman, or Yara Shahidi!
- Create a cover for André 3000 when he decides to bless us with one more rap album.

Who have been some of your favorite colleagues or clients?
Many of my best friends are either former or current colleagues, so that list would be far too long if I named everyone. My favorite job was being on staff at MTV. I got to shoot hundreds of celebrities and musicians, including some of my favorites of all time, like Snoop Dogg and Kendrick Lamar. That job was terrific because there were no rules, and my only directive was to be creative and do what I do best! I currently have a great job working at the Savannah College of Art & Design, and my favorite part is photographing the guests and exhibitions at SCAD FASH, the college's museum for fashion and film.

What are the top things you need from a client to do successful work for them?
The most important things for me to do my best work are trust, a great team, and creative freedom.

You shoot a variety of people, ranging from big-time celebrities to everyday folk. Is the shooting process the same for everyone? How do you work with all these different types of people?
No matter who I photograph, I try to treat them the same way. I try to stay friendly, humble, and complimentary, making everyone feel like superstars. Many people think that photographing celebrities must be challenging, but honestly, I think it's the easiest thing because they're so used to being in front of the camera and know their best angles, how to pose, and how to take direction. As long as I've got my equipment set and concept ready, it's hard to get a bad shot.

In your opinion, who is the most famous person you've shot so far?
Snoop Dogg or Arnold Schwarzenegger.

You also do motion work. How did you get into doing motion, and how did it influence your photography?
Long before I started doing photography, I shot and edited videos and loved it so much. In college, my focus changed to stills, and I've made a career of that since, but I've never stopped shooting motion and would love to start doing that more professionally.

What do you consider your greatest professional achievement so far?
In 2012, I got to photograph fashion icon André Leon Talley for *South* magazine, and he loved the portrait so much that he hired me for several jobs afterward, from fashion editorials to documenting New York Fashion Week with him. He trusted me

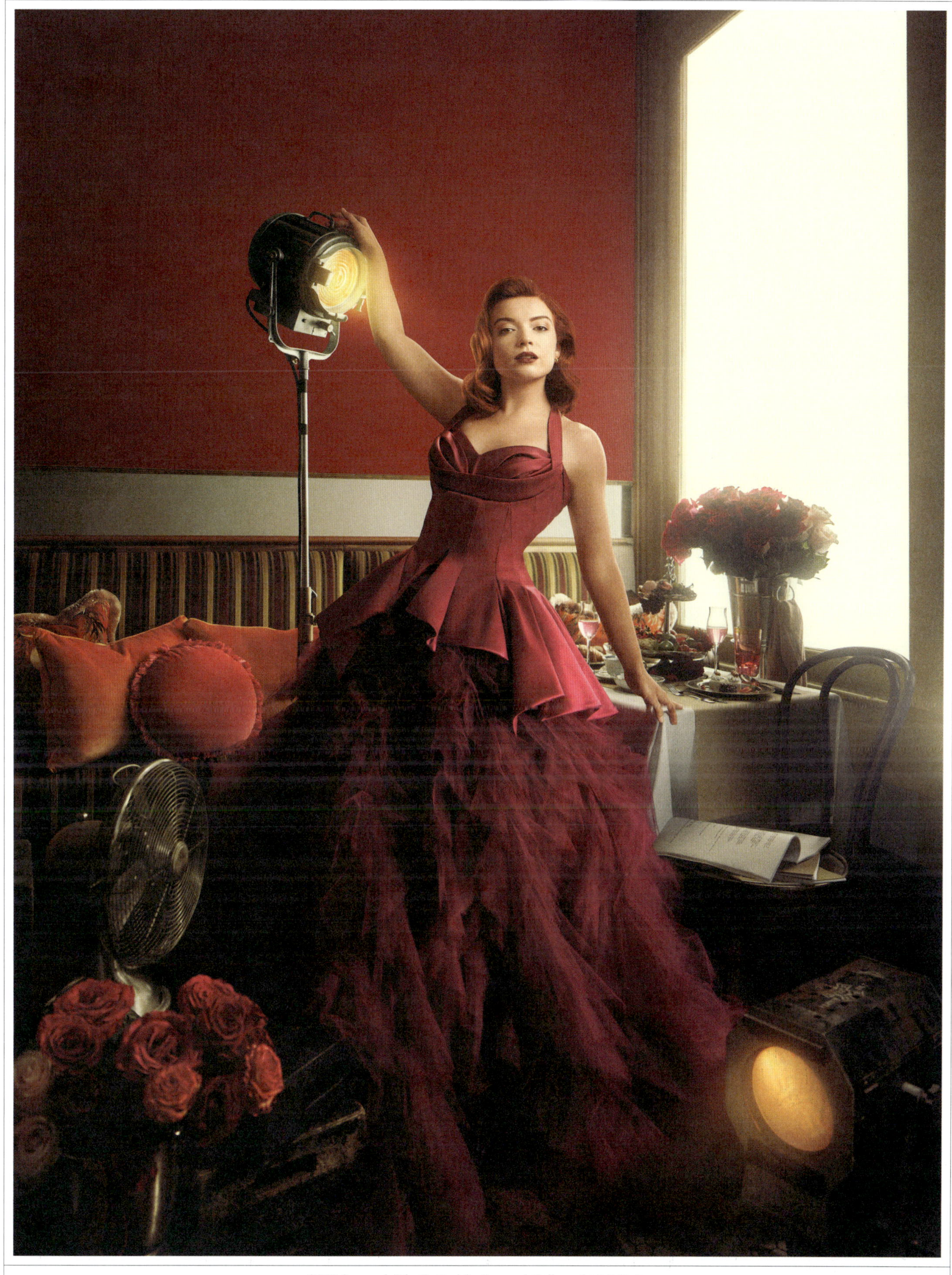

SCAD Savannah Film Festival for Savannah College of Art & Design

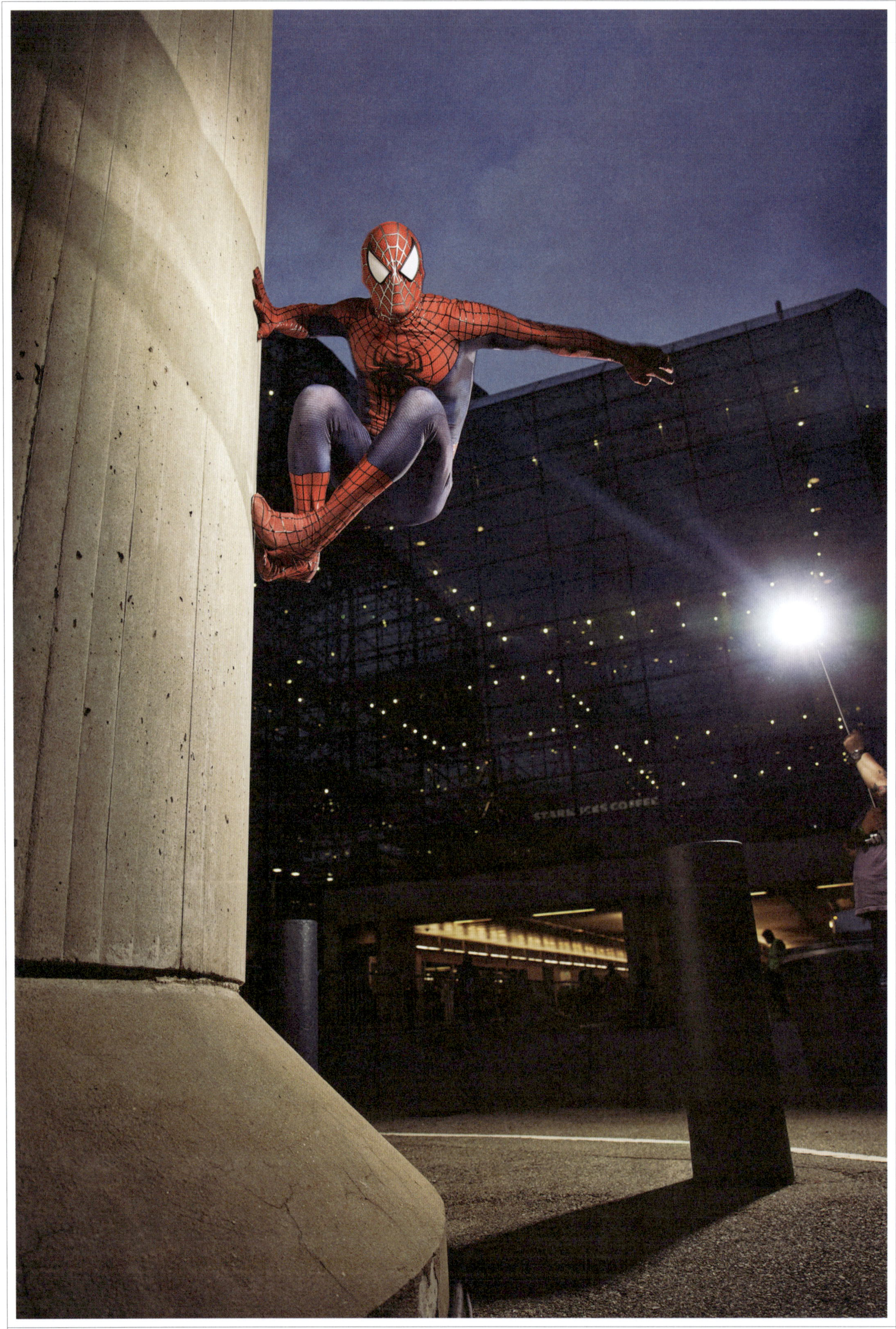

New York Comic Con 2021

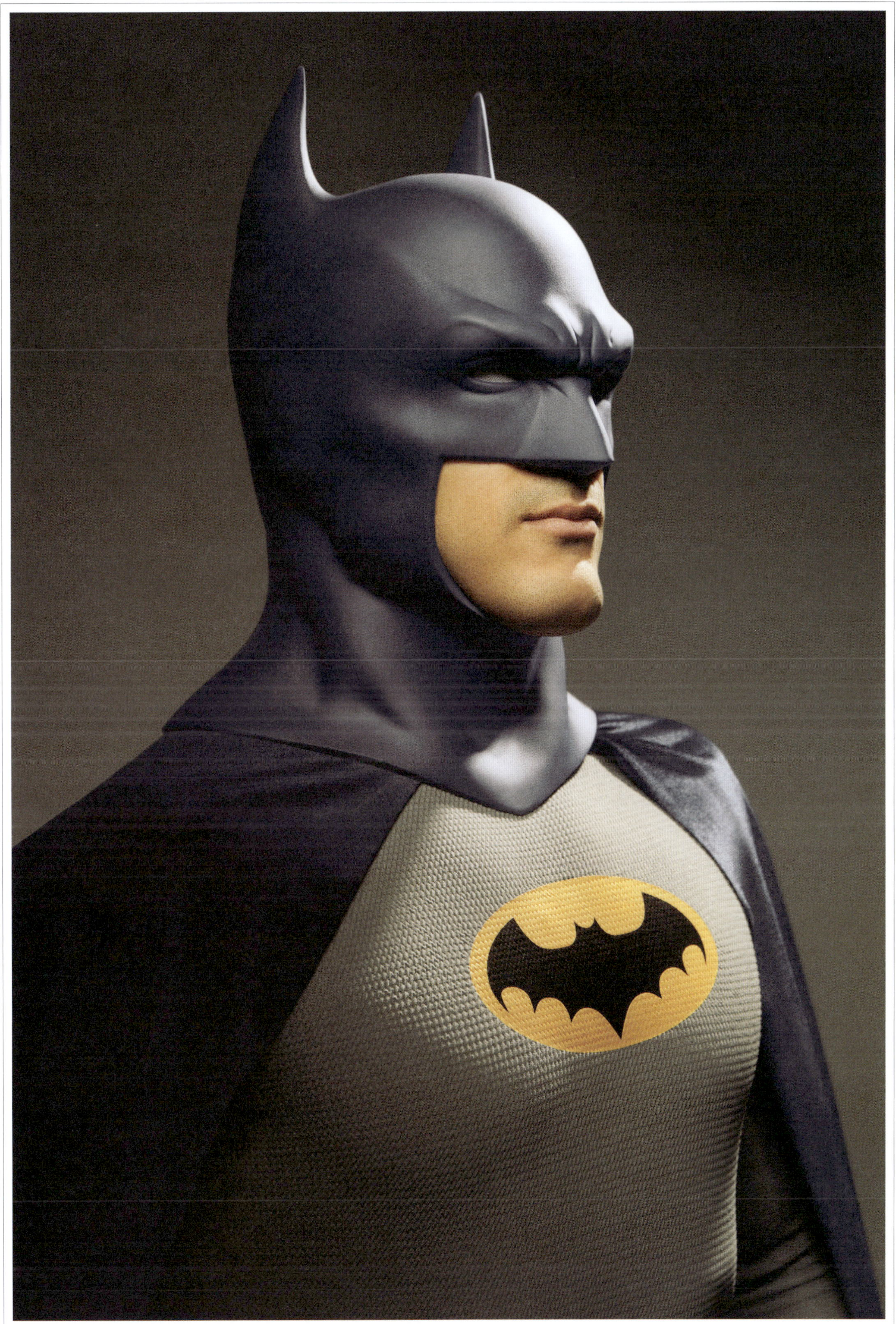

New York Comic Con 2019

enough to photograph his mother's funeral service; it meant so much to me to be asked to shoot such an emotional event for him. When it was time for his memoir to come out, he chose my image out of thousands of options, and I thought that was the biggest honor, especially now that he has passed on.

According to your website, you pride yourself on being able to "connect with a subject within moments and reflecting that connection back through the final image." How do you think you achieve that?
You generally get what you give, so I try to be as genuine as possible, smile, give honest compliments, and be enthusiastic about wanting to get the best photograph of my subject that I can.

What about your work gives you the greatest satisfaction?
As an artist, my four favorite days of the year are shooting at the New York Comic Con in October. I've been shooting portraits of the incredible cosplayers there for over a decade. The first few years, it was assignments for MTV. Years later, in 2017, I was hired by ReedPop, the company that puts on the event, to produce their posters for their marketing campaign. However, for most years, I shoot it for fun because I love it so much. Thanks to Dallas Raines and Mike Abrego of AgX Brooklyn, I'm lucky to have an amazing team that volunteers each year to help capture incredible images. I wouldn't be able to do it without them. I hope to publish a book of all the best photos we have shot within the next year or two.

What part of your work do you find the most demanding?
The photography part of being a professional photographer is easy for me, but the business end has always been a struggle, from pricing to marketing to logistics. I plan to take some business courses so that that part is not so overwhelming. I also spend far too much time sitting in an office in front of a computer when I would rather be out in the world taking pictures and exploring.

What professional goals do you still have for yourself?
There is still so much I dream of accomplishing in my career. Right now, my number one priority is to get my New York Comic Con book together and have it published by a major art book publisher like Phaidon, Rizzoli, or Taschen. I'm also working on prepping my online print shop. Past that, I would love to travel much more than I do, and I also want to photograph large-scale movie sets as well as magazine and album covers.

What advice do you have for students starting out today?
As a student, it's obviously essential to use all of the resources and teachings you can to learn and develop your craft, but even more important than that is to work on your interpersonal skills, make friends, and learn how to work as part of a team. Almost every job I've ever gotten has been through a friend or past client who knows they can trust that I'll be easy to work with and do my best to deliver an excellent product. If there is a job that I'm not able to take on for one reason or another, I will always try to pass that on to a friend of mine. Another important thing is to find what you are most passionate about shooting, but also learn how to shoot as much other stuff as you can because to make it as a professional, you will often have to shoot things that may not be your ideal assignment. It's extremely rare that somebody will graduate and immediately get to start shooting for their dream clients. It could take years or decades. Lastly, on any job, the number one priority is delivering what your clients want, but if you have the time, it's always great to shoot something exactly as you personally would like to do it. Ideally, your client would love those even more and hire you to shoot more like them. If not, you at least have new work for your portfolio.

What interests do you have outside of work?
I love being outside, walking, hiking, swimming, rollerblading, and skateboarding. My main creative endeavor outside of work is making music. My aim is to have a few completed songs by the end of the year. The visual arts are great, but I love music more than anything!

What do you value most in life?
Above all else, I value my friends and family the most. I wouldn't be here without them.

What would you change if you had to do it all over again?
If I had a do-over, I probably wouldn't have left my $1,200 a month, rent-stabilized apartment in Manhattan to move to California. I would love to move back to NYC someday, but I know I'll never find a deal like that again.

Where do you find inspiration?
I find inspiration literally everywhere. There aren't enough days in the week to be able to do all of the creative projects that I wish I could.

How do you define success?
Being able to make a living doing photography is obviously a huge success, but I find the most joy in it when I capture or create images that I love or impress me.

Where do you see yourself in the future?
I dream of being sponsored by Canon or Profoto, being hired by clients to shoot photos and videos all over the world, and spending time with my loved ones. Eventually, I want to put out an album!

How do you balance your work with your personal life if there is a distinction between the two?
As a creative, it can be hard to separate my work and personal life, and the two often blend together. I definitely struggle with doing work that I feel is strictly for the money. Making a good living is obviously very important, but the dream is to regularly be doing projects you would want to shoot even if you weren't getting paid for it. When that's the case, I feel that differentiating the two can be less critical. Either way, I definitely need a lot of downtime, whether with friends or recouping in solitude.

In what ways do you see your field changing over the years?
As long as photography has been around, technology has become better and easier to use, making it more accessible. Now, anyone with a good phone can take great pictures. This definitely has both pros and cons. It's great that so many people can easily create, document, and share their lives or what inspires them. The hardest part is that now that everyone is a photographer, the competition for jobs is even greater, and companies expect more while budgets get lower and lower. AI is also changing the game, and images that are almost indistinguishable from actual photographs are already being created. I definitely think it's important for all creatives to learn the tools of this quickly advancing technology.

Colin Douglas Gray www.ilovecolingray.com

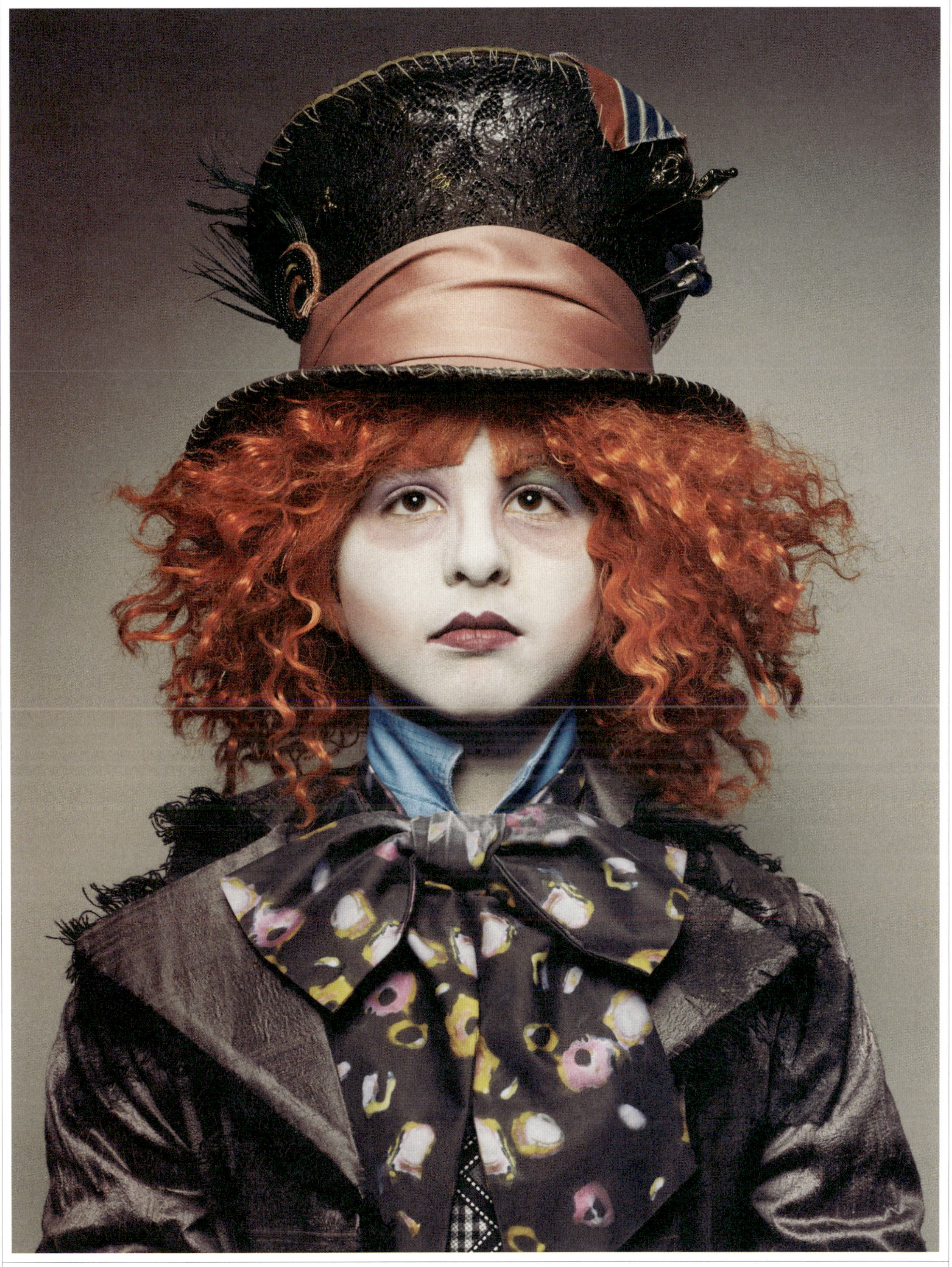

New York Comic Con 2014

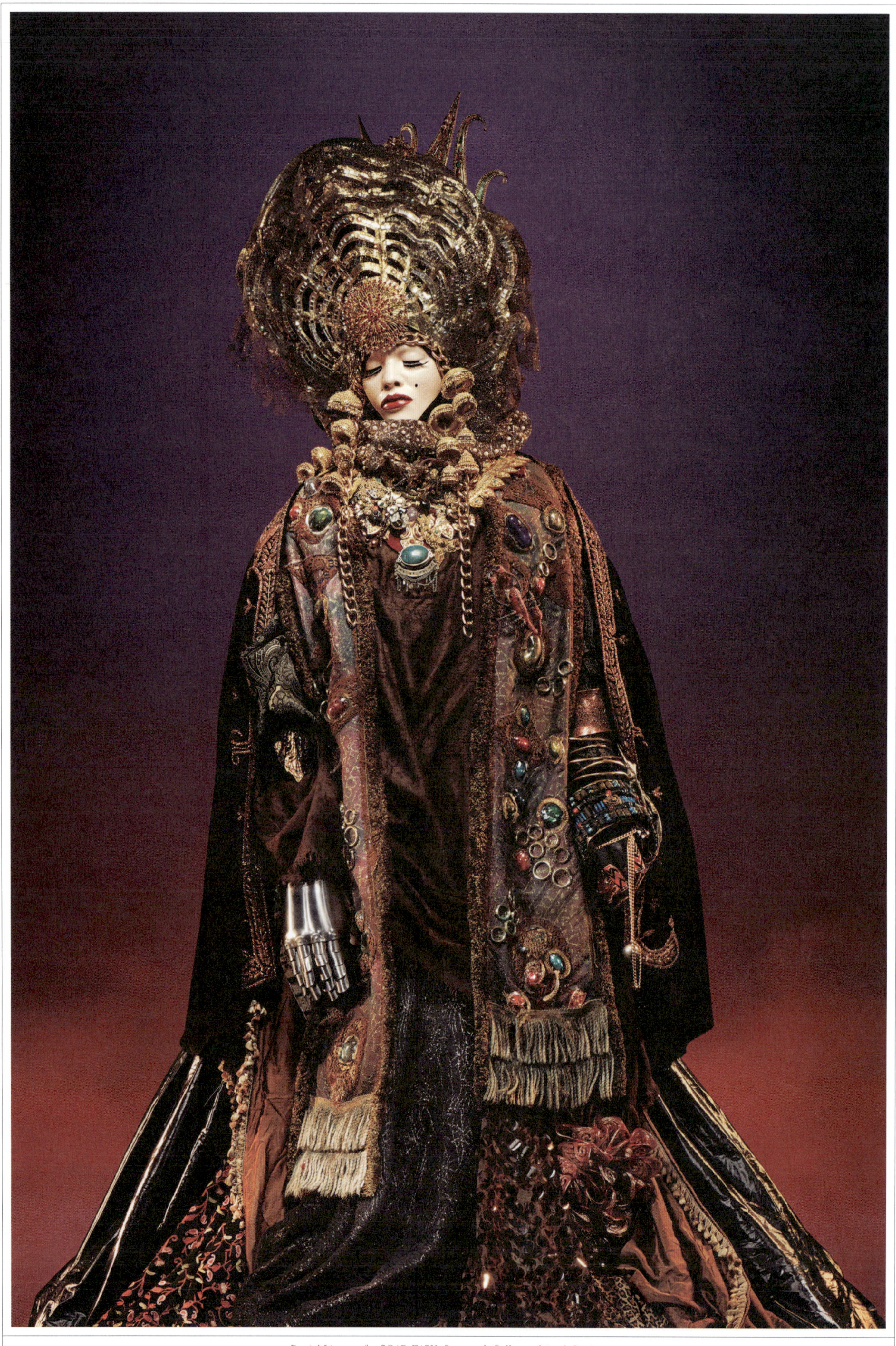

Daniel Lismore for SCAD FASH, Savannah College of Art & Design

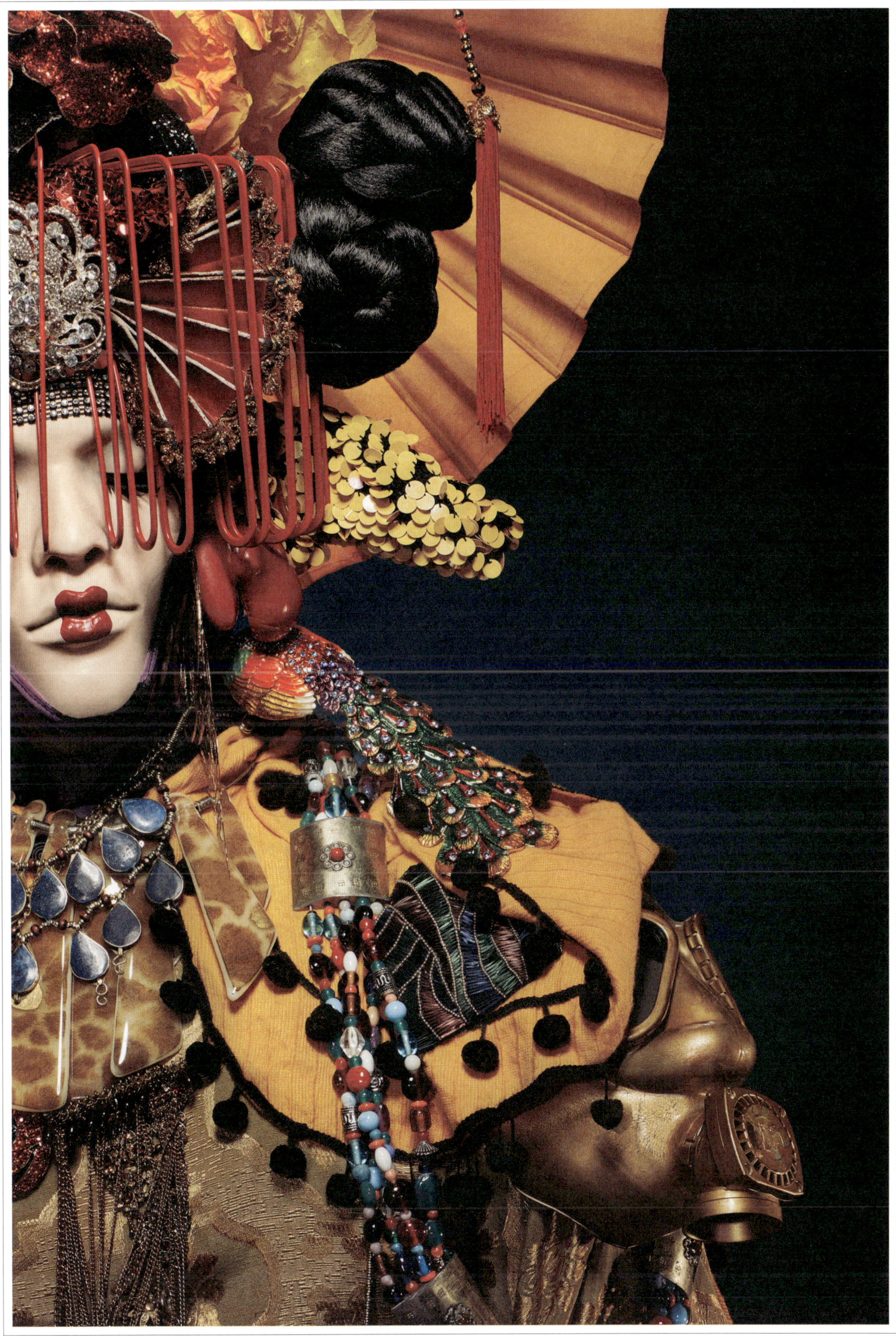

Daniel Lismore for SCAD FASH, Savannah College of Art & Design

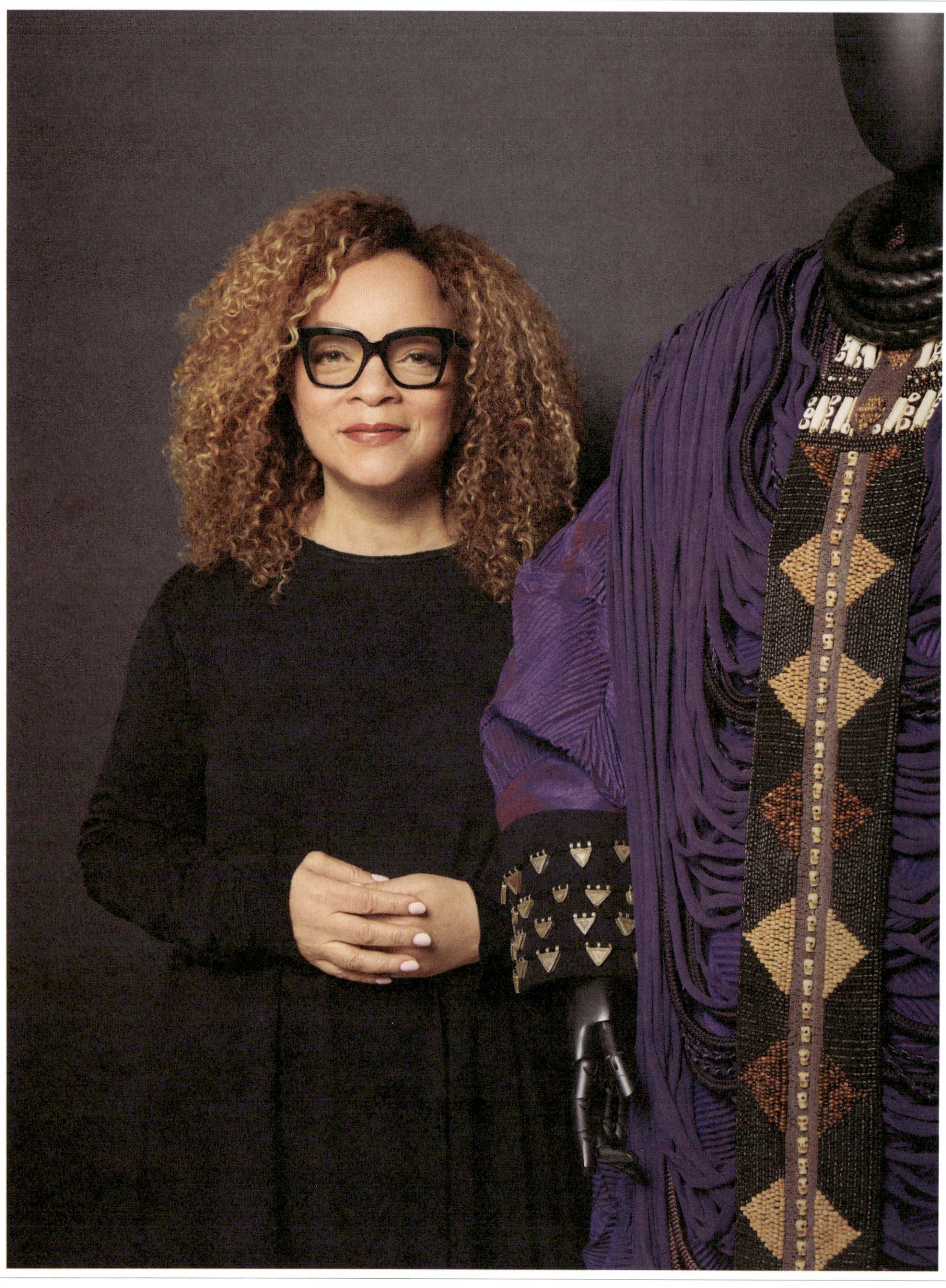

Ruth Carter for SCAD FASH, Savannah College of Art & Design

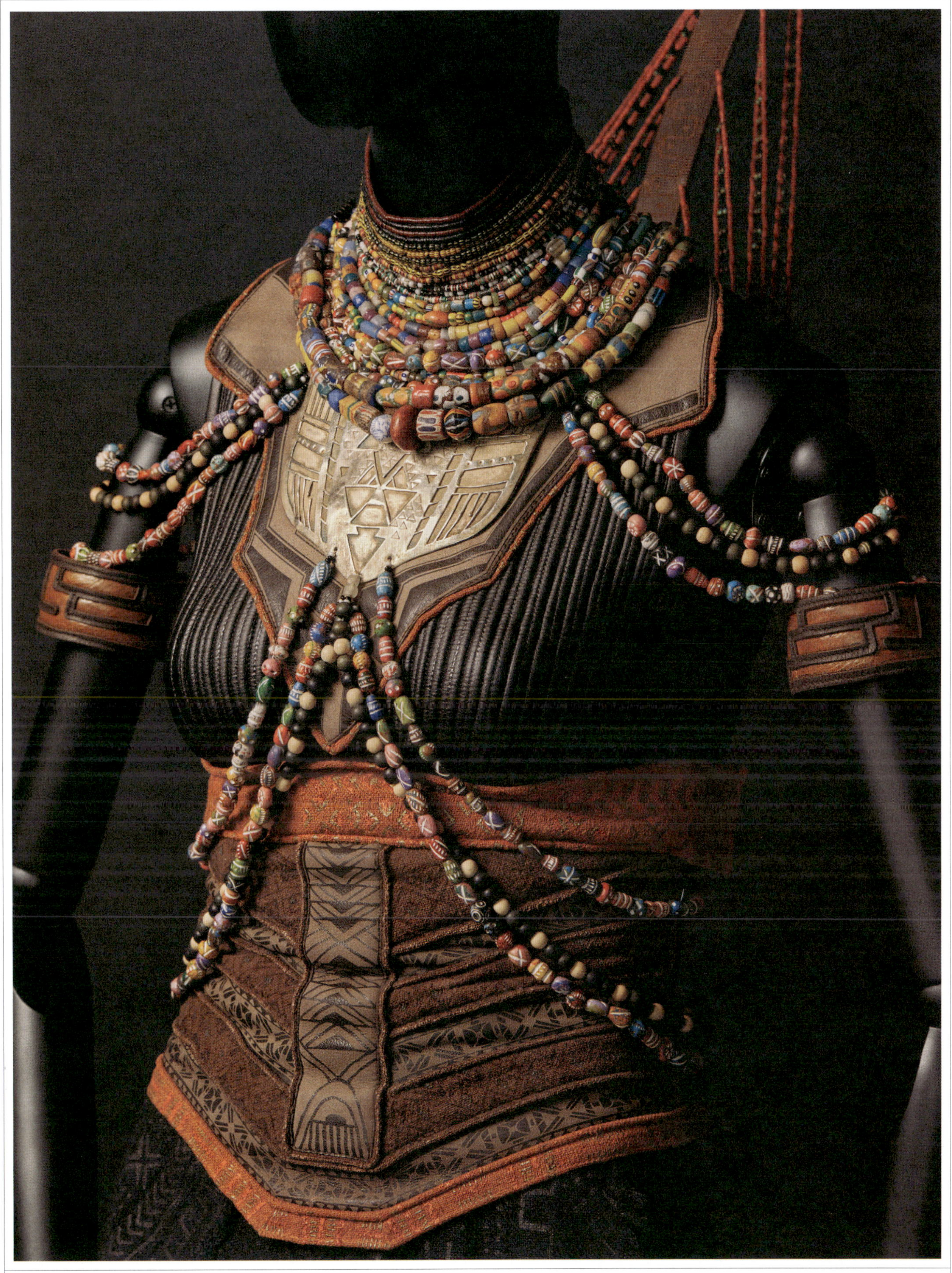

Ruth Carter for SCAD FASH, Savannah College of Art & Design

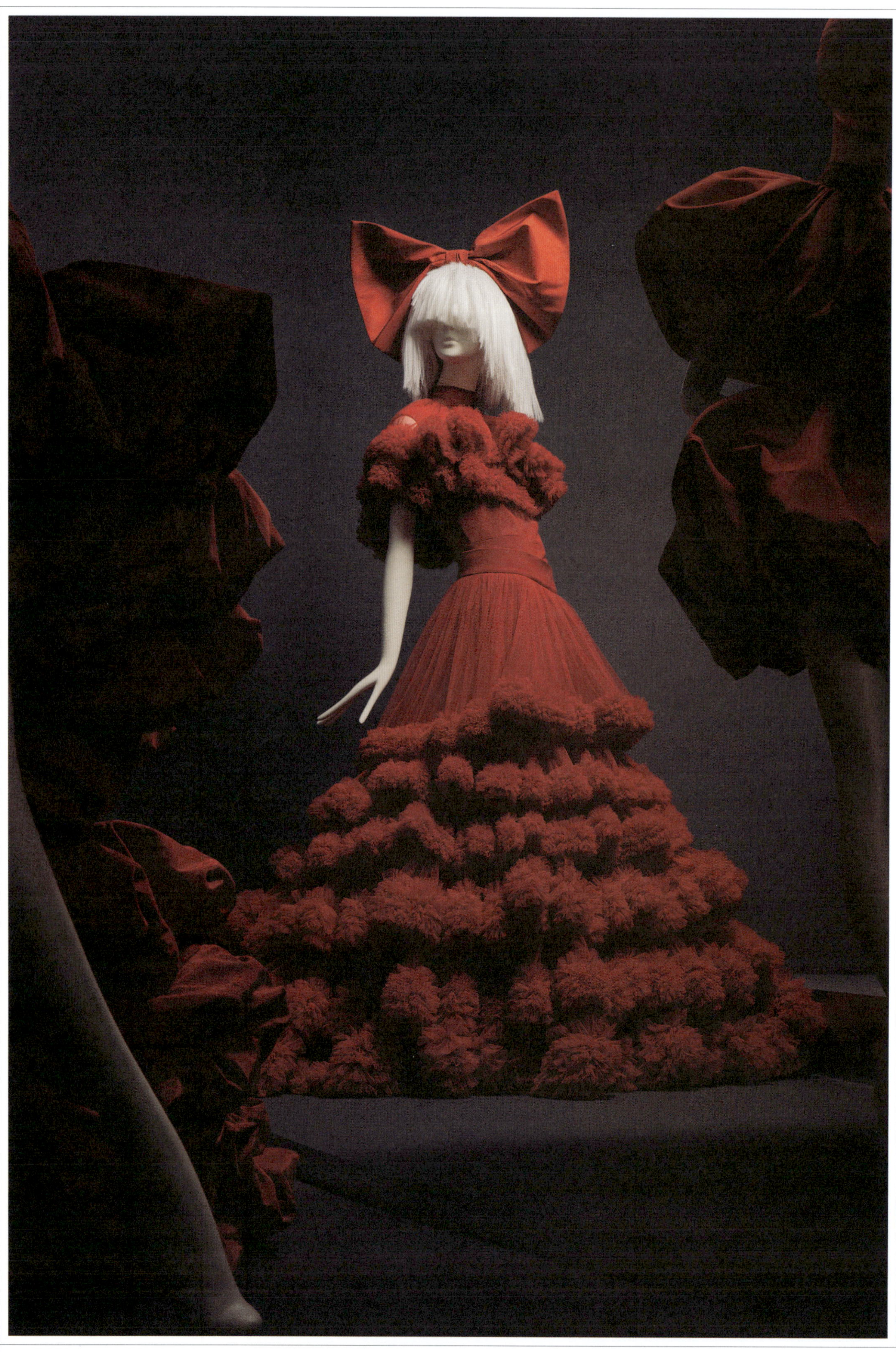

Christian Siriano for SCAD FASH, Savannah College of Art & Design

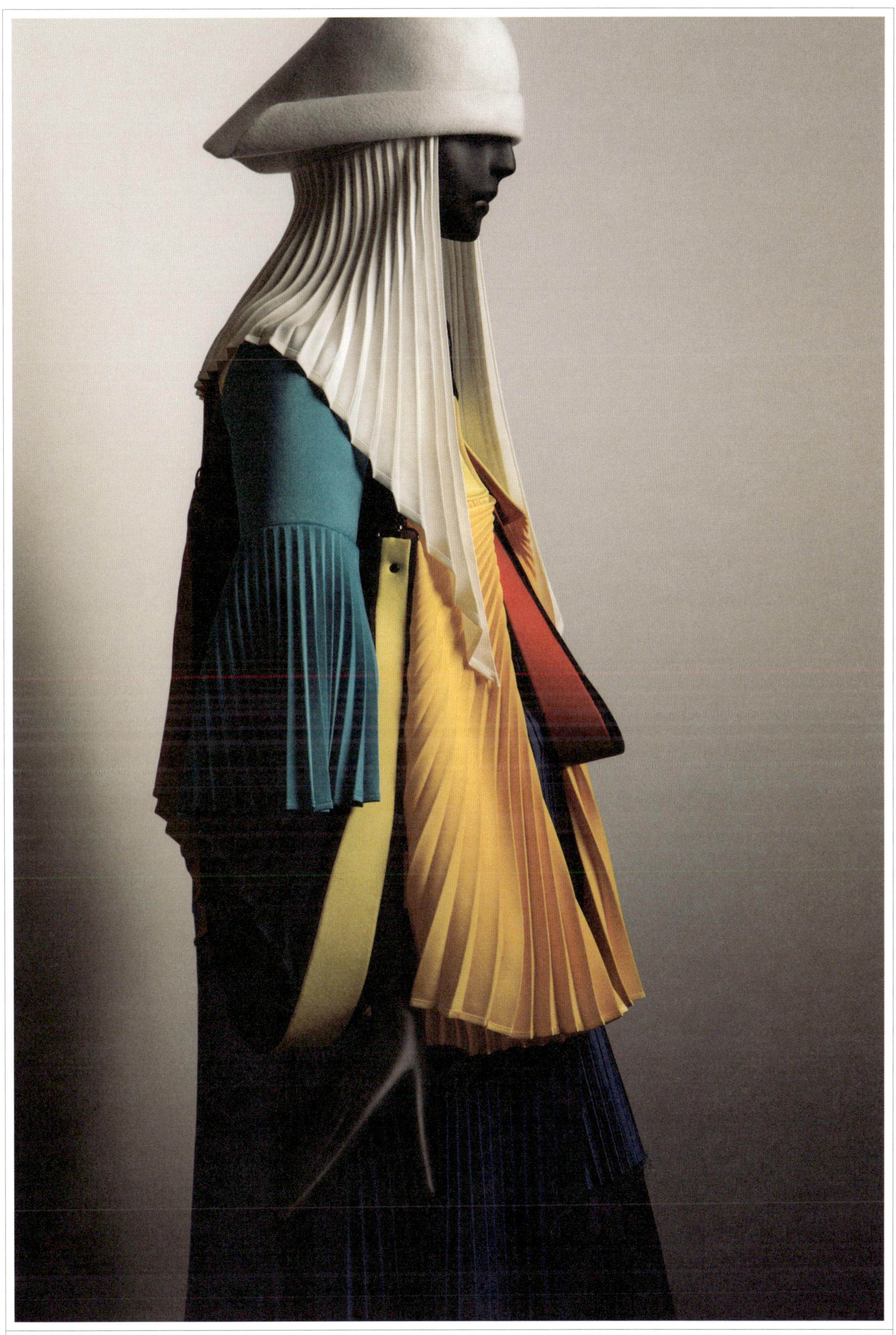

Robert Wun for SCAD FASH, Savannah College of Art & Design

Lindsay Siu: Perfect Yet Fleeting Moments

LINDSAY HAS AN AMAZING EYE FOR CAPTURING THE AUTHENTICITY OF A MOMENT IN TIME. HER LIGHTING IS EXQUISITE, HER VIBE IS CHIC, AND SHE IS THE NICEST PERSON I HAVE EVER MET.

Meredith Ott, *Founder, Alice Blue*

LINDSAY SIU'S IMAGERY LIVES AT THE INTERSECTION OF FINE ART, COMMERCIAL, AND EDITORIAL PHOTOGRAPHY, WHICH IS POSSIBLE BECAUSE OF HER PERSONAL, THOUGHTFUL, AND INTELLIGENT APPROACH TO EVERY PROJECT.

Art Streiber, *Photographer & Director, Art Streiber Photography*

IT HAS BEEN A PRIVILEGE TO SHOWCASE HER REMARKABLE PHOTOGRAPHY ON ATEDGE'S ROSTER. SHE IS A HIGHLY SKILLED ARTIST WHO MASTERFULLY BLENDS LIGHT, BALANCE, MOOD, AND ATMOSPHERE.

Francesca Galesi, *Director of Photography, AtEdge*

LINDSAY'S WORK IS A MASTERCLASS IN VISUAL STORYTELLING. AS AN ASIAN WOMAN, HER PERSPECTIVE IS INVALUABLE AND NECESSARY —BRINGING NUANCE, EMOTION, AND COMPLEXITY TO FINE ART AND COMMERCIAL PHOTOGRAPHY.

Sima Kumar, *Founder, Sima Says*

LINDSAY SIU IS AN EXCEPTIONAL PHOTOGRAPHER AND STUDIO PARTNER. HER HARD WORK, ARTISTIC VISION, AND DEDICATION MAKE EVERY PROJECT A SUCCESS. SHE'S A REAL PROFESSIONAL AND A JOY TO BE IN BUSINESS WITH!

Clinton Hussey, *Photographer & Co-founder, Elastic Studios*

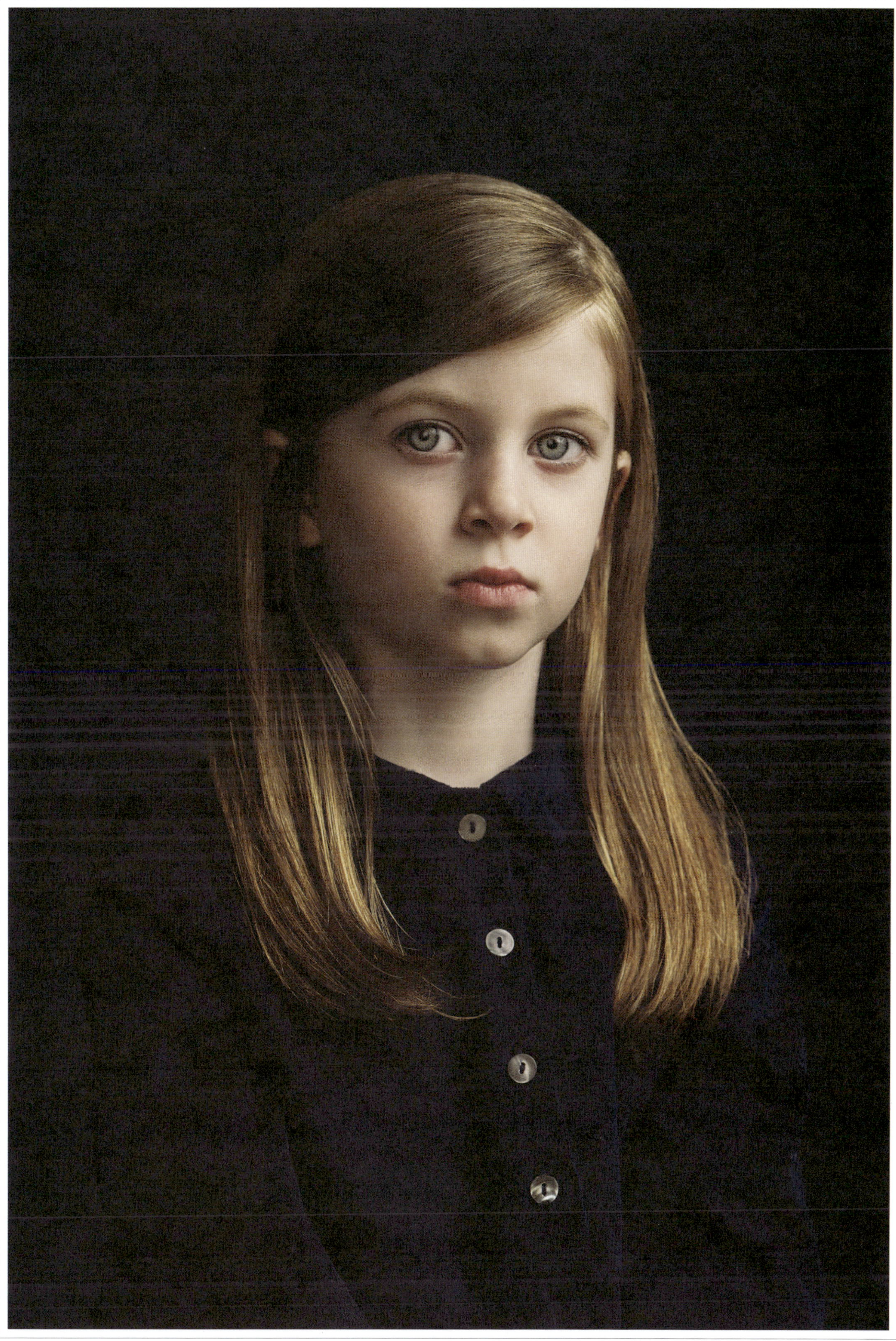

Lia, Little Women Series

As a Chinese Canadian who also makes an impact from behind the camera, I greatly admire Lindsay's contribution to representation in media—not only in her dedication to shooting diverse subjects and themes but also in allowing us to view people through an authentic lens that honors who they are. It's clear she takes her role and responsibility seriously, as it's woven with care throughout her impressive portfolio. I had the pleasure of witnessing firsthand how she connects with everyone on her set intentionally and effortlessly. Her incredible skill with the camera is rivaled only by her ability to make people feel seen, both in front of the camera and by experiencing the stories told through her masterful work.

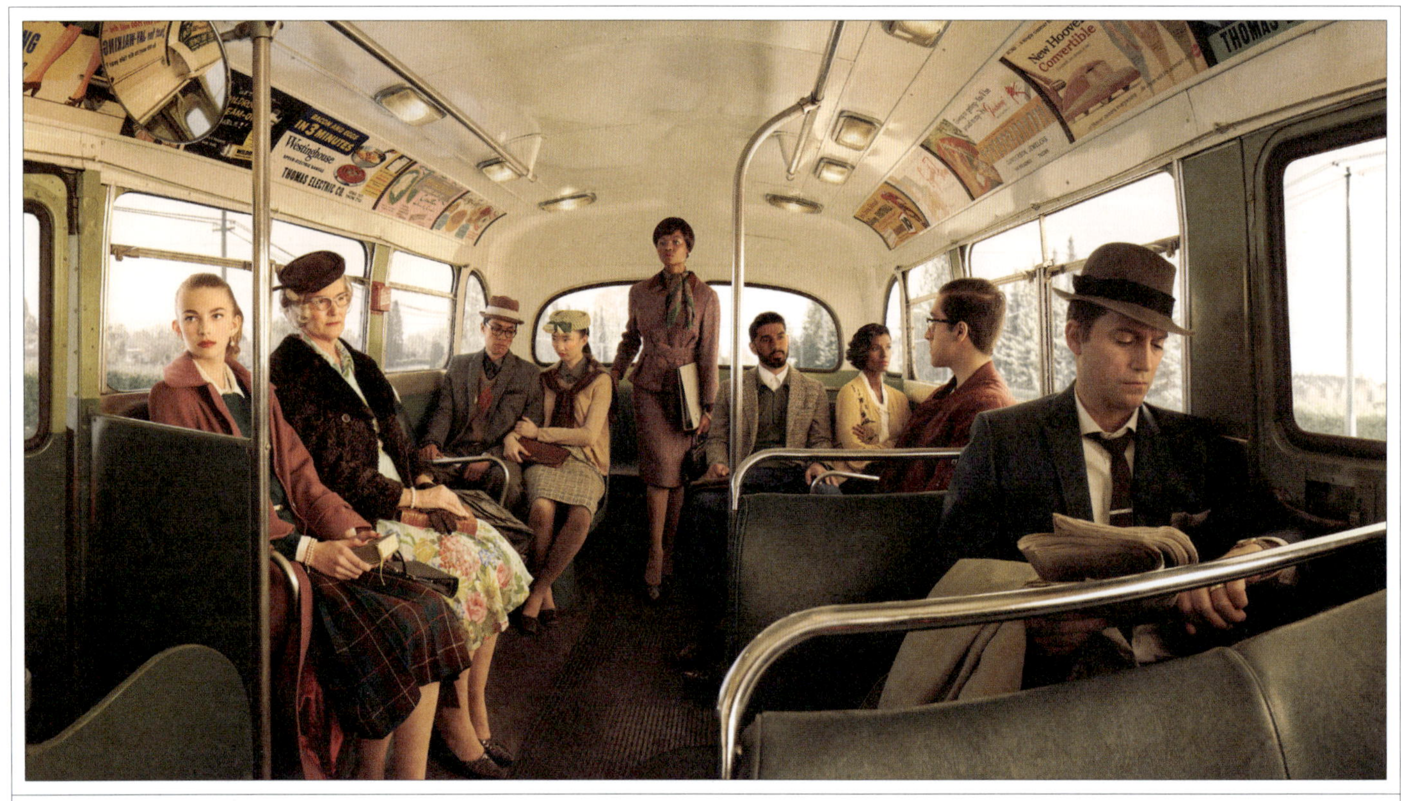

Public Transit 1957

Q&A: Lindsay Siu

What inspired you to have a career in photography?
I have always been someone who likes to imagine, make, and create. Growing up, I was initially drawn to painting and drawing, and I also loved writing and reading poetry. In high school, I enjoyed theater and improv.

It wasn't until university that I really got into photography. It was so different from the other studio art classes I was taking at the time. I loved the mix of the technical and the creative, as well as the immediacy of the results in the darkroom. I also enjoyed the experimentation. I remember incorporating my parents' old black-and-white negatives with the film I had just shot and developed.

My degree was in art history, and I was really inspired by the work of Jeff Wall. I loved the cinematographic style of his large-scale work, especially the clever nods and references to history and his social commentary. I also loved Cindy Sherman's "Untitled Film Stills" series and the portraiture of artists such as Diane Arbus, Richard Avedon, and Herb Ritts.

I was also obsessed with pop culture. I devoured fashion magazines and was drawn to the ads and celebrity portraiture. Work that mixed fine art with high commerce seemed like a fascinating challenge to me.

What about photography are you most passionate about?
It may sound cliché, but I'm passionate about capturing those perfect yet fleeting moments in time. I pored over photos when I was a kid—old family photos, *National Geographic*, fashion magazines, or posters in *Teen Beat*. Those images are burned into my mind. The idea of creating imagery that lasts as a memory of a person at a particular moment in their life feels important and meaningful.

Who is or was your greatest mentor?
Many people have influenced me and my work. In the early part of my career, I was lucky to work as a digital tech for celebrity photographer Art Streiber, who has since become a mentor and friend. He has greatly influenced my career and its trajectory, and I've learned so much from him about lighting, technical problem-solving, managing relationships, and how to lead.

My family was also a huge influence. I grew up in a home with no shortage of books, where curiosity was encouraged, and I was taught that learning never ends.

What is your work philosophy?
I love working hard, problem-solving, collaborating with

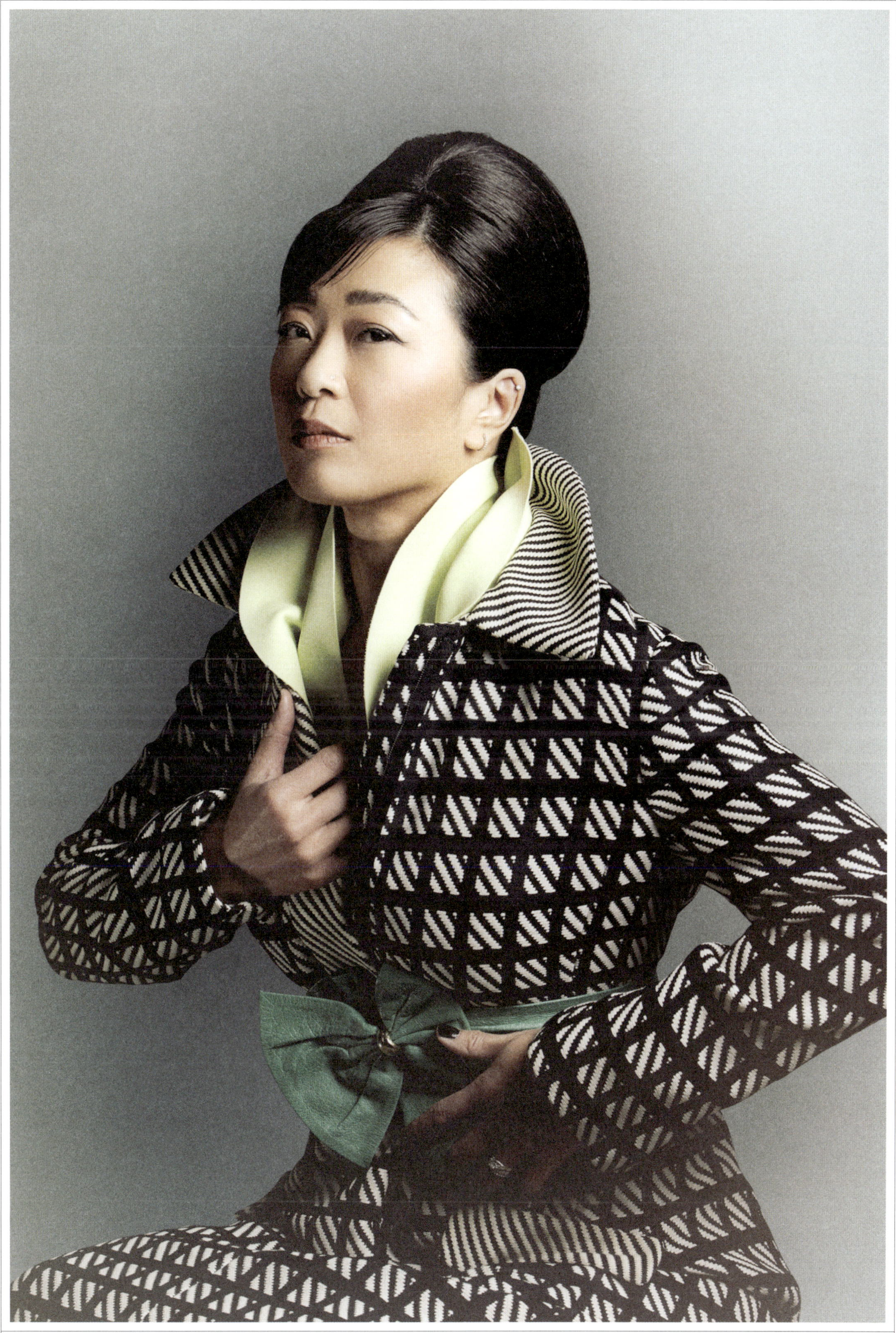

Black and White Trench Coat, Self-Portrait Series

talented people, and paying attention to details. I genuinely believe in treating others well, caring for your crew, and surrounding yourself with good people.

Most of my shoots require the efforts of many people, from digital techs and lighting assistants to my agents and producers, wardrobe stylists, hair and makeup, prop-makers, and production designers—and my clients, of course! My best work has always been a result of great collaborations with people I respect and care about.

Whose work among your contemporaries today do you admire?
There are so many incredible photographers I could name! Off the top of my head: Julia Fullerton-Batten, Brooke DiDonato, Ramona Rosales, Dan Winters, and Art Streiber.

You're primarily known for your portraits. What draws you to this type of photography?
I spent my formative years living in a relatively small town in Saskatchewan. As a first-generation Chinese Canadian, I was an obvious minority. Though I couldn't articulate it then, I constantly yearned to see someone who looked like me or had similar life experiences in mainstream culture. But my feeling of otherness also made me interested in hearing other people's stories. I'm really inspired by people and learning about their experiences in the world. Having the opportunity to sit with someone, capture their photo, and share their story can be an incredibly bonding experience.

*You also shoot a lot of entertainment work.
How is this different?*
Entertainment jobs come with a different set of logistical challenges. You're working around the (very tight) schedule of the talent and the production, often on their working stage. Creatively, there are all the typical aesthetic aspects to manage, but when it comes to celebrities, there is a need to instill confidence and trust. That means using my people skills to work with big and occasionally intimidating personalities. For me, it's about reading the emotional room. It's about finding a way to relate and engage with my subjects while inspiring and managing my crew and having open and fluid dialogue with my clients, all at the same time. It's about getting the very best that I can out of everyone in a very limited period of time.

Ultimately, the goal is to help tell a story by connecting with my subjects and directing them to bring a personality or character to life.

Who have been some of your favorite colleagues or clients?
I won't name names because there are too many, and I'd hate to leave someone out. I've been fortunate to work with many great, talented people. Generally speaking, I was initially drawn to advertising photography by the energy of the creatives. I appreciated how thoughtful, diverse, and funny most of them were. I really appreciate those with a great sense of humor.

*What are the top things you need from a client to do
successful work for them?*
In advertising, great creative concepts, strong visions, and clear briefs win the day. When I know and understand the client's and agency's overarching objectives and the parameters of the production, it informs the decisions made along the way (lighting, mood, compositional approach, etc.) that will bring it to life and make it great. I aim to always stay true to my vision while ensuring the client's message is clear and compelling.

With editorial, portrait, or entertainment work, having as much background information as possible about the subject is critical. I always do my homework and learn everything about any job before stepping on set, but being able to read a script or the first draft of an article sets me, my clients, and my subjects up for success. Really understanding the nuances of the story I'm trying to bring to life can lead to interesting and meaningful choices in front of the camera.

What is the most difficult challenge you've had to overcome professionally?
Finding my way as a young woman in a male-dominated industry that I knew very little about was quite a difficult challenge.

When I first started out, I had the opportunity to assist with many different types of commercial shoots. I was pretty naive back then and quickly found myself in some eye-opening and occasionally uncomfortable situations. It could be frustrating to be one of the only female assistants in Vancouver when the type of jobs I wanted to experience were big ones, but some of the photographers I worked for assumed I lacked physical strength.

It took a long time to be taken seriously, but eventually, I figured out how I best contributed to successful productions (it wasn't by being the strongest). In the end, these experiences helped me to focus on my strengths and to find my voice.

Having won multiple awards for your work, which one is the most meaningful to you?
It's really an honor when my personal work is well received. My self-portrait series meant a lot to me because of the link to my family's history. It's gratifying when people ask about it and want to learn more.

What about your work gives you the greatest satisfaction?
I love that every day on set is different and that there are new and different challenges with every job. I get an immense amount of satisfaction bringing an idea or concept to life, especially when I'm pushed outside my comfort zone or encounter challenges to work through and problems to solve along the way. Seeing the first sketch and the finished product side by side is really, really satisfying.

What professional goals do you still have for yourself?
I'd love to direct a short film one day.

What interests do you have outside of work?
I love great design, interior decor, fashion, and film. My husband and I both run our own businesses, and we have two busy teenagers, so my time outside of work is limited these days. We spend a lot of nonwork time driving our kids to sports and activities, but it's awesome watching them discover and chase their own dreams. When we can, our family loves traveling, cheering on our favorite teams (go Dodgers!), going to live music, and checking out galleries and new cool restaurants.

How do you define success?
Work-wise, success is creating and executing ideas I love and collaborating with people I like and care about. In life, the goal would be to give back more than I've taken and maybe inspire others to do the same.

Lindsay Siu www.lindsaysiu.com

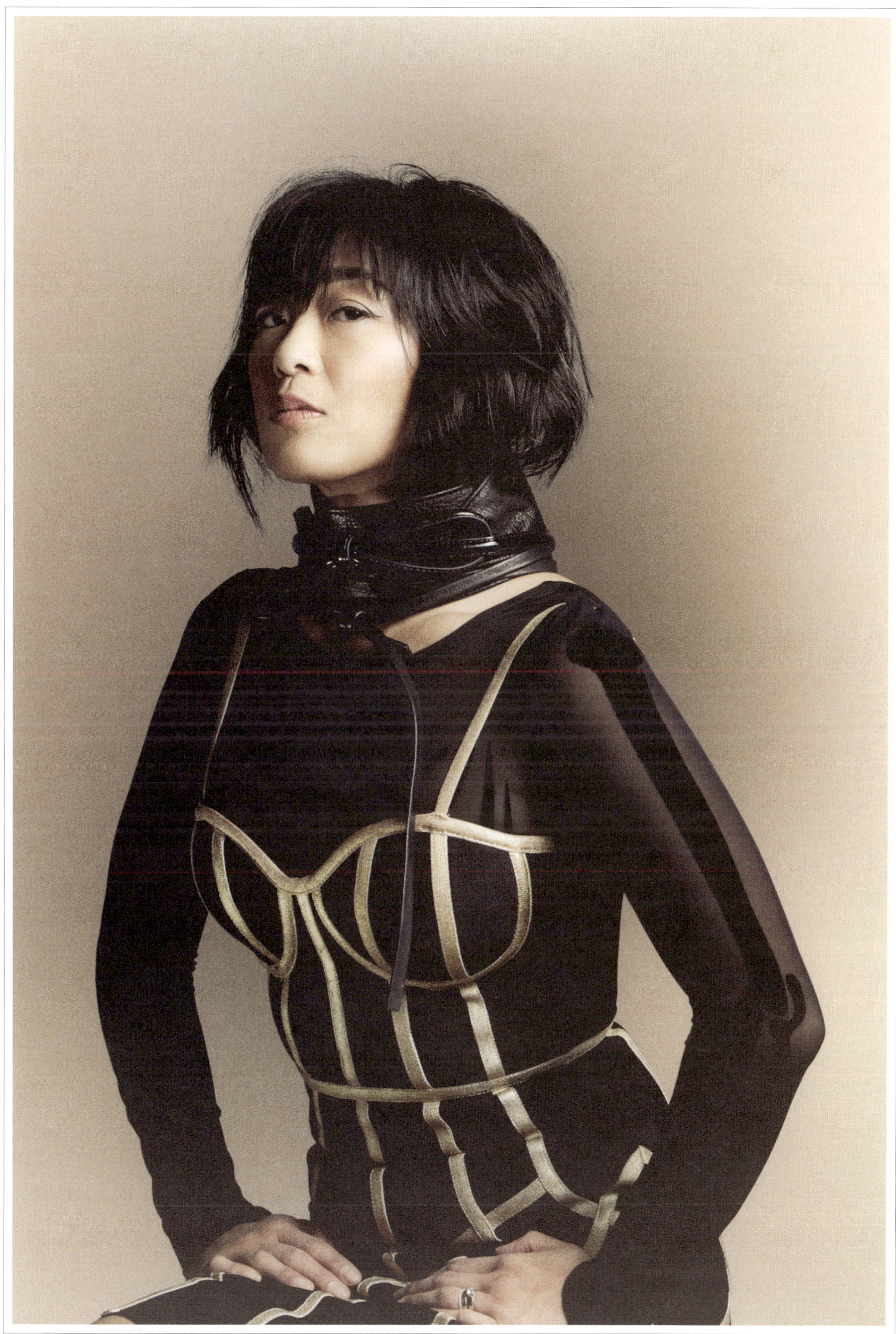

Gold Corset With Leather and Bones, Self-Portrait Series

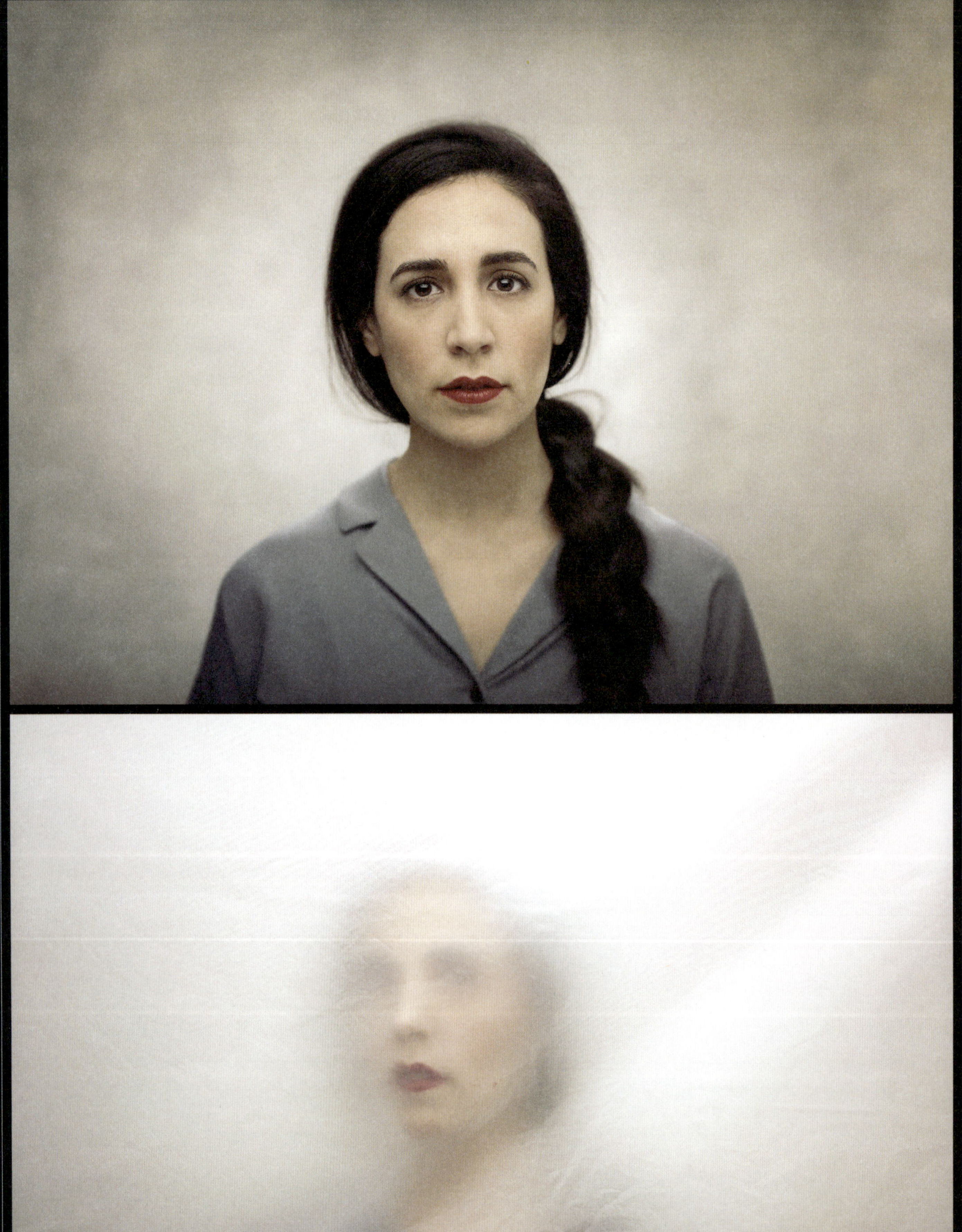

From Invisible to Invincible, BC Women's Hospital

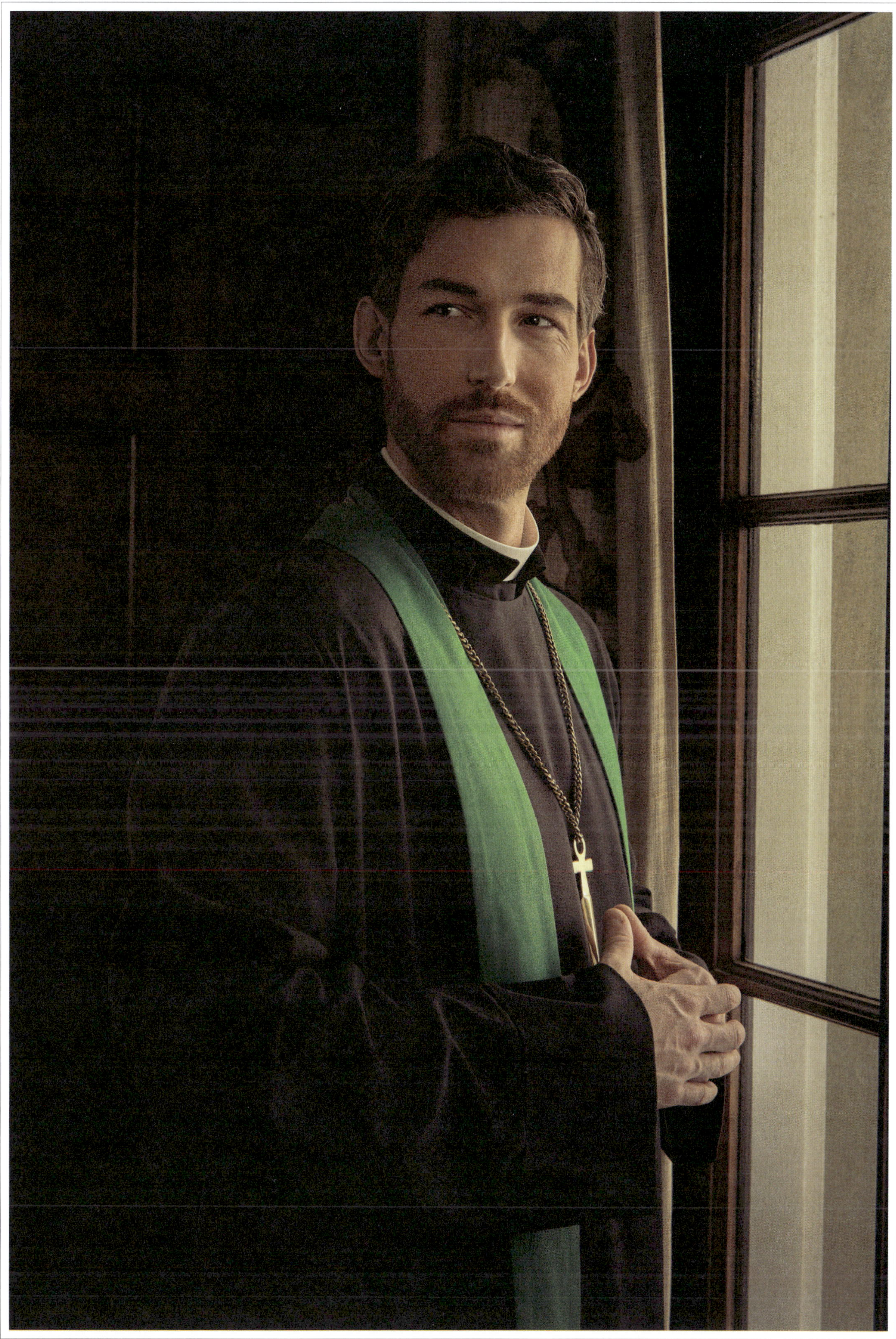

Reverend Green, Clue Series

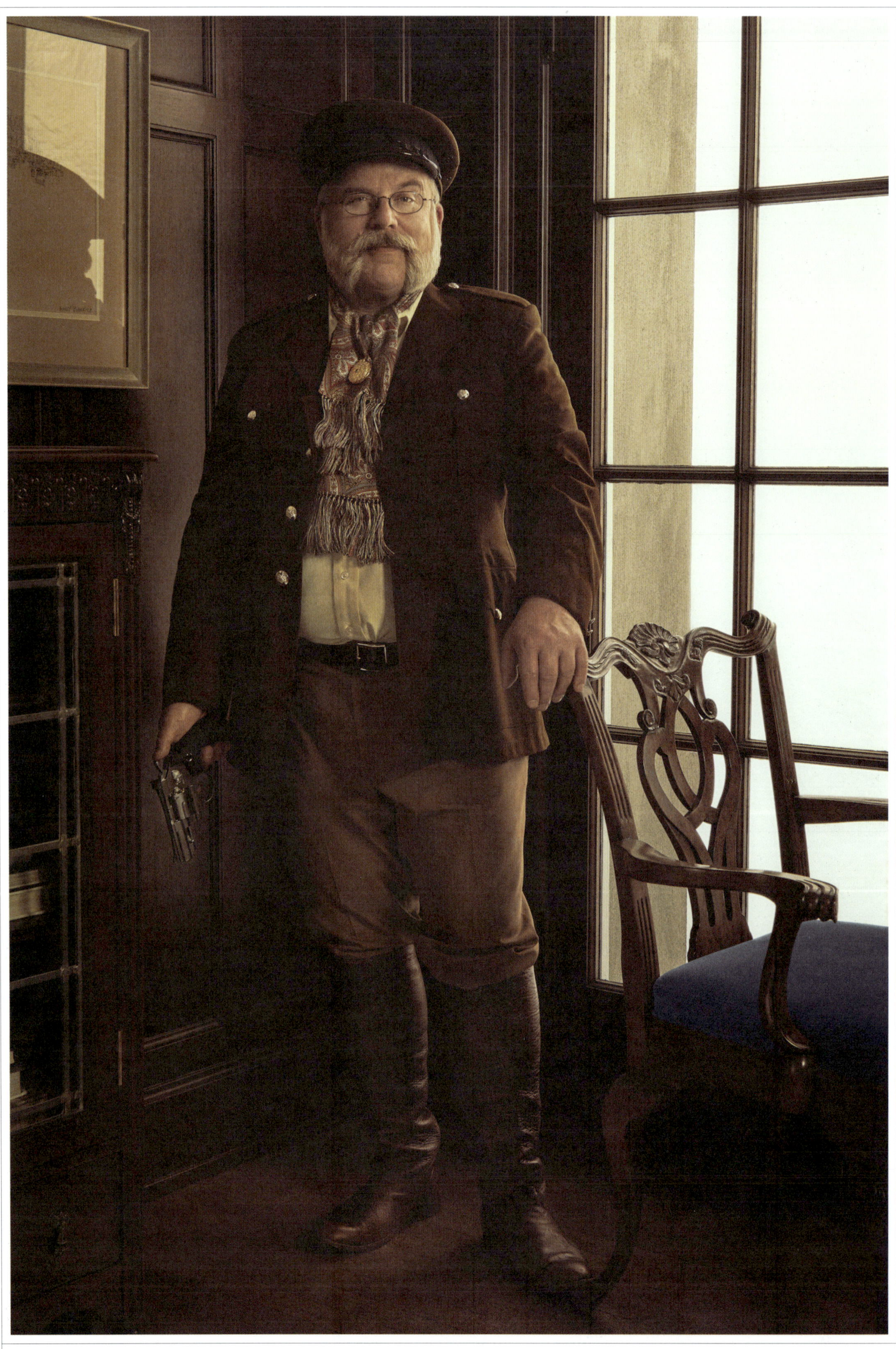

Colonel Mustard, Clue Series

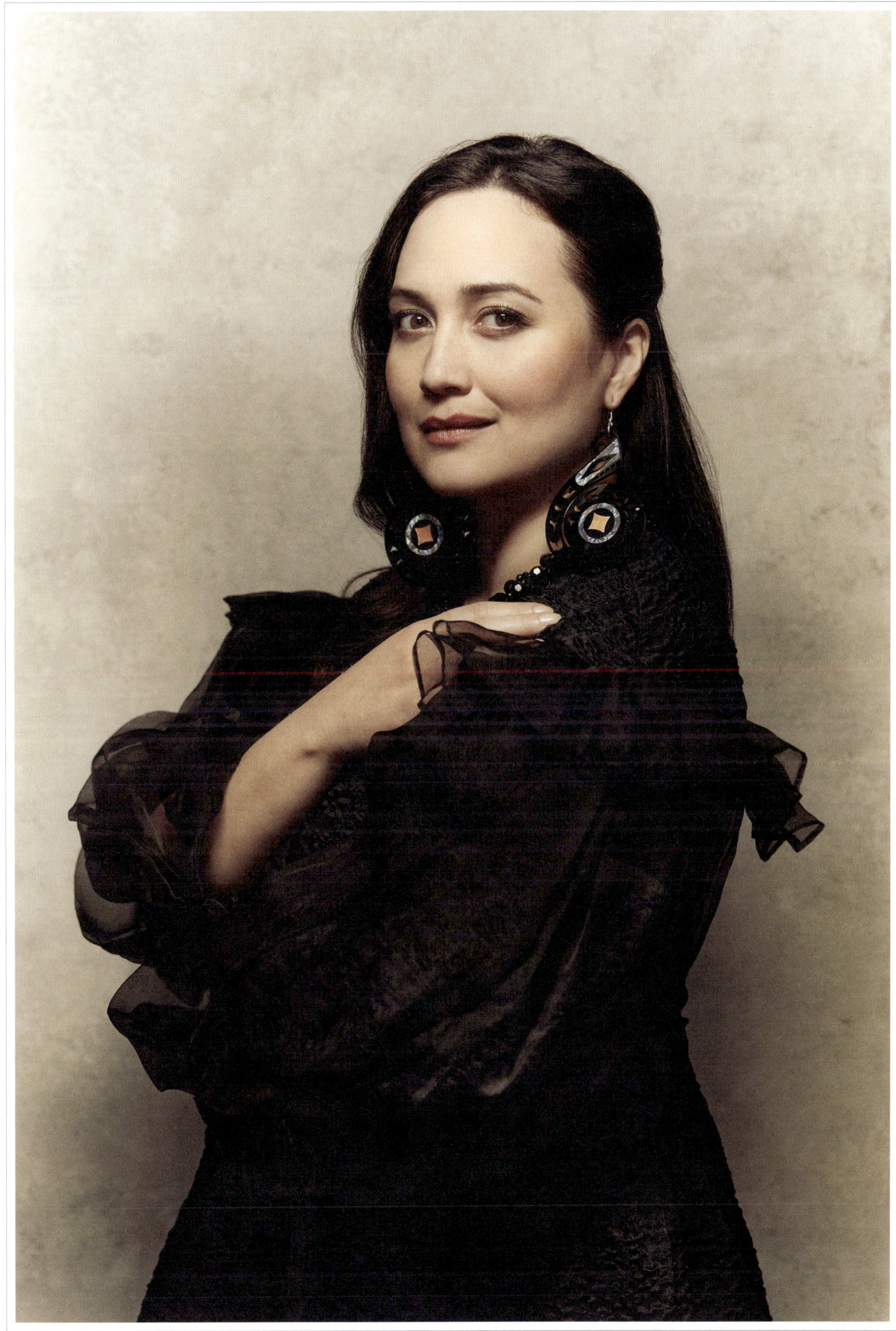

Lily Gladstone

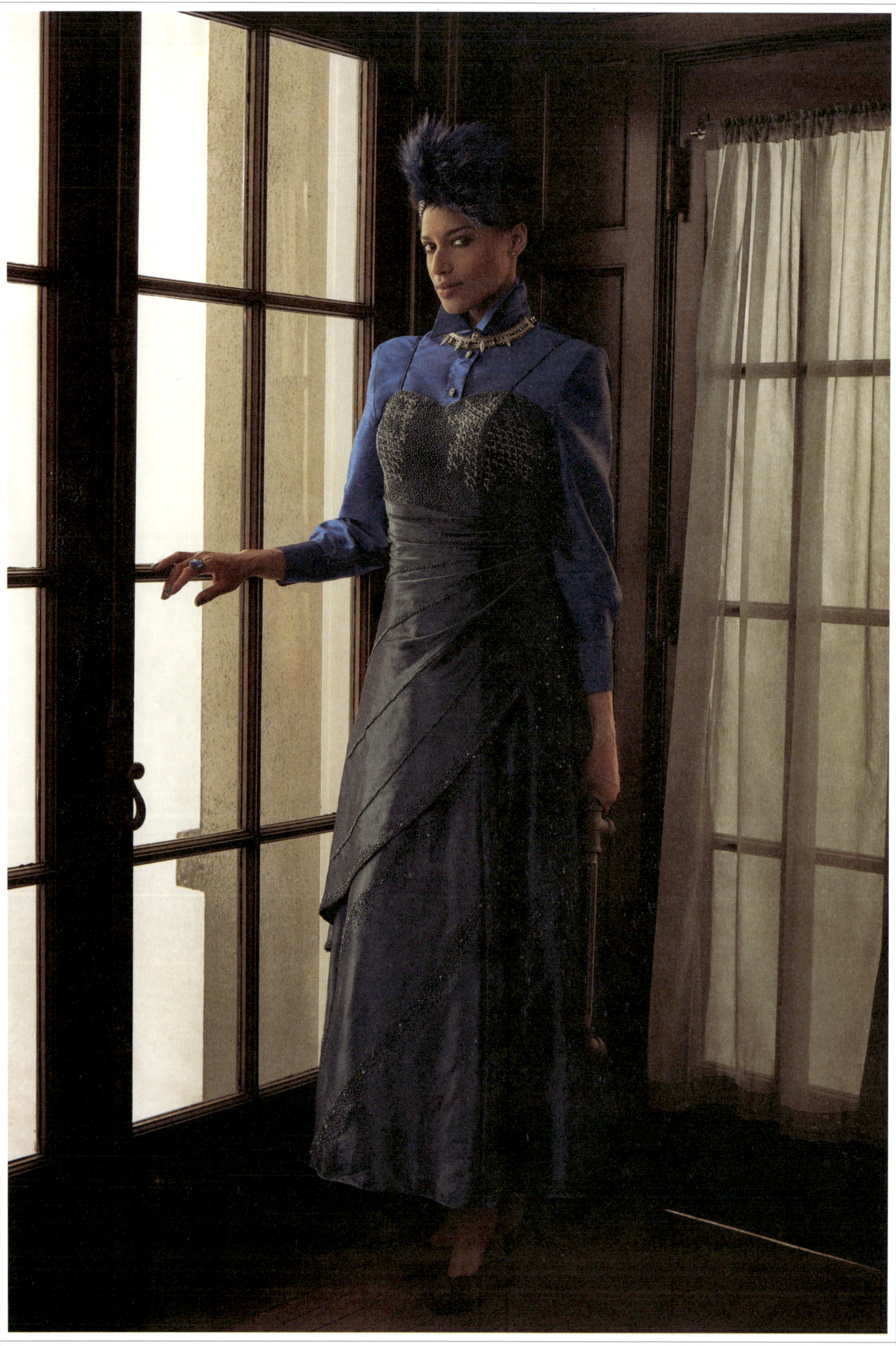

Mrs. Peacock, Clue Series

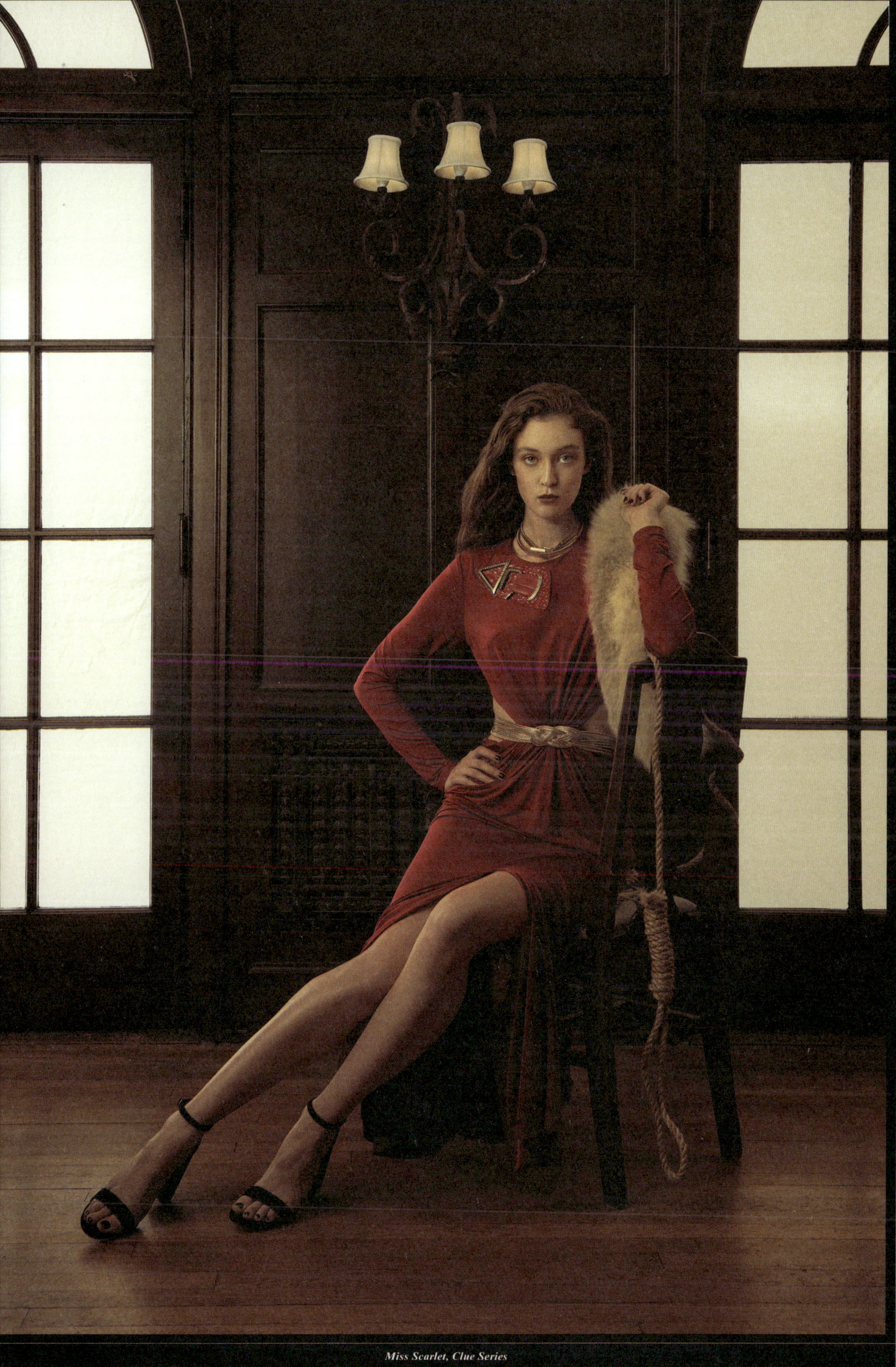

Miss Scarlet, Clue Series

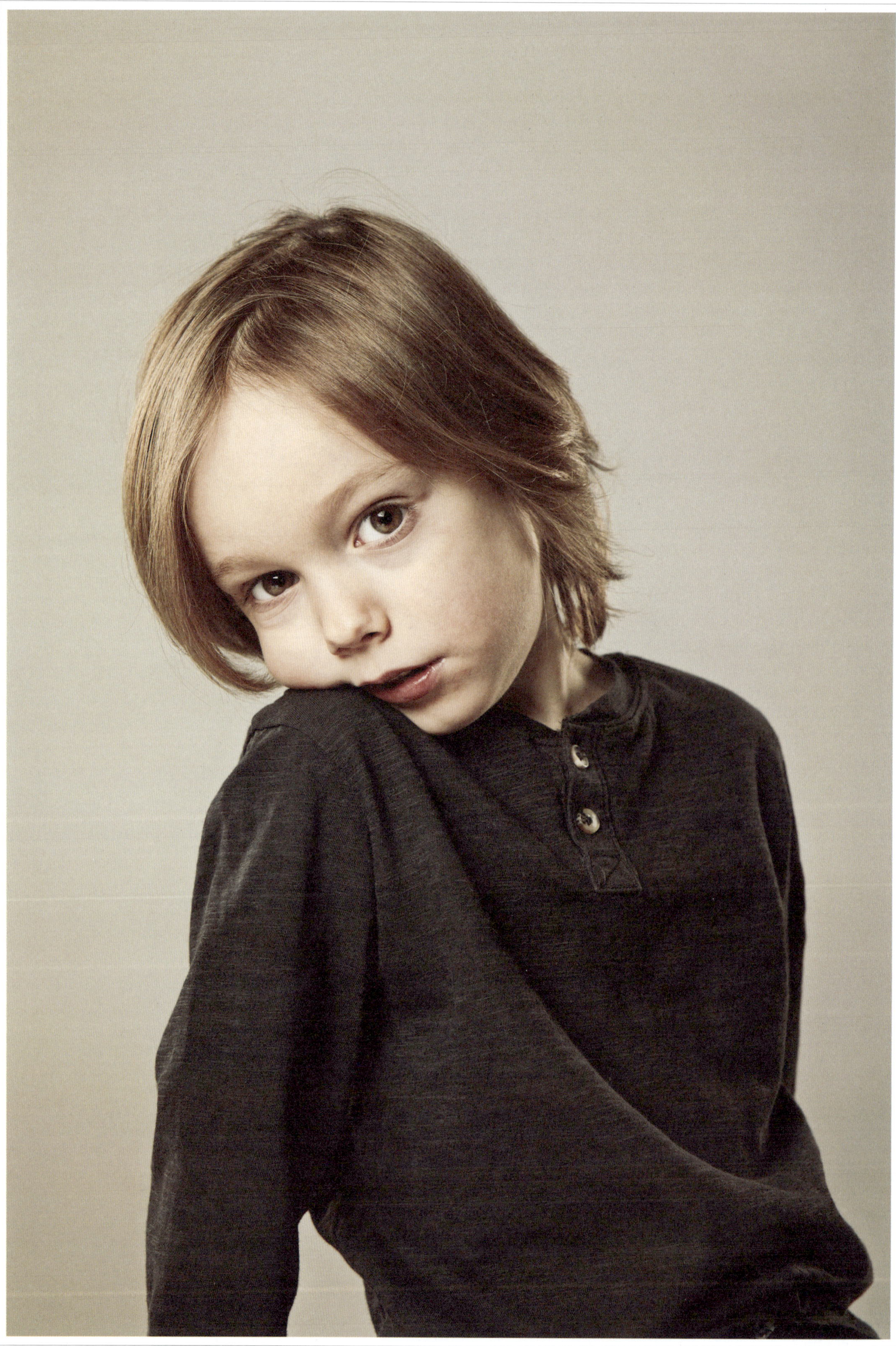

Locke

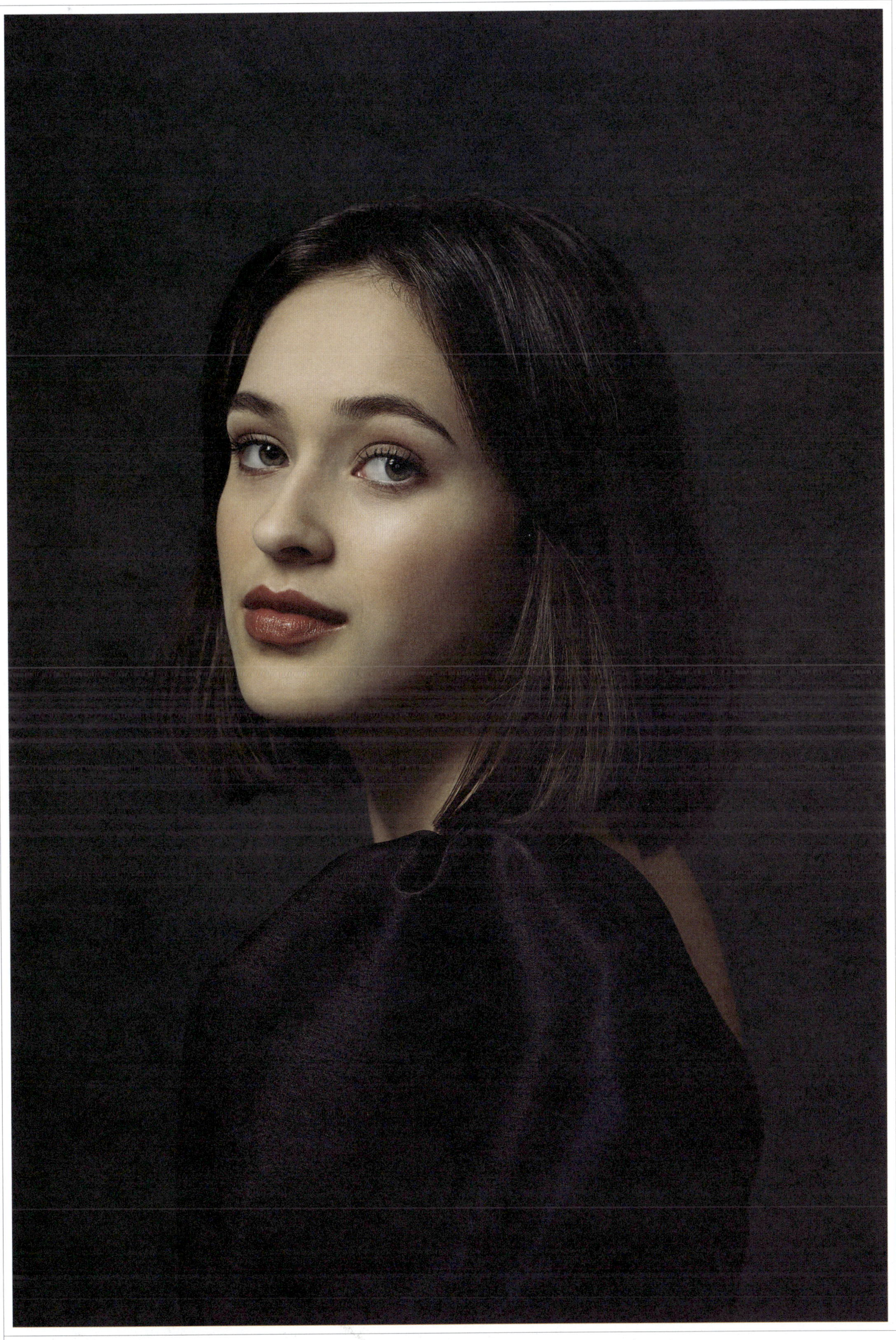

Bella Roces

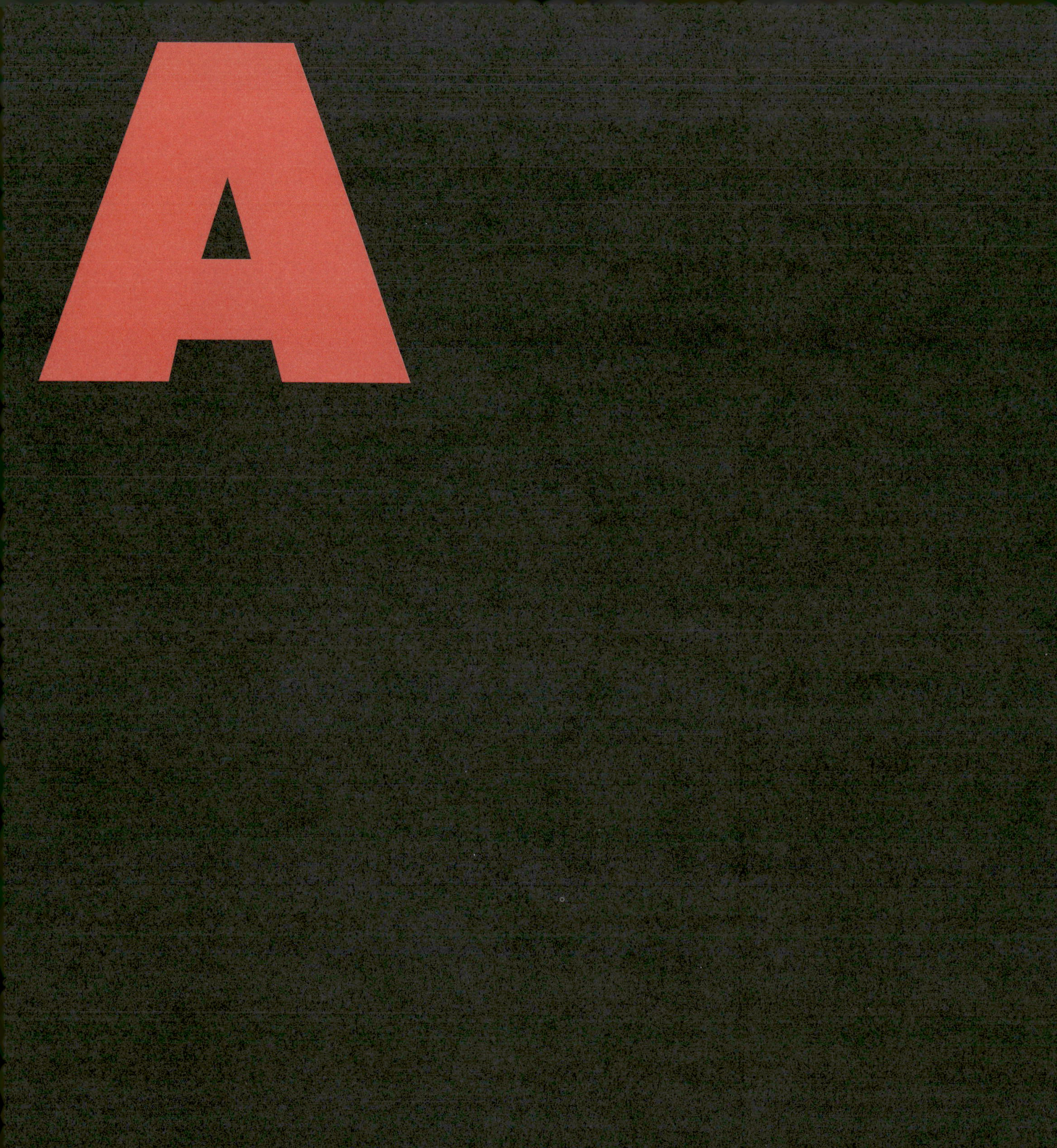

A

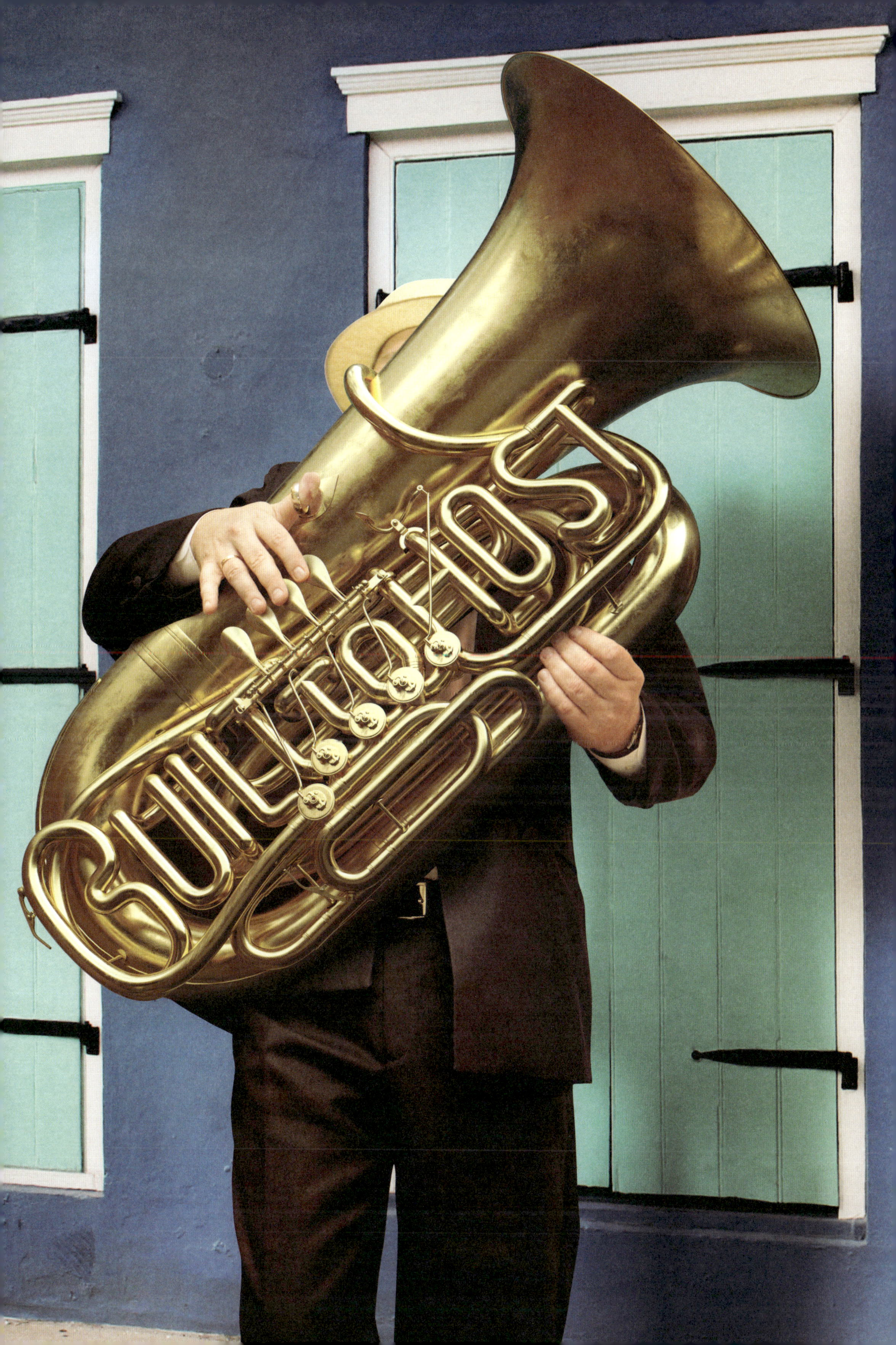
GUILT TO HOST

WHAT SETS EVE AND SEAN APART IS A SHARED PASSION FOR THE PERFECTION OF EVERY DETAIL OF A PROJECT—AN ABSOLUTE JOY TO WORK WITH.

David Onessimo, *Creative Director, Connelly Partners*

SEAN & EVE ARE LIVING PROOF THAT CRAFT STILL EXISTS IN OUR INDUSTRY.

Zak Mroueh, *Founder & Creative Chairman, Zulu Alpha Kilo Inc.*

DRIVEN BY THEIR ENDLESS CURIOSITY AND A LOVE FOR CREATING, SEAN & EVE COMBINE DESIGN, TEXTURE, AND EXPERIMENTATION TO CRAFT UNIQUE, EYE-CATCHING WORK.

Liz Leavitt, *Agent, LEVINE/LEAVITT*

SEAN & EVE'S CRAFT IS A TRUE EXPRESSION OF CREATIVE FREEDOM AT THE SERVICE OF DESIGN NEEDS. THEIR WORK IS AN INSPIRING REMINDER OF HOW CREATIVITY AND TECHNICAL MASTERY CAN FORM SOMETHING UNIQUE AND TIMELESS.

Alex Trochut, *Typography Artist*

SEAN & EVE ARE AT THE TOP OF THEIR GAME AS TYPE ARTISTS. THE WORK WE DID TOGETHER WAS A TRUE PASSION PROJECT, AND THE END RESULT EXCEEDED MY EXPECTATIONS IN EVERY POSSIBLE WAY.

Mario Kerkstra, *Creative Director, AMV BBDO*

SEAN & EVE'S FUSION OF DESIGN, TYPOGRAPHY, AND CREATIVITY HAS YIELDED DYNAMIC AND COMPELLING ILLUSTRATIONS FOR *TIME*. THEIR CONTRIBUTIONS HAVE ENHANCED AND ENRICHED THE STORIES FEATURED IN *TIME*.

Rich Morgan, *Senior Art Director, TIME Magazine*

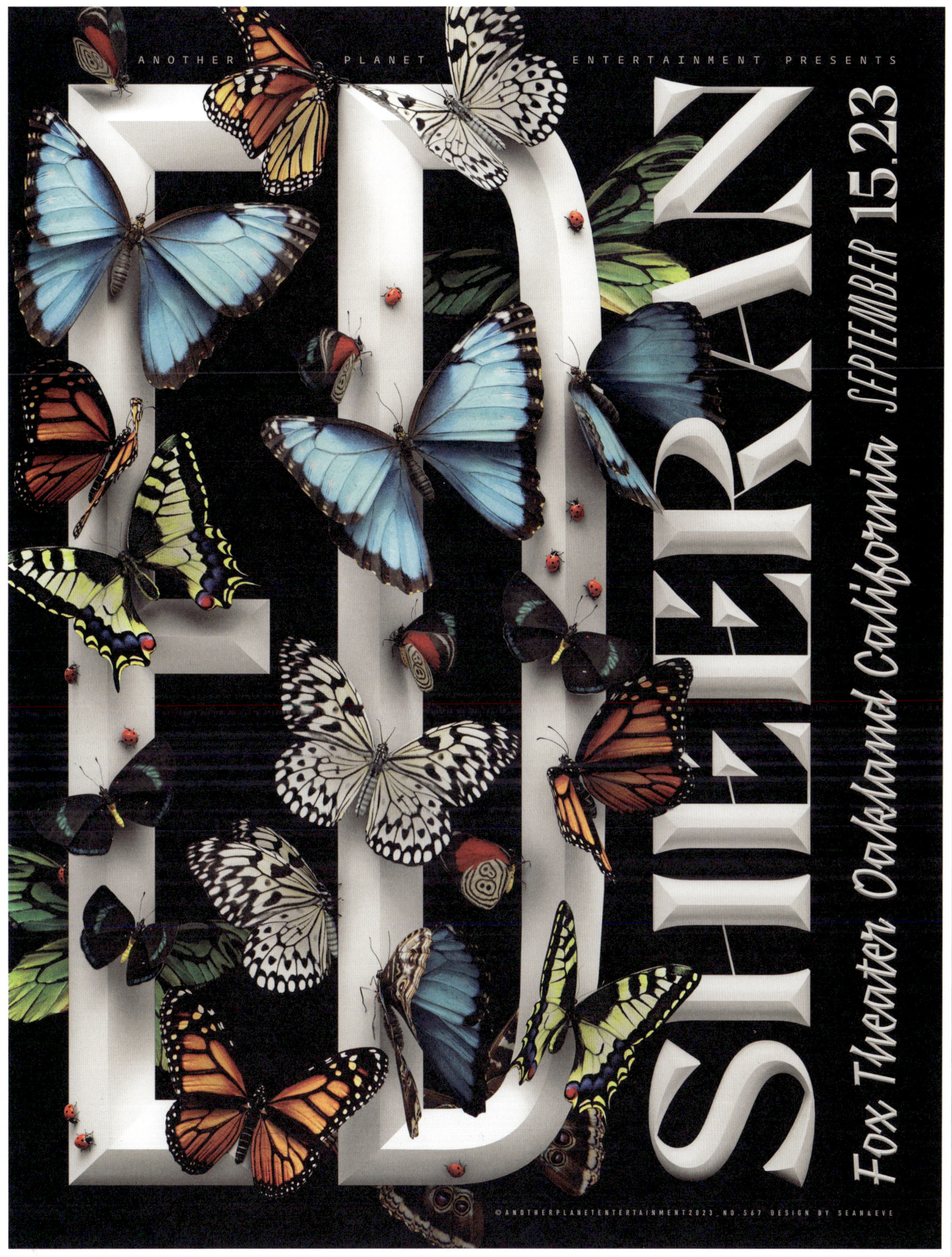

(Page 93) Client: New Orleans Tourism. Campaign: NOLA, Built to Host. Agency: 360i. Design Firm: THERE IS STUDIO. Creative Director: Andrew Hunter Creative Producer: Eve Steben. Typographers: Sean Freeman & Eve Steben. 3D Modeling: Albert Zablit
(Above) Client: Another Planet Entertainment. Project: Ed Sheeran Concert Poster. Design Firm: THERE IS STUDIO. Art Director: Jessica Rogers Creative Director: Eve Steben. Typographer: Sean Freeman. Digital Artist: Sean Freeman

Working with Eve and Sean is an immense joy! They are kind, open, and gracious. They are fast and efficient. But honestly, don't let their calm demeanors fool you—the best part of having them aboard a project is that it's like stepping into any creative ring with Muhammad Ali in your entourage. The work will be polished and honed sharp, and it always packs a punch. They're big-picture thinkers who meticulously drill down into the minutiae to render visual solutions full of subtext and knockout pow. That's a rare combination. To be sure, they've put in the reps and, in my opinion, are the undisputed heavyweight champs when it comes to executing complex creative solutions that must, well, float like a butterfly and sting like a bee.

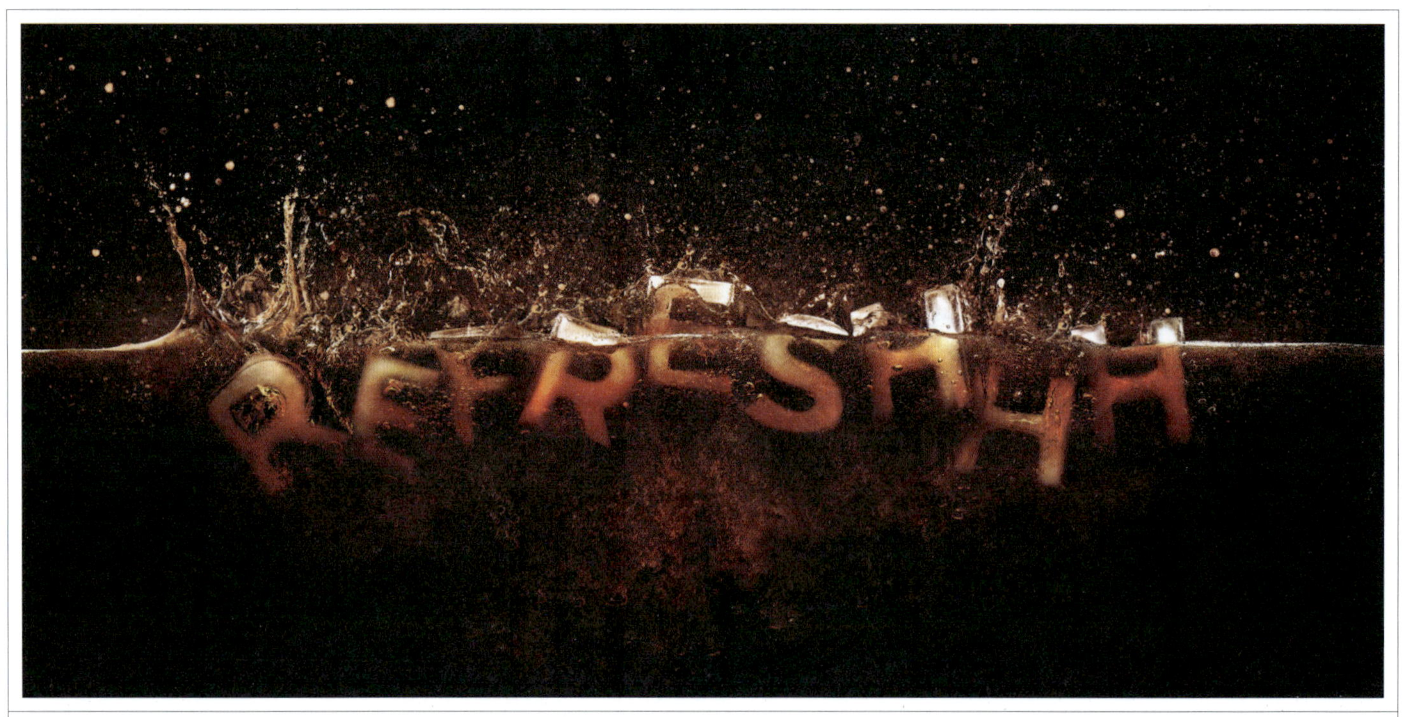

Client: Coke Zero. Campaign: Tastes Too Good For Words. Agency: Ogilvy NYC. Design Firm: THERE IS STUDIO. Creative Director: Chris Rowson
Creative Producer: Eve Steben. Photographer: Sean Freeman. Typographer: Sean Freeman. Drink Stylist: Eve Steben

Q&A: Eve Steben & Sean Freeman, Co-founders & Illustrators, SEAN & EVE (AKA THERE IS STUDIO) 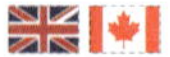

What is your work philosophy?
Quality over quantity?... Nurturing the joy in craft and collaborations while embracing challenges, happy accidents, new methods, and aiming for the stars.

What is it about illustration that you are most passionate about?
Our favorite part of the work is developing textures that we then manipulate to create something greater, really embracing the whole process... The thinking, the making, the discoveries, and the incredible details that come from that kind of approach. During these sessions, time is suspended—it's pure exploration, raw creativity, that we pour ourselves into. Each session and material can go in so many directions; it keeps the work exciting and ever-evolving.

Besides illustration, your studio also does art direction, typography, CGI, and photography. What's your favorite type of project to work on?
We love analog and digital artistic methods equally, as well as everything in between. It's always mesmerizing how wonderfully things can blend together and the specific aesthetics you can achieve using various techniques. That said, it's not so much about the nature of the project but the output and the journey to get there. We love the speed and happy accidents you get with photography. Being on set, shooting things—it's all very hands-on and sometimes experimental in how you can bring effects to life. There's an incredible buzz and rush of energy that comes with that. Contradicting the speed and immediacy we love about photographing projects, we love the time you can spend crafting elements in 3D and the mathematical yet abstract nature of this approach. It comes with its own hurdles and sometimes crazy, unexpected learning curves, but you have to take the rough with the smooth. Pixels are wild little things.

Your work spans advertising, editorial, food and drink, music, and film. Is there a particular category you like best?
It's all about good balance, as working across industries keeps things fresh from a creative standpoint. Eating your favorite meal every day can make you sick, and this is what we actively try to avoid in our work. Projects that are nourishing and fulfilling are the ones we're most passionate about, either from a creative, production, or personal perspective. To answer the question, the best part of the work is the variety of projects and industries we come across: the techniques, treatments, results, and basically the whole process of bringing ideas to life... With a focus on tailoring our approach to the message, the weaving of each project is unique.

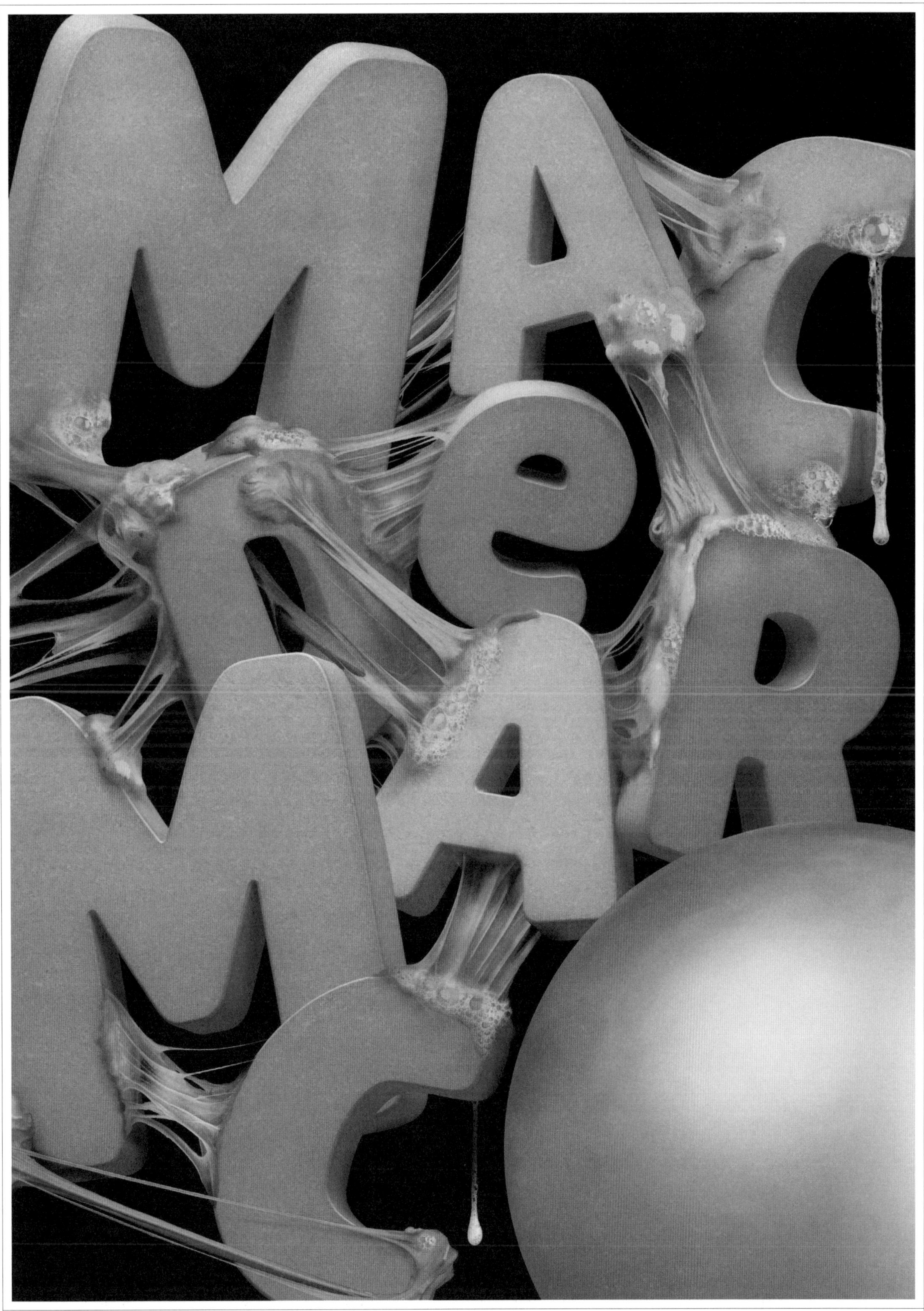

*Client: Another Planet Entertainment. Project: Mac DeMarco Concert Poster. Design Firm: THERE IS STUDIO. Art Director: Jessica Rogers. Creative Director: Eve Steben
Creative Producer: Eve Steben. Photographer: Sean Freeman. Typographer: Sean Freeman. Digital Artist: Sean Freeman. Food Stylist: Eve Steben*

We really like the advertising work at large: The idea is bold, and it must be executed beautifully. We enjoy the intensity of the process, the craft that goes into it, and the excitement of seeing it out there in the world, giant and glorious. We love music, film, and editorial because of the evocative, conceptual nature of the work and the unique opportunity to develop treatments with a different layer of storytelling into the mix. We love working with food and drink for its unique, ultra-textural, playful, and physical nature. One day, we can shoot an amusing and textured liquid piece for an ad campaign, followed by a floral arrangement for a music poster—next, a burger, chocolate, ladybugs, or something entirely different... Never a dull moment! That's the best thing.

What is the most difficult challenge you've overcome to reach your current position?
Finding personal balance while pushing the practice. When you're so passionate about your hobby that it becomes your work—and that you're two in that tango—lines can be blurred between life, ambition, and time. As a side angle to this theme, another challenge is overcoming the worry of work drying up and embracing the flow. It's probably healthy to always have a little bit of that fear that keeps you on your toes and makes you evolve in your practice.

Who were some of your greatest past influences?
We've always been big fans of contemporary art and various other art forms—more so than design, strictly speaking. We love the work of the YBA's: Tracey Emin, Damien Hirst, Marc Quinn... Also, Yayoi Kusama, James Turrell, Olafur Eliasson, David Shrigley, Jeff Koons... Going back a shade further, Francis Bacon and Mark Rothko show how they managed to capture so much emotion with paint. Design-wise, in the early days, the work of Non-Format was a considerable influence, as was Stefan Sagmeister and everything he was doing.

Who among your contemporaries today do you most admire?
In the typography department, we really admire Alex Trochut. His work has been brilliant ever since we first came across it so many years ago. His typography work is exceptional, varied, and well-thought-out. It's been inspiring to see his work evolve and develop. On top of all that, he's also a genuine and lovely guy.

Who have been some of your favorite people or clients you have worked with?
The human side of things and relationships play a big role in the creative process and are something we value in our work. We've been fortunate to collaborate with fabulous clients and people through the years. Many of them have become regulars or actual friends over time. In that department, we must throw some flowers to our incredible agents at LEVINE/LEAVITT, with whom we've had the joy and privilege to work since the studio's infancy and who have collectively been a vast provider of good vibes.

What are the most important ingredients you require from a client to make successful work?
As a start, fun projects for fun brands are always sweet ingredients. Then, Sean enjoys a well-wrangled concept for working within a brief and executing an idea, no matter how abstract it might be. The combination of a tight deadline, a blank page, and an open brief makes him break out in a cold sweat. At the other end of the spectrum, Eve absolutely loves an open brief, room for artistic freedom, and getting involved with conceptualization and is amazing at running with it. Good communication, providing concise feedback, and carrying a vision are also vital to a successful recipe. Overall, collaborating with trusting, enthusiastic clients who embrace the development process, supported by budget and time to execute ideas at the right level, is definitely the cherry on top.

What part of your work is most demanding, considering your position?
As stated previously, finding personal balance while pushing the practice is important. When you're so passionate about your hobby that it becomes your work—and that you're two in that tango—lines can be blurred between life, ambition, and time. There's the need to do personal work and learn new techniques and tools alongside keeping on top of and consistently delivering quality commissions in an ever-evolving industry landscape, not to mention putting time aside for all that important life stuff and maintaining energy levels. I guess you can't complain about being busy, but the nature of freelance work can sometimes make this a tricky exercise where the pace can get a little unpredictable.

What professional goals do you still have for yourself?
Working on projects we love, staying passionate about the work, and having fun. Traveling again for commissions, working on physical installation pieces, and more in situ collaborations would also be fantastic. We find that working in a totally different cultural environment is very stimulating, and producing public work is always a great experience. This side of things changed a bit for us, especially with the increase in remote work over the last few years... We miss it!

What advice would you have for students starting out today?
Obviously, today is a very different landscape than when we started out, but in the beginning, the approach was to be lightly aware of what's going on in the scene (perhaps harder to achieve today with the omnipresence of Instagram) but to do personal work being almost oblivious to what's happening. Do your thing, get it out there, and find your niche. Also, as fellow typographer Anthony Burrill famously quoted on his iconic poster, "Work hard and be nice to people."

What would you change if you had to do it all over again?
Taking the importance of social media more seriously and getting on board with it sooner.

What interests do you have outside of your work?
Cooking, eating, traveling, theater, music concerts, walks in the forest, friends, and family—in no specific order.

Where do you seek inspiration?
Music has always played a big part in finding inspiration through moods and lyrics, perhaps less now than before, but it certainly was a big part of what kickstarted Sean's love affair with typography... Creative juices can start flowing in so many ways: by actively or passively researching elements for a project—online, in bookshops, museums... It can also be

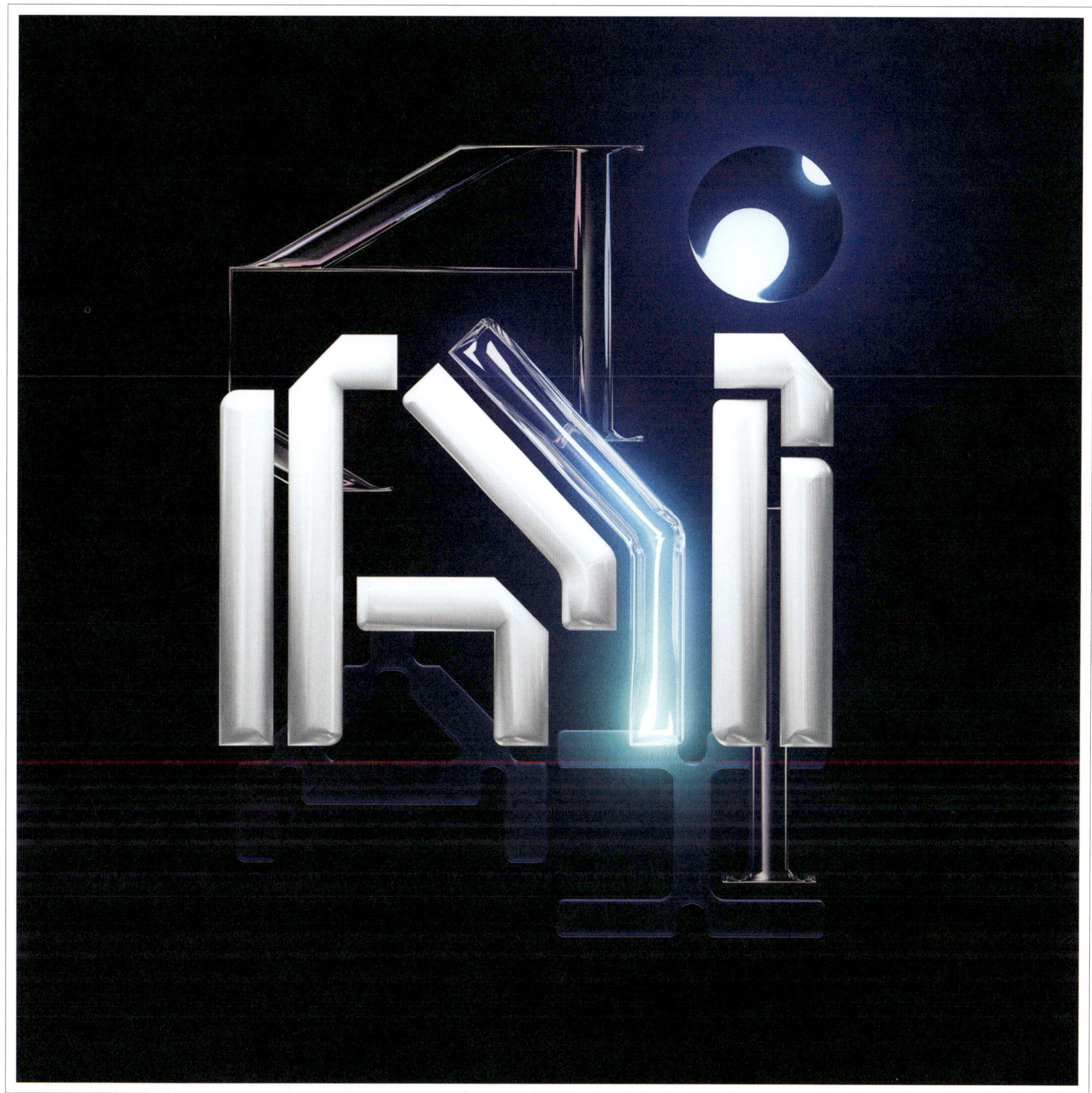

Client: TIME Magazine. Project: TIME 100 / AI. Design Firm: THERE IS STUDIO
Art Director: Rich Morgan. Typographers: Sean Freeman & Eve Steben. Digital Artist: Sean Freeman

totally random, for instance, when you get that eureka flash in the middle of the night. Inspiration often comes through a multitude of things and actions: enjoying art and design, playing with materials, contemplation, discovering weird textures or unusual applications, reflecting on mundane things, traveling, being on set together, cooking, floristry, ceramics, crafts at large... From that, we build up our creative wishlists, boards, collections of images, and material, all of which keep the wheel spinning.

Where do you see yourself in the future?
Working on projects we love (which fulfills our creativity),

being passionate about the work, and still learning, experimenting, and having fun. Other than that, we're somewhere nice, near a wild beach or a village, sharing a bottle of wine with our feet in the sand and looking out over the sea.

How do you define success?
Being able to work like we do, year in and year out—every year, we thank our lucky stars.

SEAN & EVE sean-eve.com
See their Graphis Master Portfolio at graphis.com.

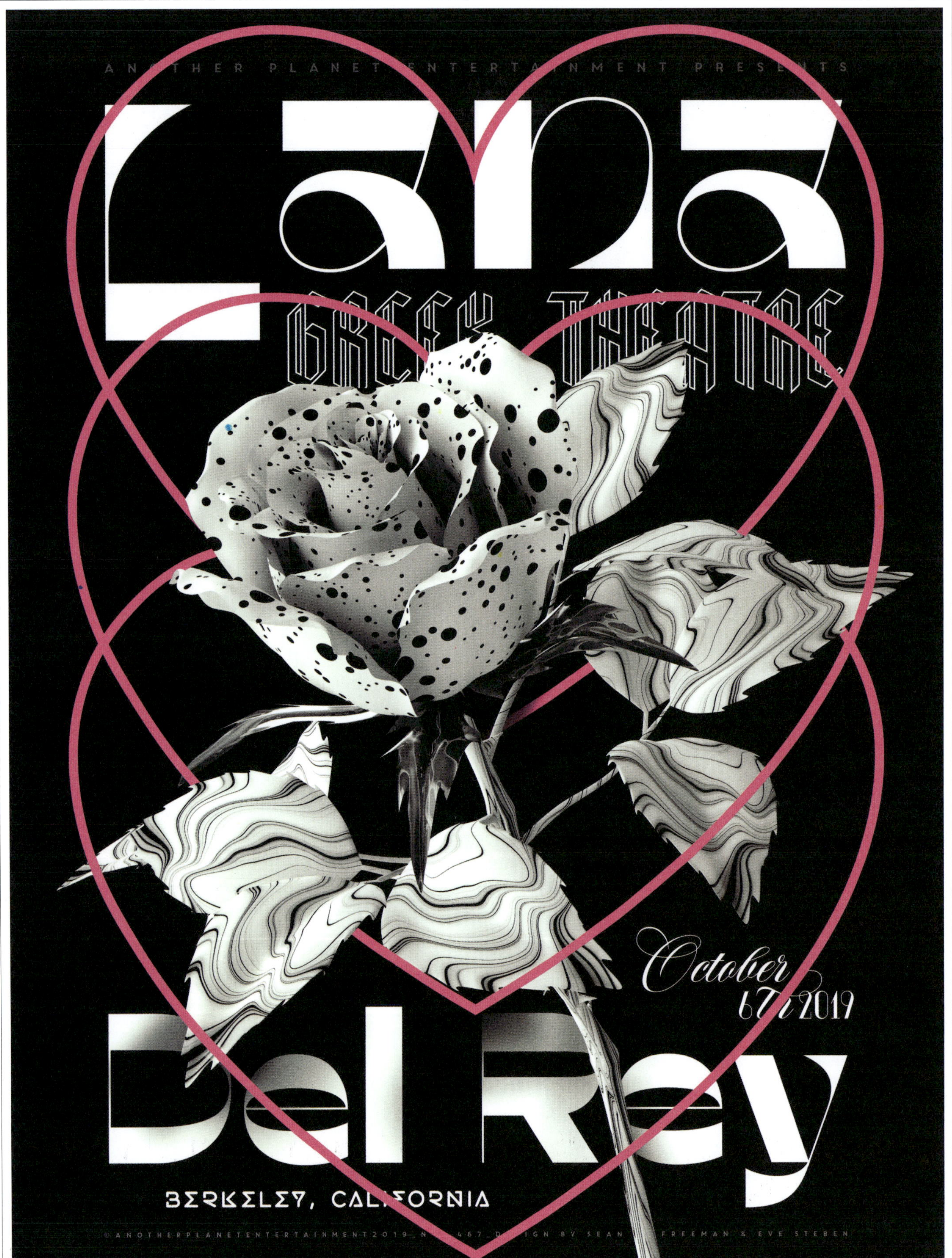

Client: Another Planet Entertainment. Project: Lana Del Rey Concert Poster. Design Firm: THERE IS STUDIO. Art Director: Jessica Rogers
Creative Director: Eve Steben. Typographers: Sean Freeman & Eve Steben. Digital Artist: Sean Freeman. Designers: Eve Steben & Giada Pieropan

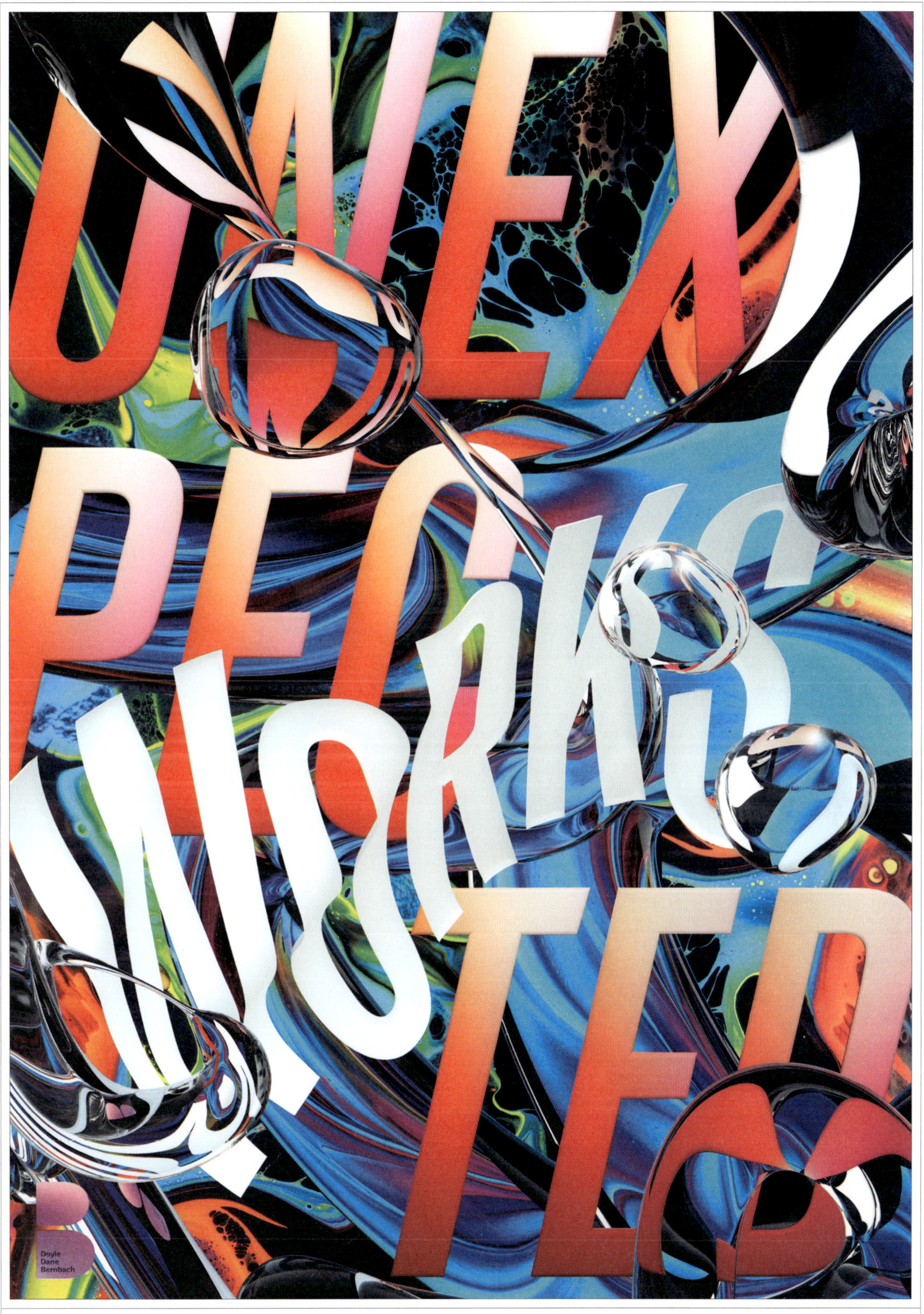

Client: *DDB World*. Project: *Unexpected Works*. Design Firm: *THERE IS STUDIO*
Creative Director: *Maximilien Guibert*. Typographers: *Sean Freeman & Eve Steben*. Digital Artist: *Sean Freeman*

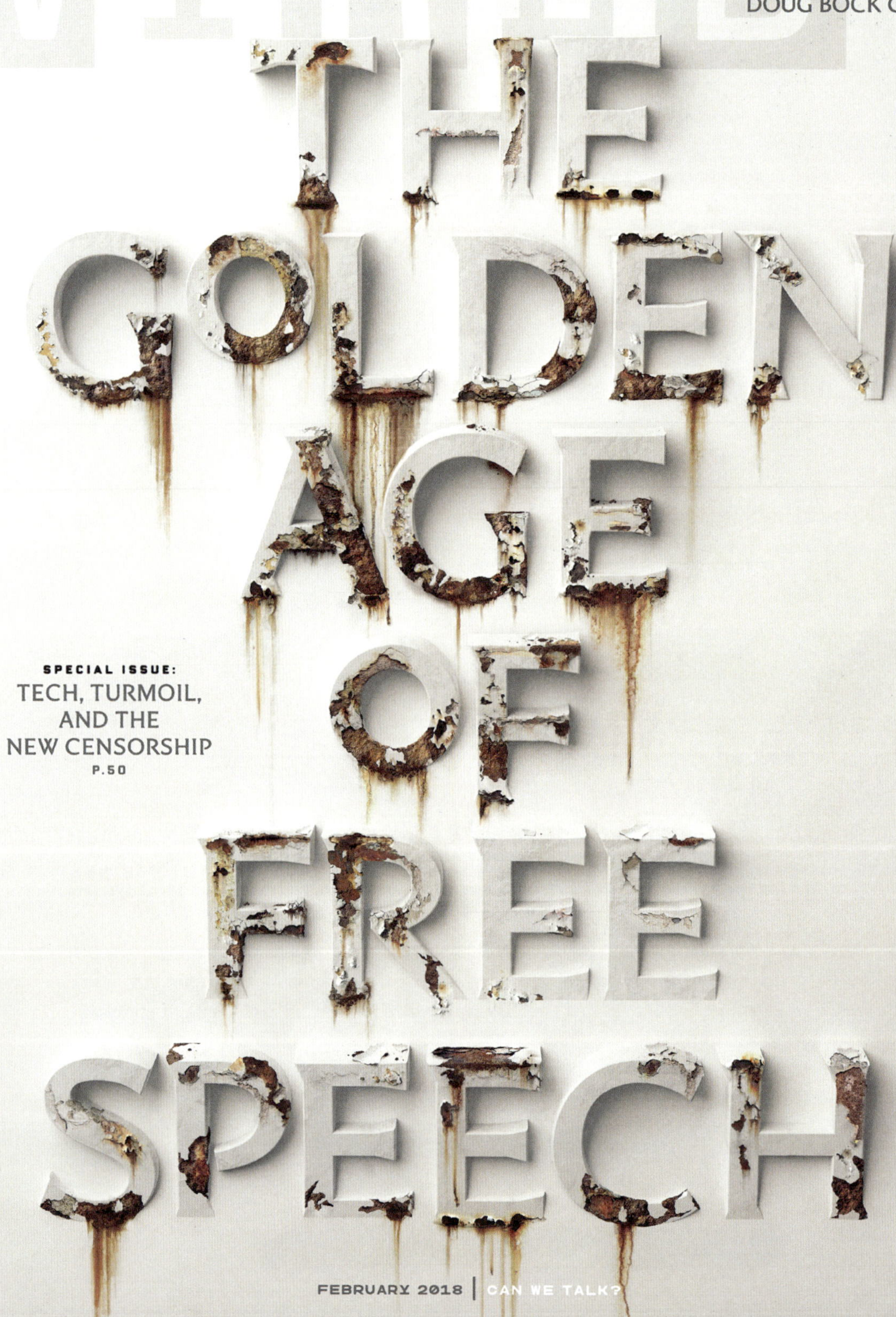

WIRED
WIRED-26.02
CREATE. CONNECT. CONDÉ NAST.
FEATURING:
ZEYNEP TUFEKCI
ALICE GREGORY
VIRGINIA HEFFERNAN
STEVEN JOHNSON
DOUG BOCK CLARK
THE GOLDEN AGE OF FREE SPEECH
SPECIAL ISSUE:
TECH, TURMOIL, AND THE NEW CENSORSHIP
P.50
FEBRUARY 2018 | CAN WE TALK?

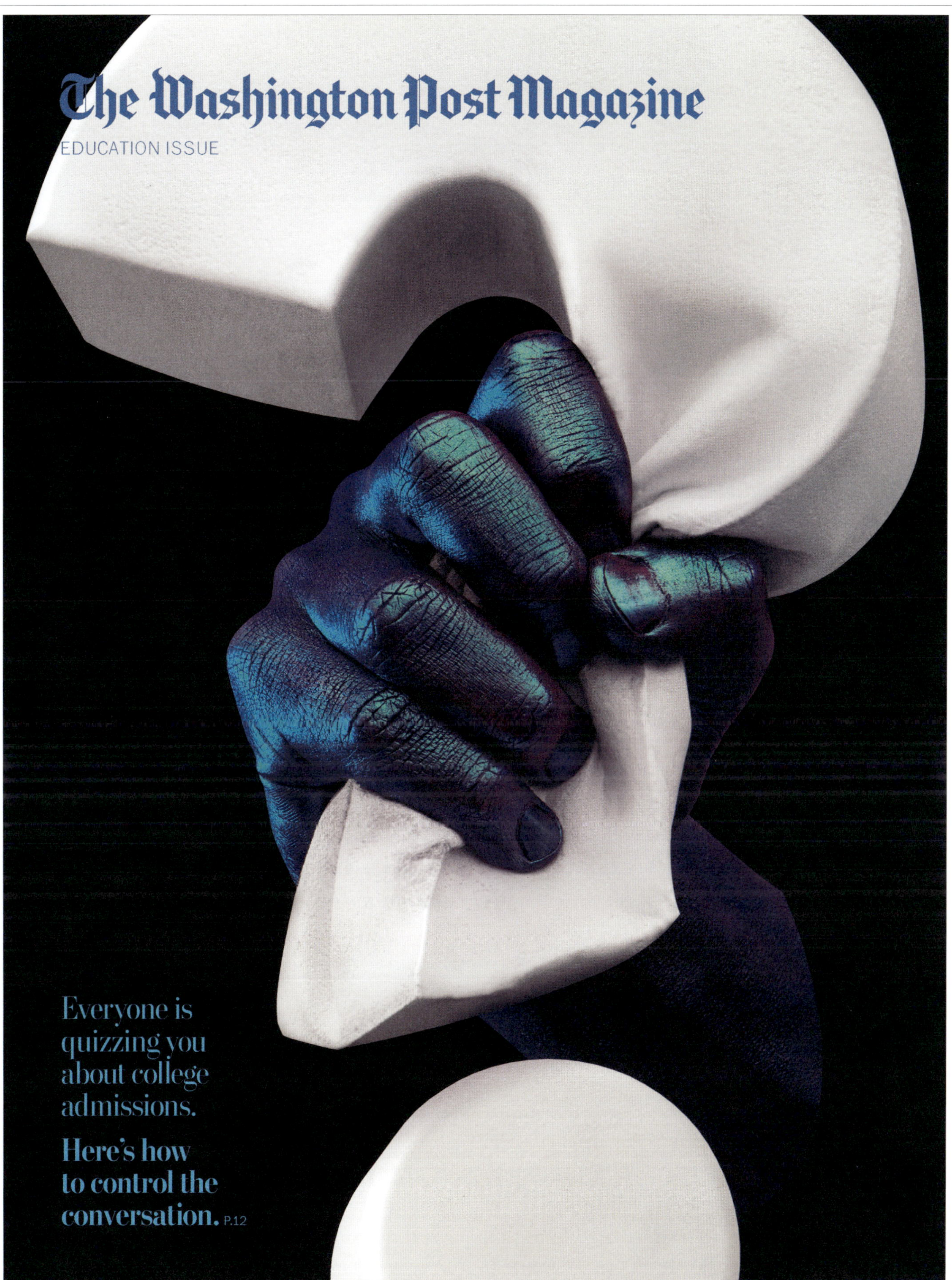

Client: *Washington Post.* Project: *Higher Education Anxiety.* Design Firm: *THERE IS STUDIO.* Creative Director: *Christian Font*
Creative Producer: *Eve Steben.* Typographer: *Sean Freeman.* Photographer: *Sean Freeman.* Assistant: *Oliver Clyde.* Prop Stylist: *Eve Steben.* Special FX Makeup: *Eve Steben*

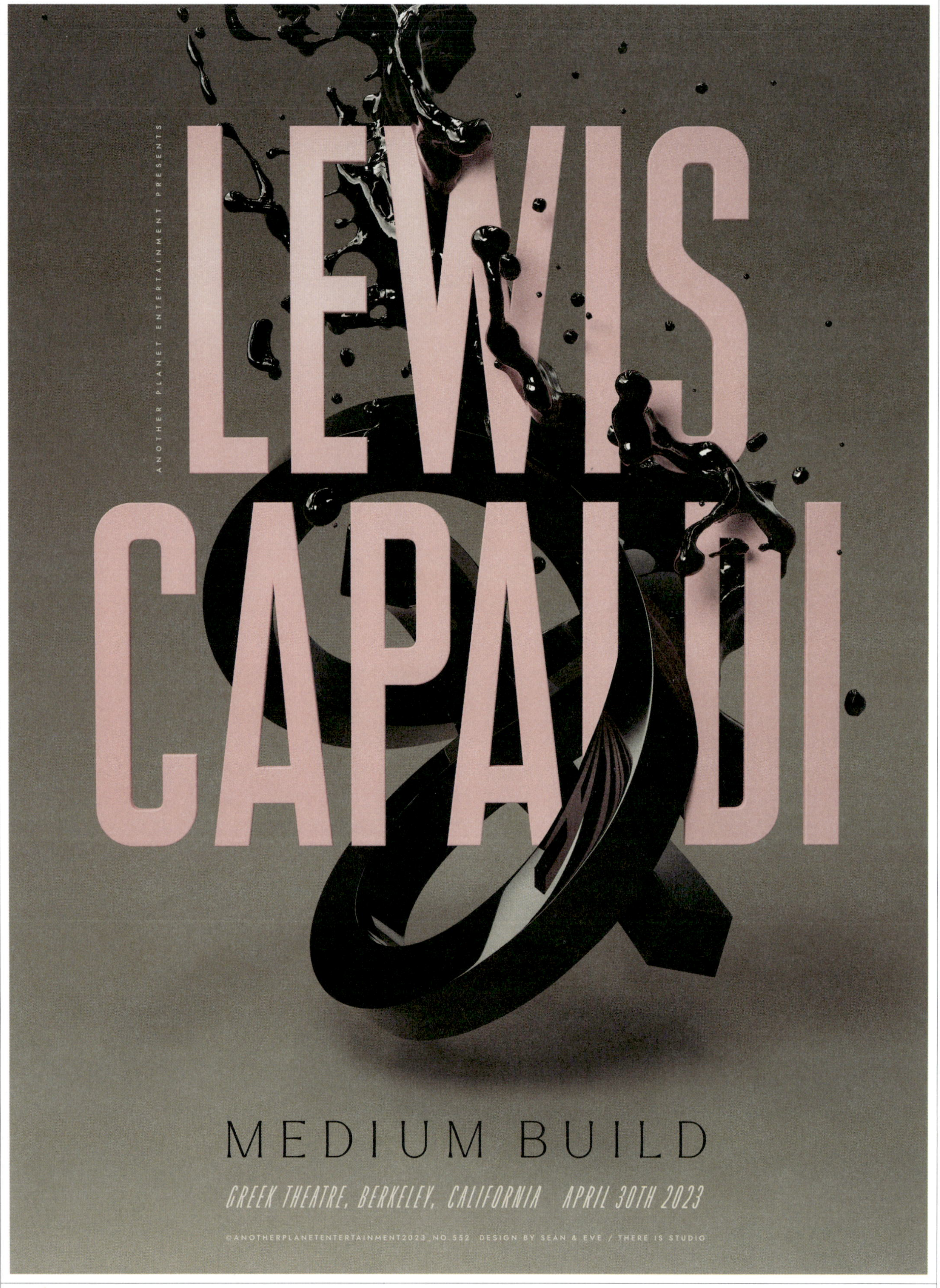

Client: Another Planet Entertainment. Project: Lewis Capaldi Concert Poster. Design Firm: THERE IS STUDIO. Art Director: Jessica Rogers
Creative Director: Eve Steben. Typographer: Sean Freeman. Digital Artist: Sean Freeman

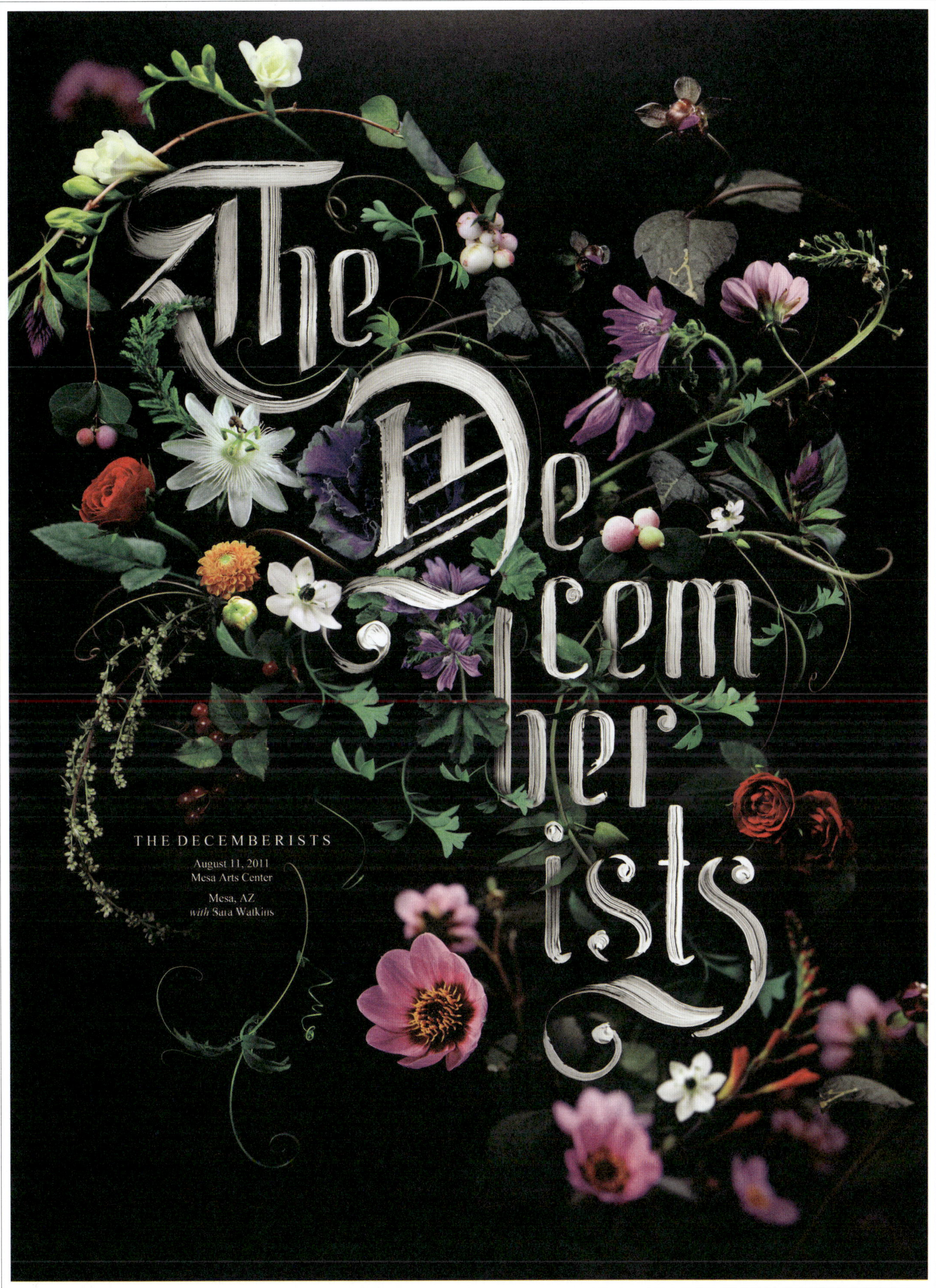

Client: *Another Planet Entertainment*. Project: *The Decemberists Concert Poster*. Design Firm: *THERE IS STUDIO*. Art Director: *Jessica Rogers*
Creative Director: *Eve Steben*. Photographer: *Sean Freeman*. Typographers: *Sean Freeman & Eve Steben*. Prop Stylist: *Eve Steben*. Digital Artist: *Sean Freeman*. Designer: *Eve Steben*

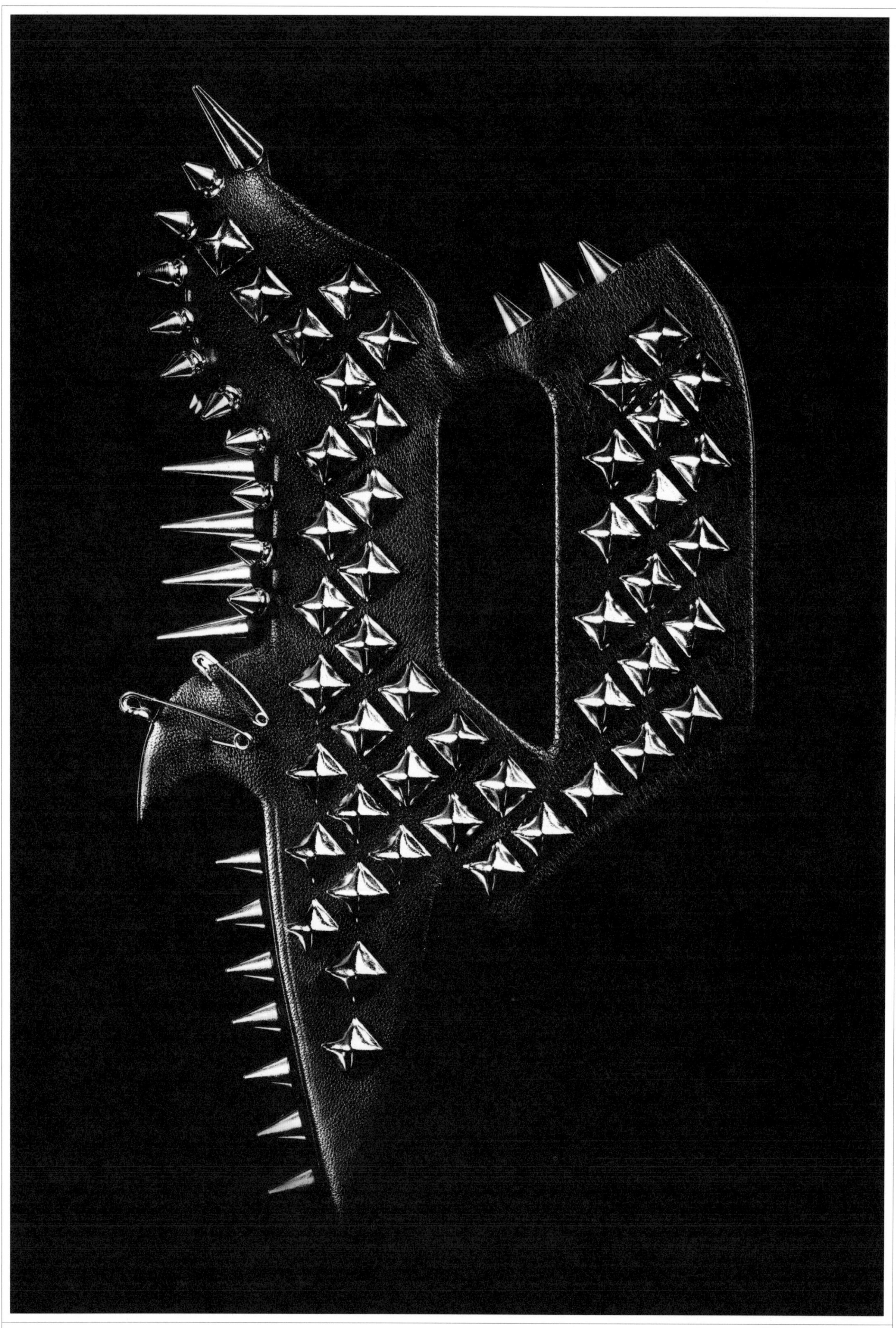

Client: Self-initiated/Personal Project. Project: Describing Words, P for Punk. Design Firm: THERE IS STUDIO
Typographer: Sean Freeman. Photographer: Mathieu Fortin. Prop Stylist: Eve Steben

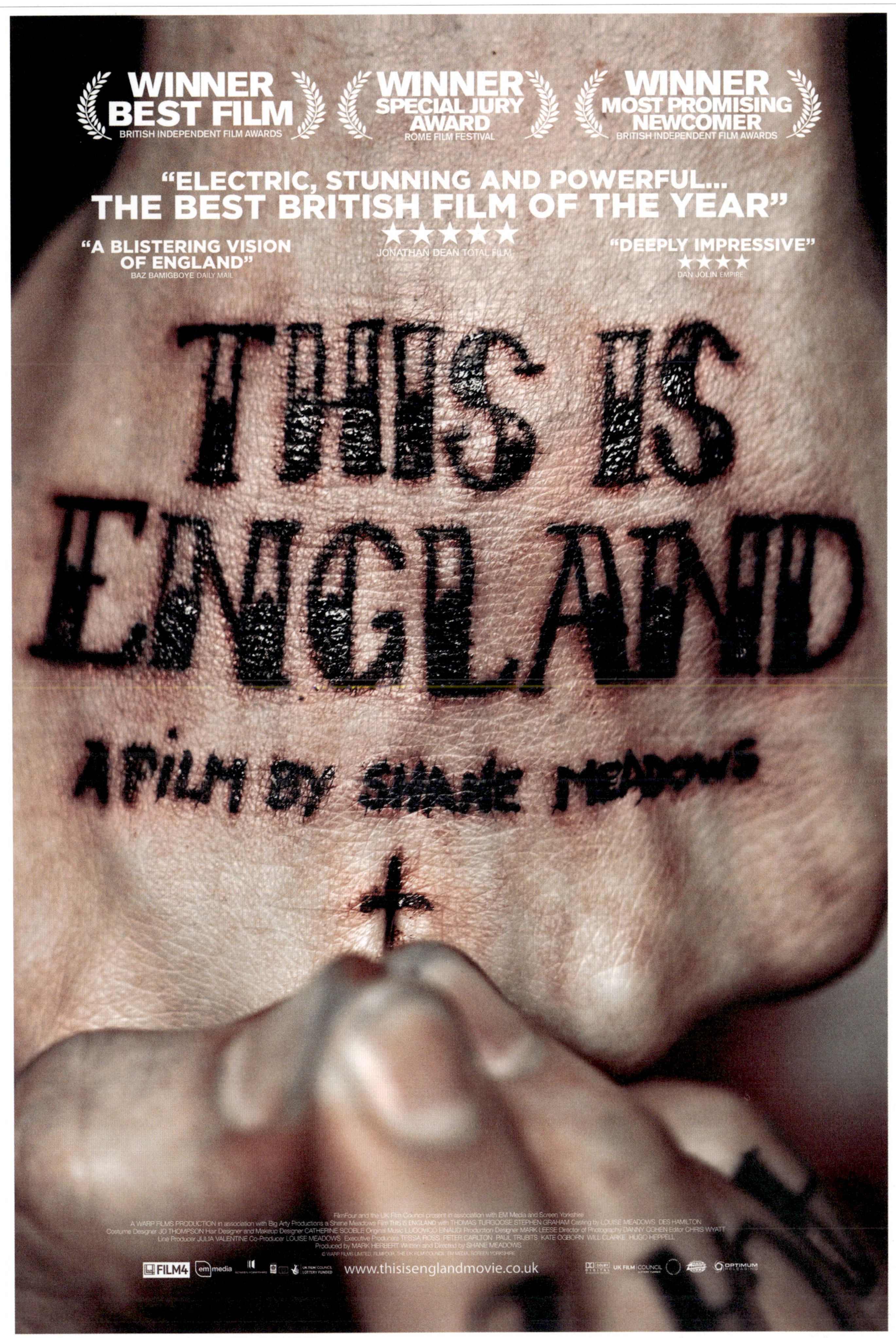

WINNER
BEST FILM
BRITISH INDEPENDENT FILM AWARDS

WINNER
SPECIAL JURY
AWARD
ROME FILM FESTIVAL

WINNER
MOST PROMISING
NEWCOMER
BRITISH INDEPENDENT FILM AWARDS

"ELECTRIC, STUNNING AND POWERFUL...
THE BEST BRITISH FILM OF THE YEAR"
★★★★★
JONATHAN DEAN TOTAL FILM

"A BLISTERING VISION
OF ENGLAND"
BAZ BAMIGBOYE DAILY MAIL

"DEEPLY IMPRESSIVE"
★★★★
DAN JOLIN EMPIRE

THIS IS
ENGLAND

A FILM BY SHANE MEADOWS

www.thisisenglandmovie.co.uk

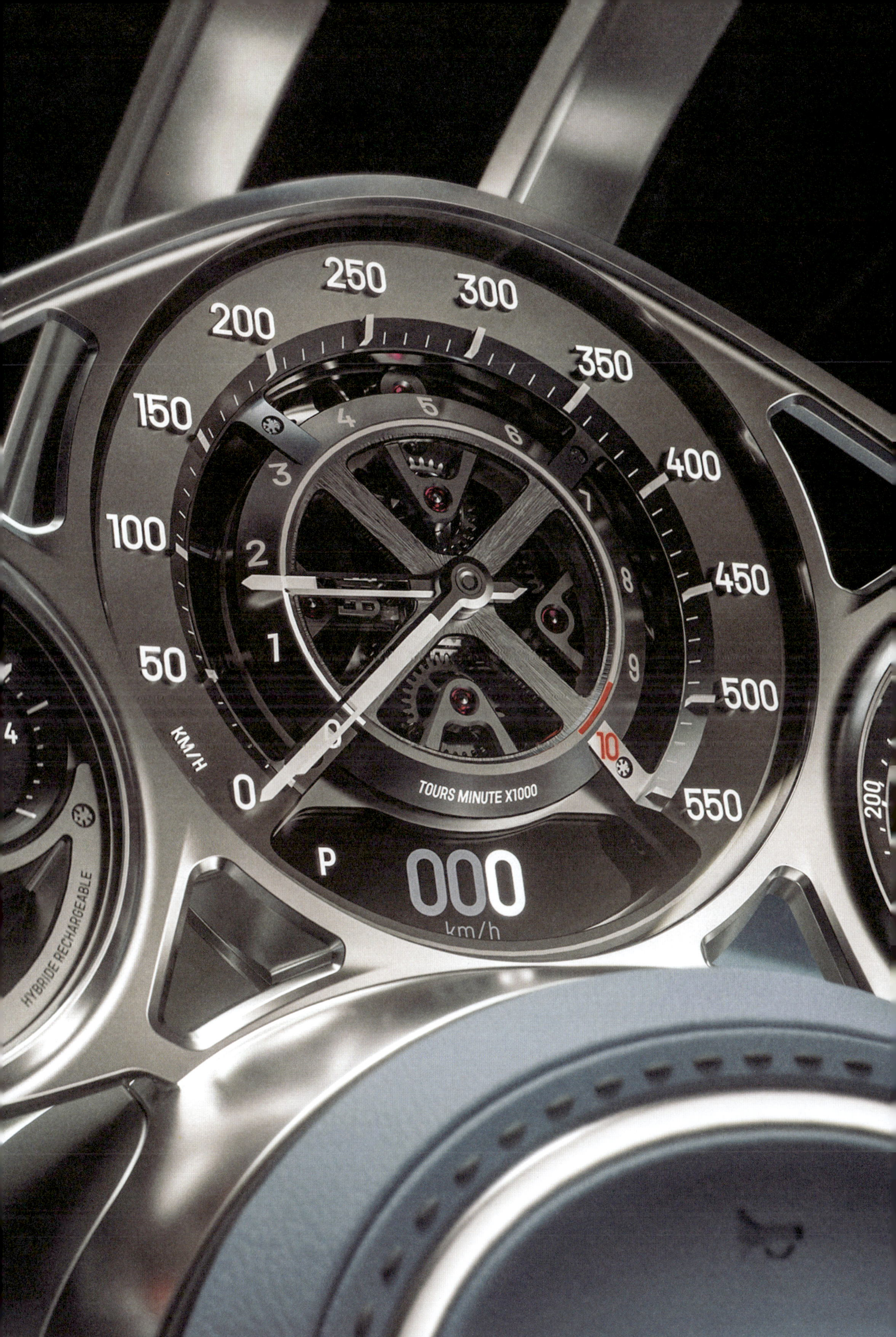

250
300
200
350
150
400
100
450
50
500
550
KM/H
0
P
000
km/h
TOURS MINUTE X1000
3
4
5
6
2
7
1
8
9
10
HYBRIDE RECHARGEABLE
4
200

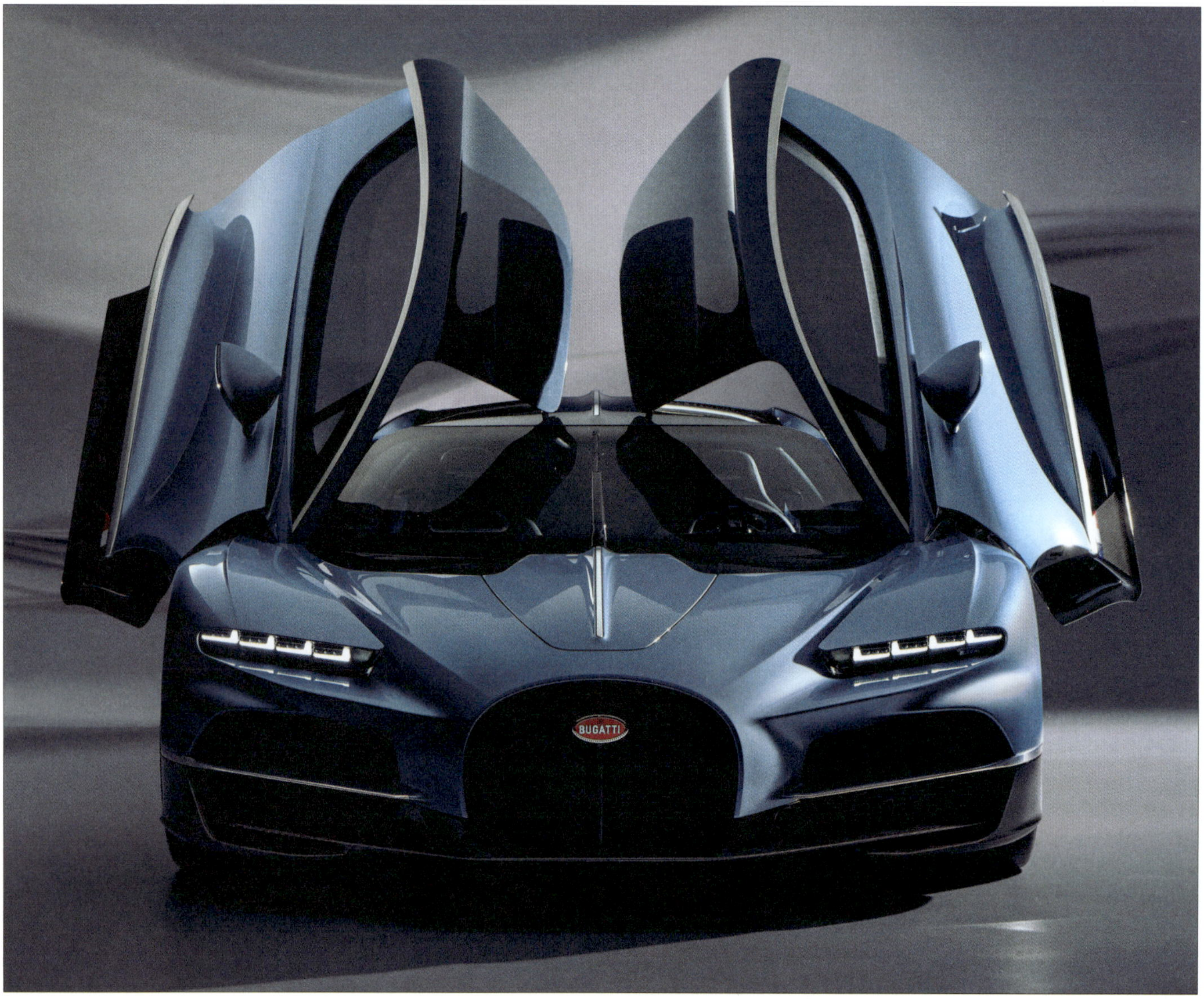

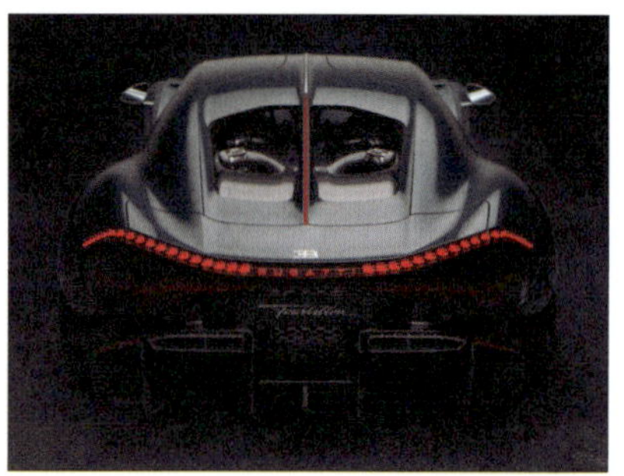

BUGATTI World Premiere Press Kit Images

Power output: 1,800 horsepower	**Engine:** V16 naturally aspirated	**Acceleration:** 0-62 mph (100 km/h) in 2 seconds	**Width with side mirrors:** 7.1 ft (2.2 m)
Maximum speed: 236 mph (380 km/h) limited	**Maximum torque:** 900 Nm	**DIMENSIONS:**	**Height:** 3.9 ft (1.2 m)
276 mph (445 km/h) with speed key	**Maximum rpm:** 9,000 rpm	**Length:** 15.3 ft (4.67 m)	

If the words "Announcing the new Batmobile" accompanied an image of the Bugatti Tourbillon, how many people would doubt, even for a second, that this was true? I'd wager that zero out of 100 individuals would do so. The car just captures that menacing, gothic comic book feel so effortlessly that it's difficult to believe this is an actual automobile that can be purchased in real life.

If you were left with any doubt regarding just how bold and brave the Tourbillon is, then ask yourself the following question: How on earth has it managed to make rotating dihedral doors, which hark back to kitsch gull-wing "DeLorean" doors, look so stylish? By all rights, these doors should invite mockery. But with the Tourbillon, it's almost as if, when those doors are raised, the vehicle is staring you down and warning that there'll be dire consequences for any insult.

Inside, the Tourbillon looks similarly larger than life, with the unique dashboard layout and upholstery having a distinctively modern, essentially chrome, punk-like feel. Clearly, Bugatti, with this fantastical exterior and interior, is unashamedly targeting those among us who long to be like Bruce Wayne!

Bugatti takes credit for the very concept of the hypersports car and claims that the Tourbillon completely redefines this conceptualization. For instance, one novel approach is, in lieu of turbochargers, to combine a combustion engine with an incredibly high-performance powertrain, consisting of an electric motor in the rear, two electric motors in the front, and a 25-kilowatt-hour battery pack.

Bugatti's director of design, Frank Heyl, states that a core philosophy that influences the entire concept-to-completion process of one of the company's cars is to create something timeless. This approach has certainly contributed to the uniqueness of the Tourbillon. An example that Frank notes is the lack of screens within the interior. Instead, every aspect of the dashboard conveys a sturdiness and physicality that eschews the typical stereotypes of futuristic interiors while still looking ultra-modern.

Both Frank and Bugatti Rimac's CEO, Mate Rimac, state that design choices were influenced by the emotions that the Tourbillon could evoke, whether it was the sound of the engine or the extreme proportions of the vehicle. Of course, we can't hear the ferocious roar of the engine on this page, but who can deny that, judging by the images alone, this outstanding vehicle conjures up a specific sensation of vigilantism, making us want to jump behind the wheel and save the day?

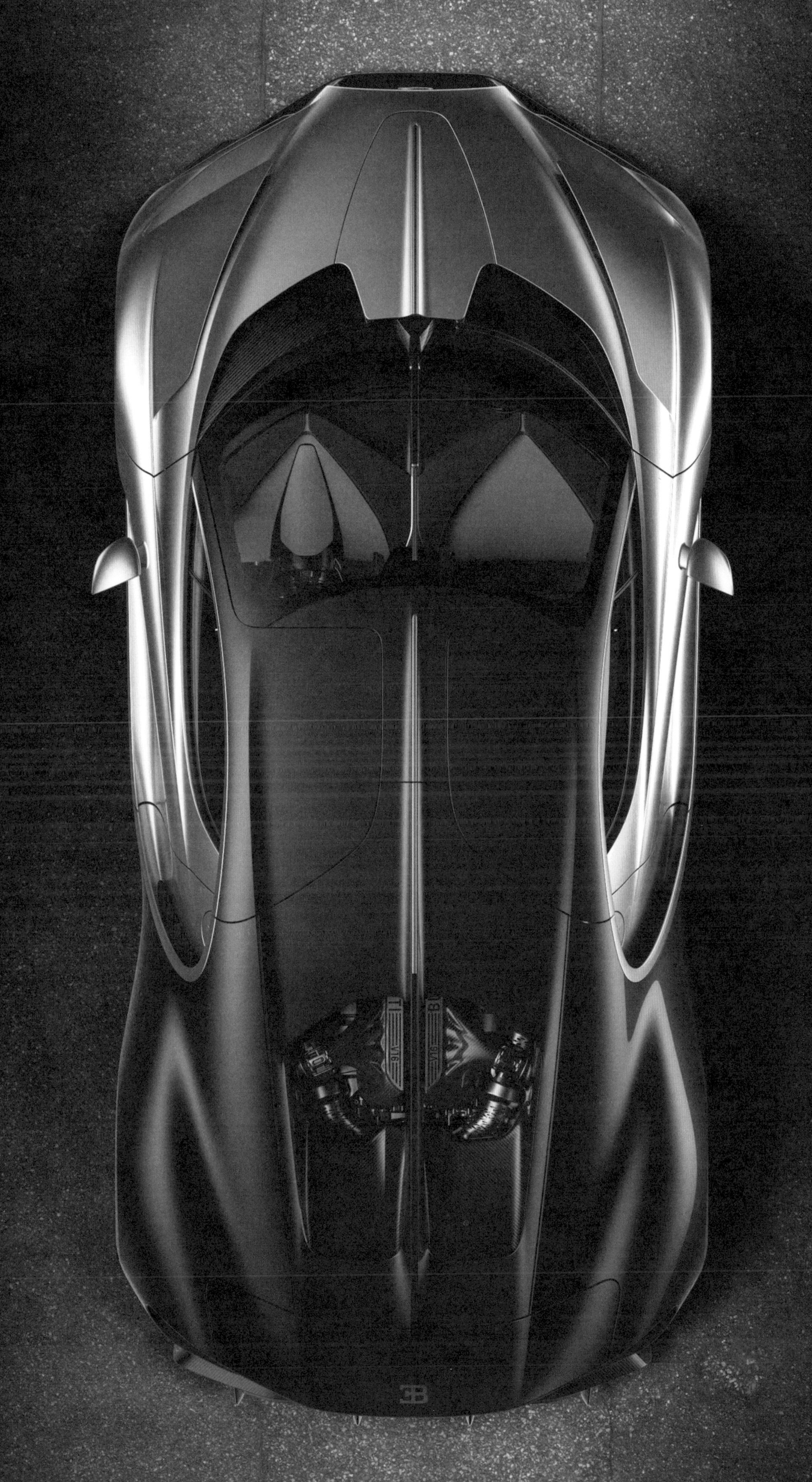

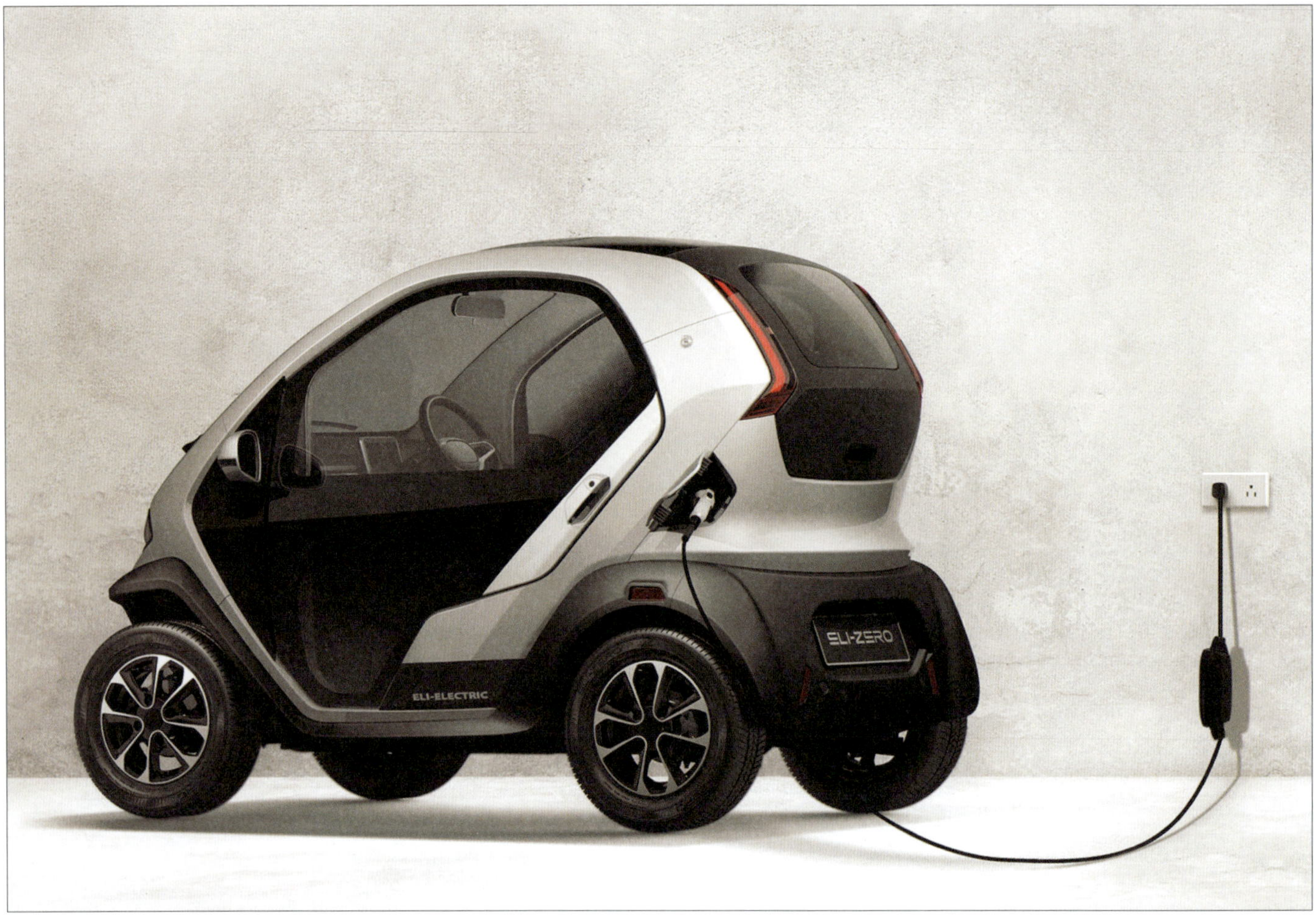

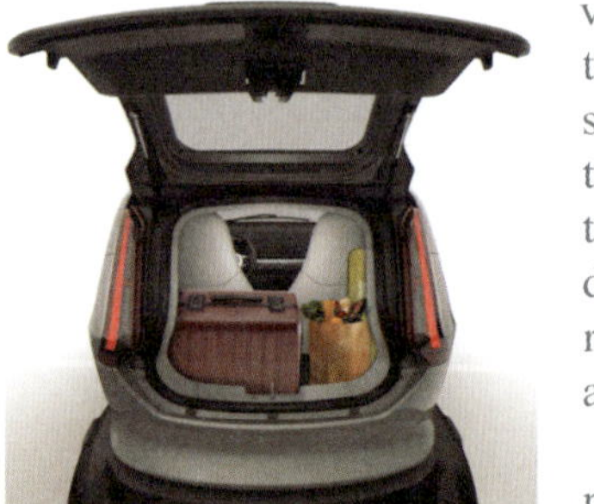

Eli Electric Vehicles

DIMENSION:	Height: 5.2 ft (1.6 m)	Battery type: 8 kWh lithium iron phosphate	Trunk capacity: 5.65 cu ft (160 L)
Length: 7.4 ft (2.3 m)	Top speed: 25 mph (45 kmh)	Charging time: 2.5 hours at 220-240 volts.	
Width: 4.5 ft (1.4 m)	Range: 60 miles (100 km)	5 hours at 110-120 volts	

A guiding principle of Eli Electric Vehicles is to bridge the gap between two- and four-wheel vehicles, with its micro-automobiles combining the nimbleness of motorcycles and the smoothness and stability of cars. After taking Europe by storm, the company is now branching out to the US market with a suitably larger new model of the Eli Zero.

The car brand Smart, which brought the compact electric vehicle to the masses, may have enjoyed strong sales in Europe for the last quarter century, but they've also received harsh criticism for their design, with their appearance being compared to "a baby's pram crossed with a Pokémon" and other cruder things. This less-than-warm reception would discourage many from creating a similar product, but Eli Electric Vehicles has instead embraced the general concept of the Smart car's shape, enacting a few small but crucial innovations with the proportions and angles. The result is a vehicle that subtly modernizes the clunky, boxy original concept into what feels like the year 2034. The diagonal shape of the doors may be the perfect example of how this electric vehicle is essentially the visual equivalent of the "20 minutes into the future" storytelling subgenre. By making these doors flow along the pod-like frame, the Eli Zero is saying that this is a streamlined reimagining of a familiar design. Some may still be put off by the Zero's resemblance to Smart cars, but many more will appreciate that this is the concept done right.

The interior carries this theme along with a page lifted from Apple's minimalistic approach to design. The dashboard has few buttons and knobs, mainly consisting of a smooth surface with just two small screens, one behind the steering wheel and one that can be flipped shut into the dashboard, acting as the primary informational focal points, simplifying the driving experience in the process.

Despite these clearly well-thought-out design decisions, the Eli Zero will almost definitely divide public opinion, with those who think that cars should be macho scoffing at its compact size. Luckily, the rest of us, who can appreciate both the vision and the convenience that the Eli Zero offers, will find plenty of joy in seeing them whizz across cities.

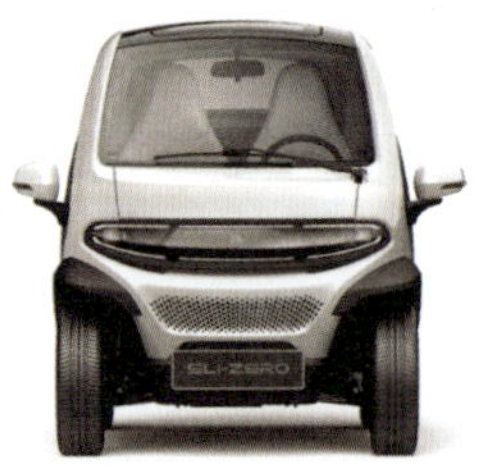

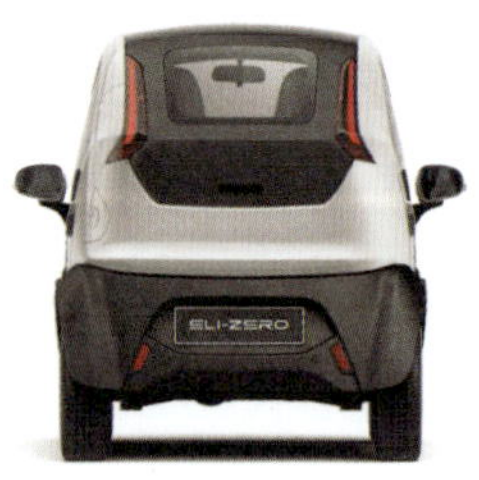

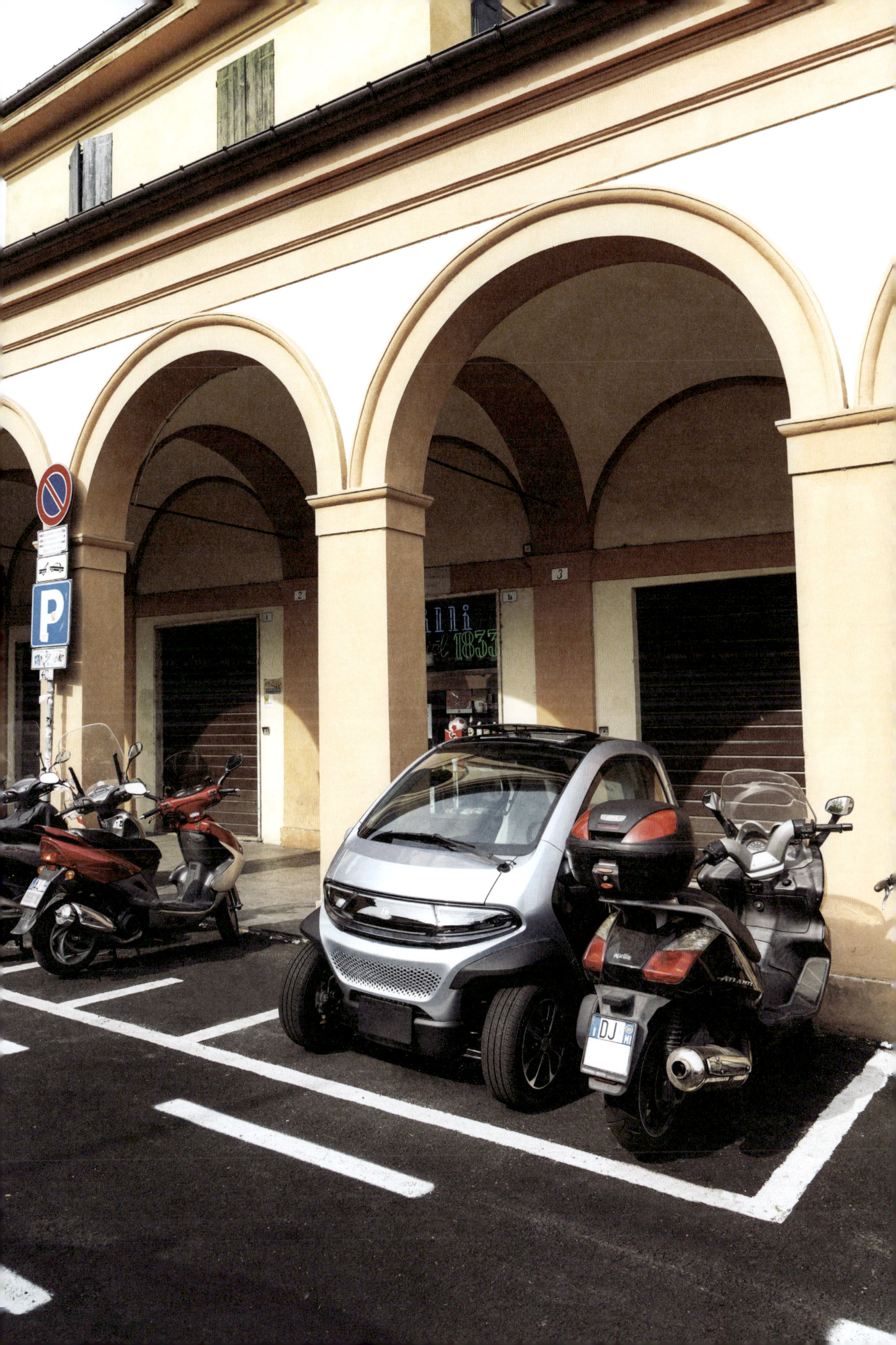
P
dal 1833

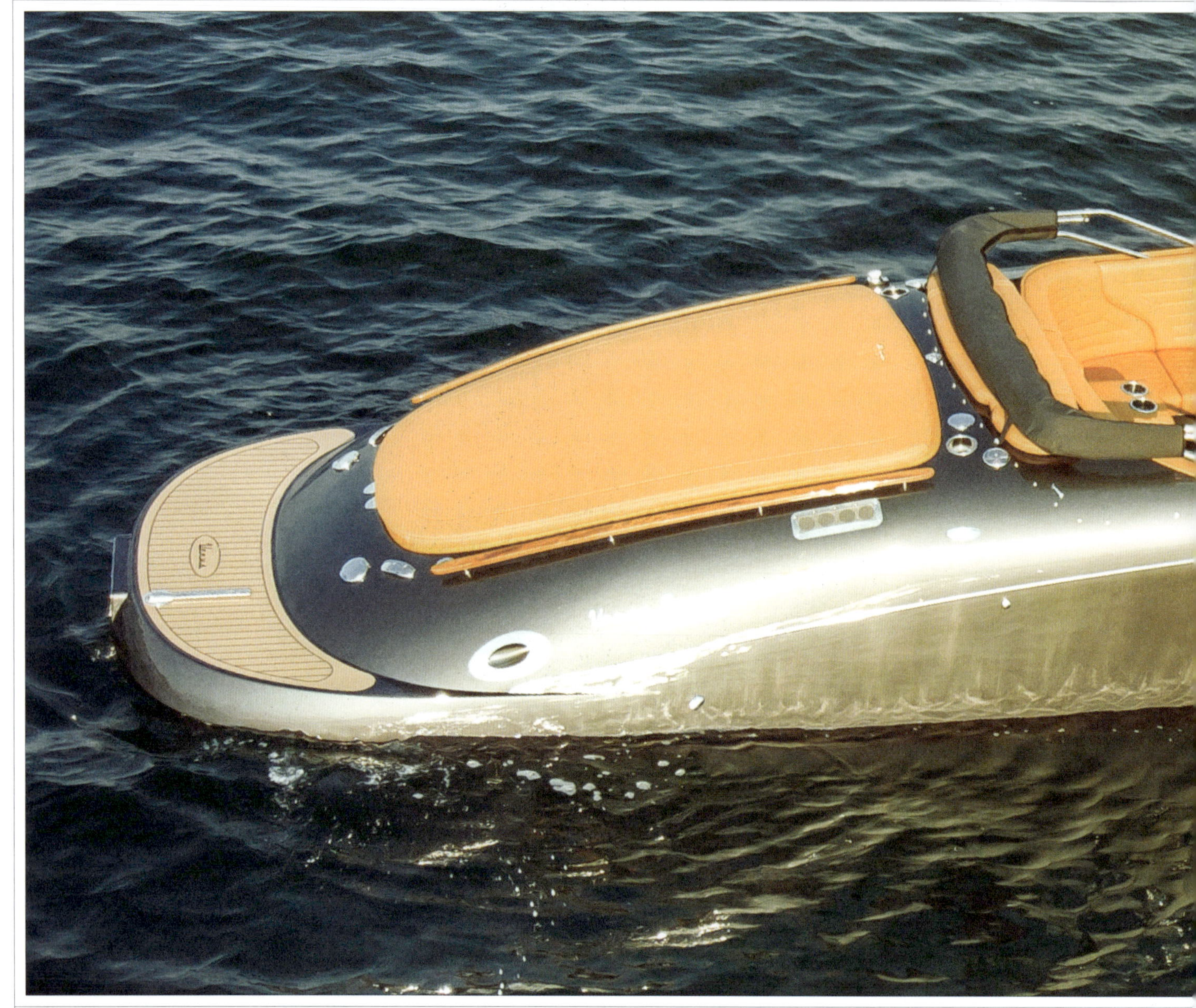

Any company that names a product after the Roman goddess of beauty needs to hold its design acumen to an extremely high standard. Luckily, Seven Seas Yachts has now twice produced a boat worthy of this deity's moniker, with the Venus Speedster's new larger variant, the Venus Speedster X, launching in 2024.

When docked among a throng of white angular vessels, both Venuses are instantly eye-catching, providing a blast to the past that will surely make some onlookers wonder which century they were crafted in. Yet, when zipping elegantly along the waves, their bygone-era personality truly shines, seeming like they're on a mission to take their passengers back to a more carefree time.

And yes, the Venuses do look smoother in motion than their competitors. Their sharp entry angles work with the unique hull designs to cut through waves smoothly, resulting in a ride that features no pounding. Or, to put it another way, the craftsmanship that has gone into the Venus Speedsters not only makes them look sleek but also ensures they feel just as smooth when charging across the open seas.

From afar, the Venus Speedster X would turn heads in destinations as lavish as Monaco. Yet, up close, a range of small touches elevate it even further. Even the beverage holders contain small LED lights, conveying an air of luxury that only those on board can genuinely appreciate. And yes, these beverages will be cold, thanks to a hidden refrigerator located behind the driver's seat within what initially appears to be humble storage space.

WITH THE VENUS SPEEDSTER X, YOU CAN ENJOY AN ENTIRE DAY ON THE WATER IN COMPLETE COMFORT, TAKING ADVANTAGE OF ITS EXPANDED FEATURES AND LUXURIOUS DESIGN. **Seven Seas Yachts**

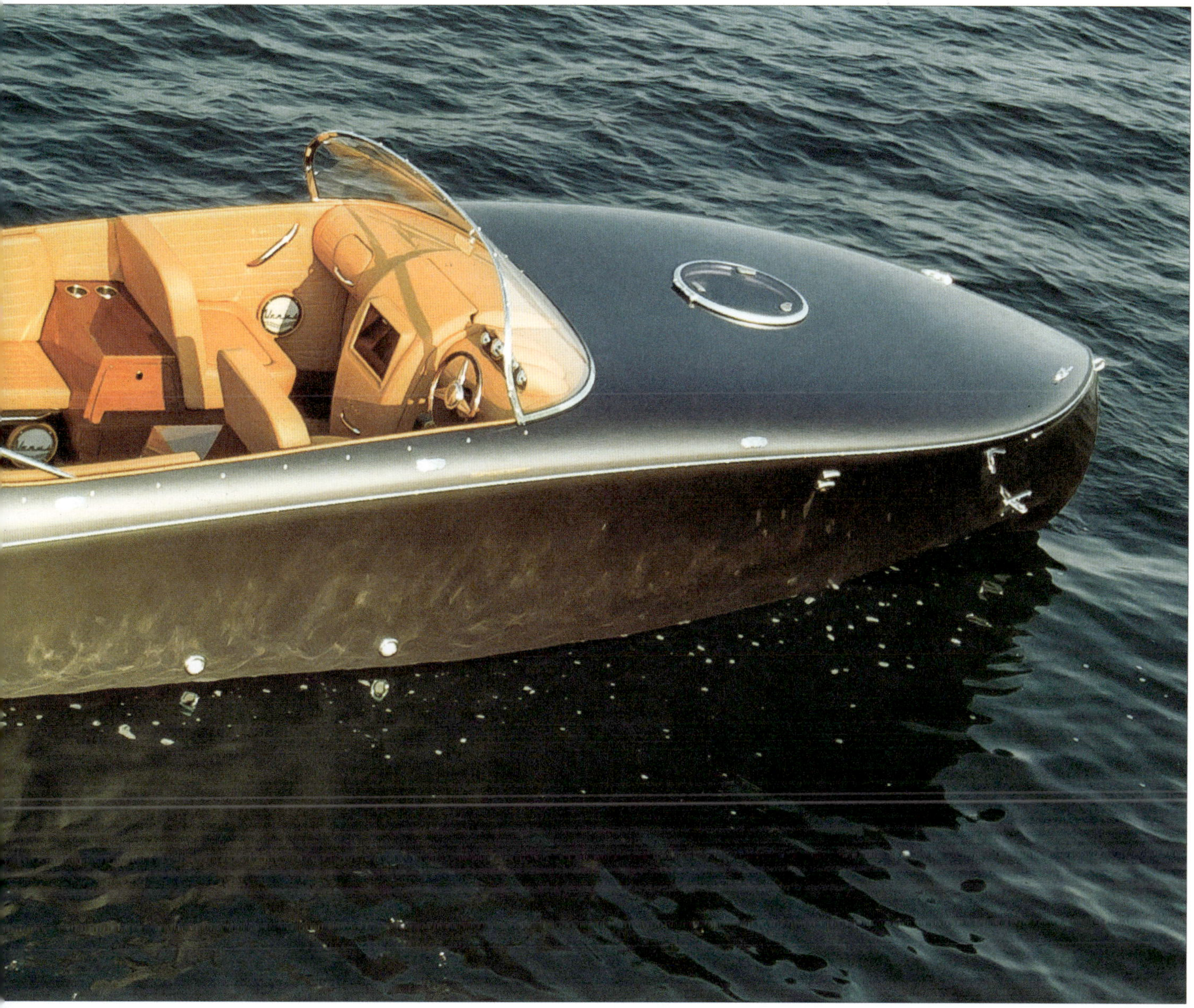

Venus Speedster X

| **LOA:** 31.66 ft (9.65 m) | **Draught:** 1.10 ft (0.30 m) | **Maximum crew:** 8 people | **Power:** 350 horsepower |
| **Beam:** 7.61 ft (2.35 m) | **Displacement:** 5,510 lbs (2,500 kg) | **Engine:** Mercury Mercruiser 6.2 V8 | |

But perhaps the most impressive hidden feature of this boat lies below deck. Within the Venus Speedster X's bow is a cabin housing a double bed with a nifty, small, circular skylight above, giving those resting within the opportunity to gaze up at a starry night. Concealed elsewhere on board are a toilet and a shower, ensuring that it's possible to live comfortably on board for an extended period of time.

Surprisingly, for a product that is so clearly an homage to the aesthetics of the middle of the 20th century, the Venus Speedster X is available with a zero-emission electric option.

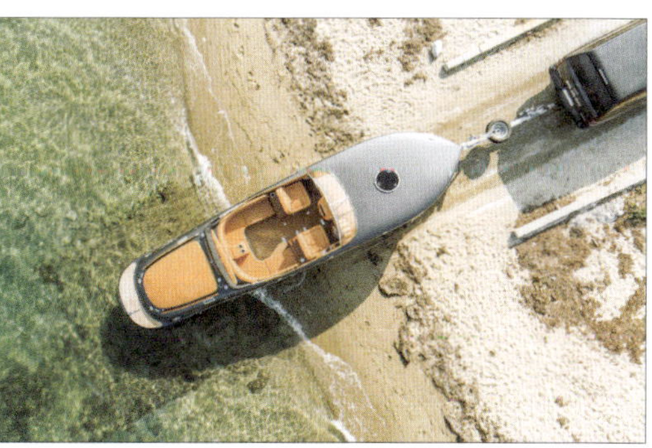

Even the version with conventional combustion uses "smaller engines than similar sized boats while still being faster than its competitors." In fact, this efficiency and a video screen in the center of the dashboard appear to be the only two exposed design elements to have noticeably come from the 21st century.

How many boats of this size on the market combine superb living amenities, stellar speed, superior efficiency, and a stunning appearance this well? The Venus Speedsters are exactly what the phrase "in a league of their own" was coined for!

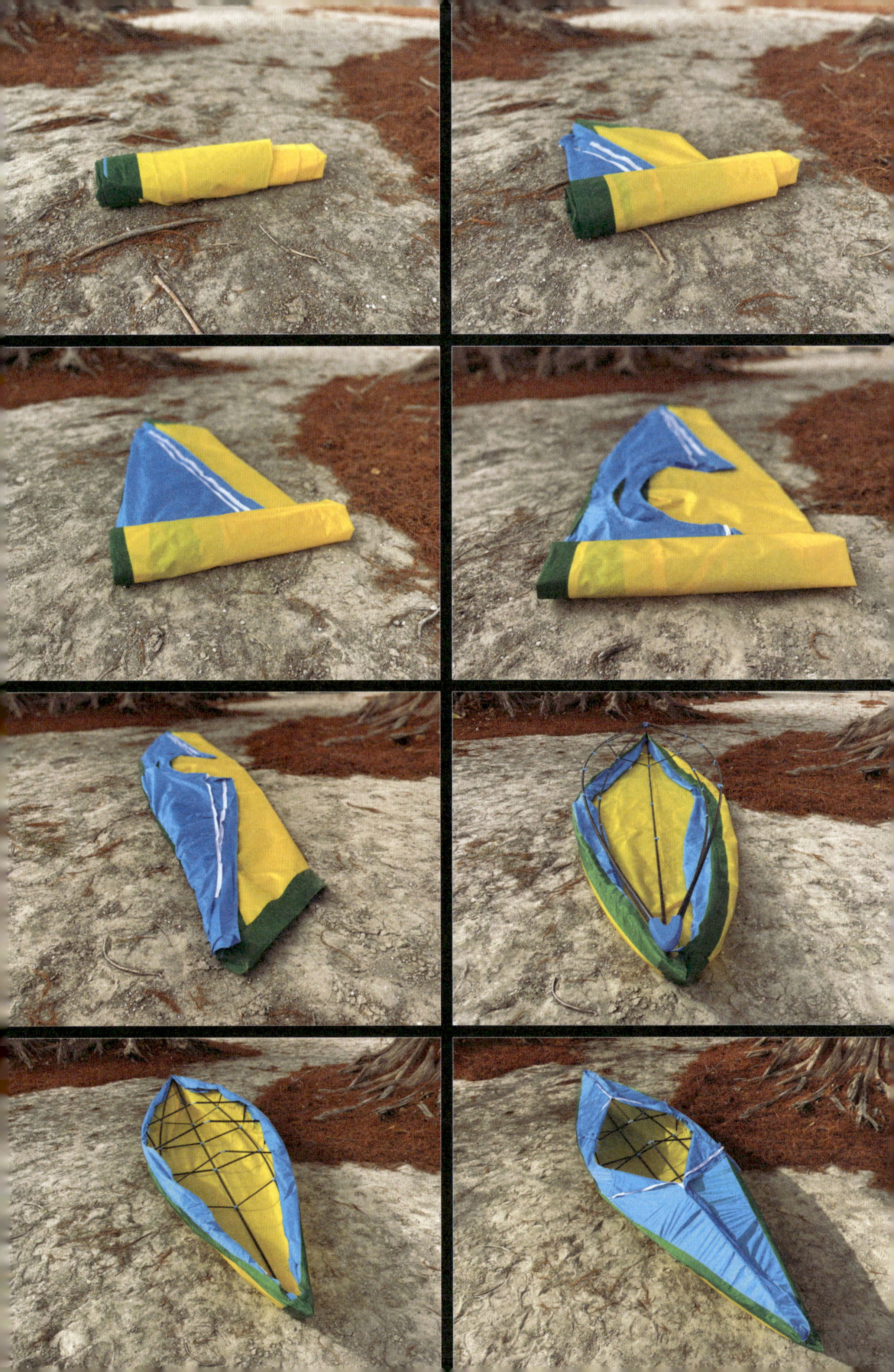

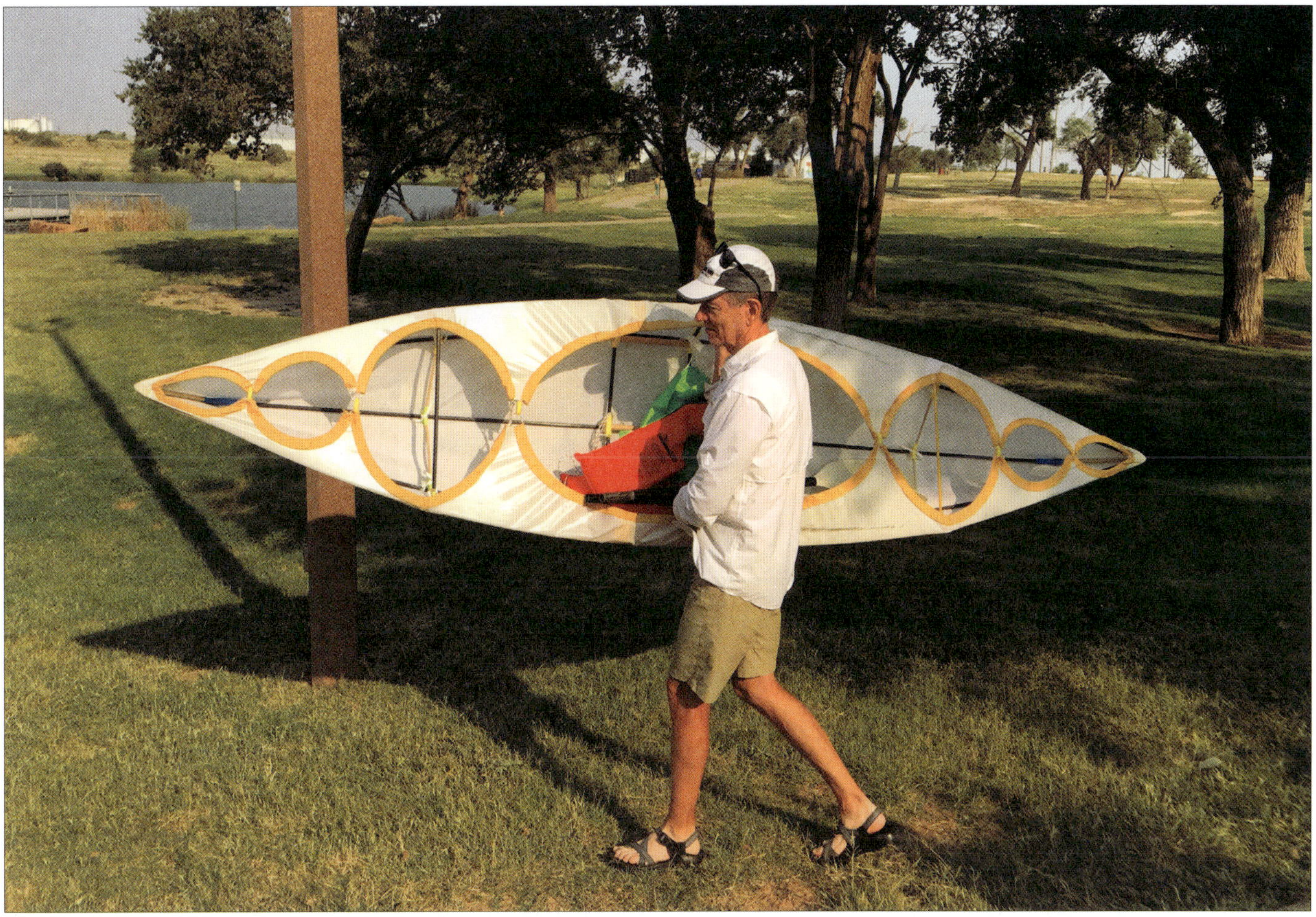

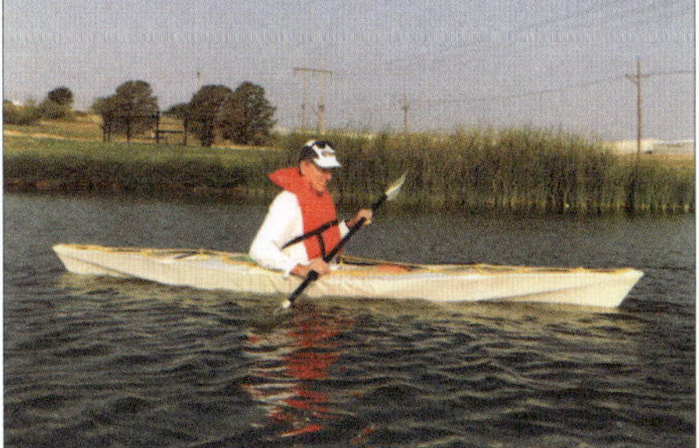

Packable Kayak

DIMENSIONS:	Width: 2.4 ft (0.7 m)	MATERIAL:	connected with shock cord	hull of 210 denier nylon
Length: 10.5 ft (3.2 m)	Weight capacity: 300 lbs	Frame: Lightweight carbon fiber	Shell: TPU bonded nylon and a lower	

This time last year, Graphis featured a folding kayak, the Oru Kayak. Now, a similar product, the Pontos Packable Kayak, has caught our attention. These two differing products initially sound the same, but a number of interesting differences show that there are endless ways to realize a concept.

In terms of inspiration, the Oru Kayak and the Pontos Kayak vary significantly. While the former applies the elegance of origami to watersports, the latter enacts the rugged escapades that tents inherently convey. Pontos is certainly being brazen by claiming that its product "is the first truly packable kayak," but the company justifies this statement by citing its ability to reduce down to a size comparable to that of a deconstructed two-person tent and having a weight of just seven pounds. For comparison, when folded, the Oru Kayak is the size of a check-in suitcase, and the lightest possible variant weighs 17 pounds. These size and weight differences may seem insignificant, but for those with a passion for outdoor exploration, it makes all the difference, as the Pontos Packable Kayak can be taken on any length of expedition with ease.

Price-wise the Pontos is only nominally more expensive than the cheapest Oru Kayak—$76 more, to be precise. This similarity is apt, considering that both products have been designed to accommodate specific niches in the market, with neither niche being "preferable" to the other. Some want to be weekend warriors who take out the graceful Oru Kayak on road trips to nearby rivers. Others find more appeal in the ability of the Pontos Kayak to always be readily available, even when hundreds of miles out in the wilderness.

Possibly the most telling difference between these two brands is the way they ensure the purchase will pay off. Oru offers customers a three-year warranty, while Pontos offers extra patch material for performing repairs. Anyone who would rather repair a product than return it is likely to find much more satisfaction from the Pontos than the Oru!

WE WANTED TO CREATE A BOAT THAT FITS INTO YOUR LIFE, SUITCASE, CAR, CLOSET, BACKPACK, AND BUDGET WHILE STILL GIVING YOU EVERYTHING YOU EXPECT FROM A KAYAK ON THE WATER.

Adam Muslow, *Founder, Pontos*

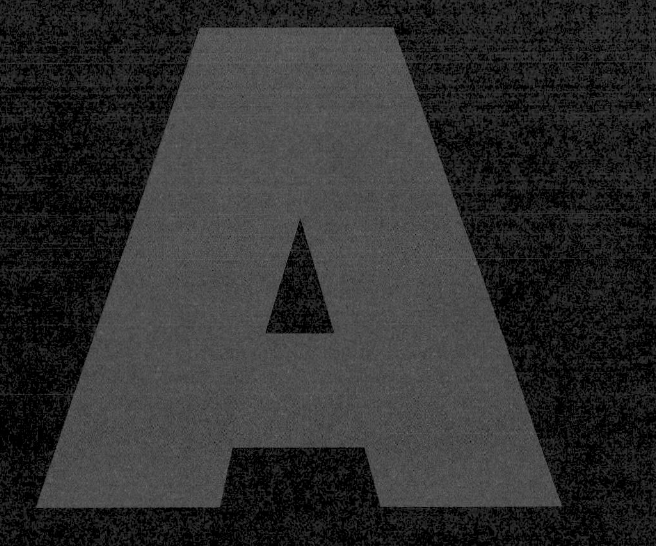

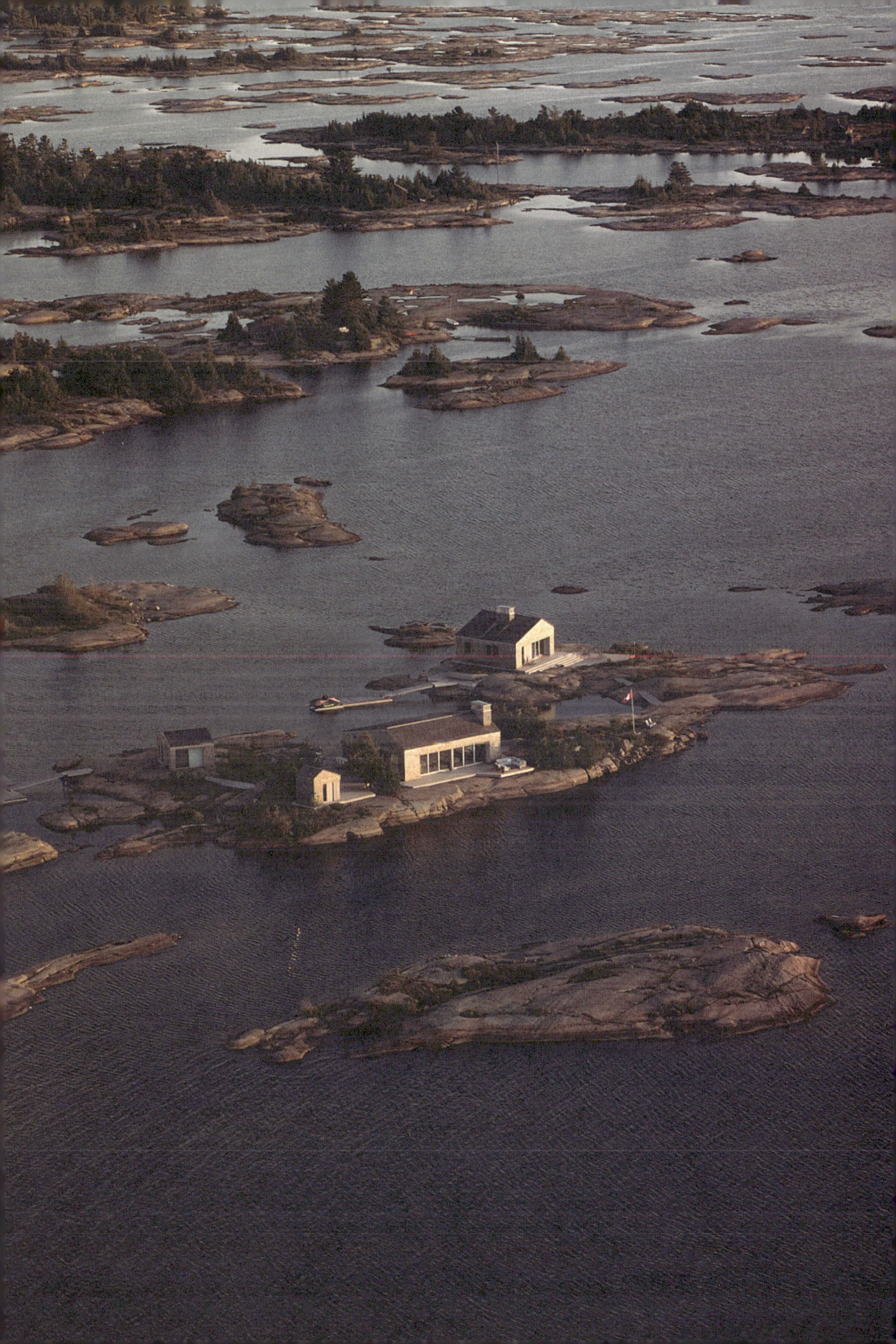

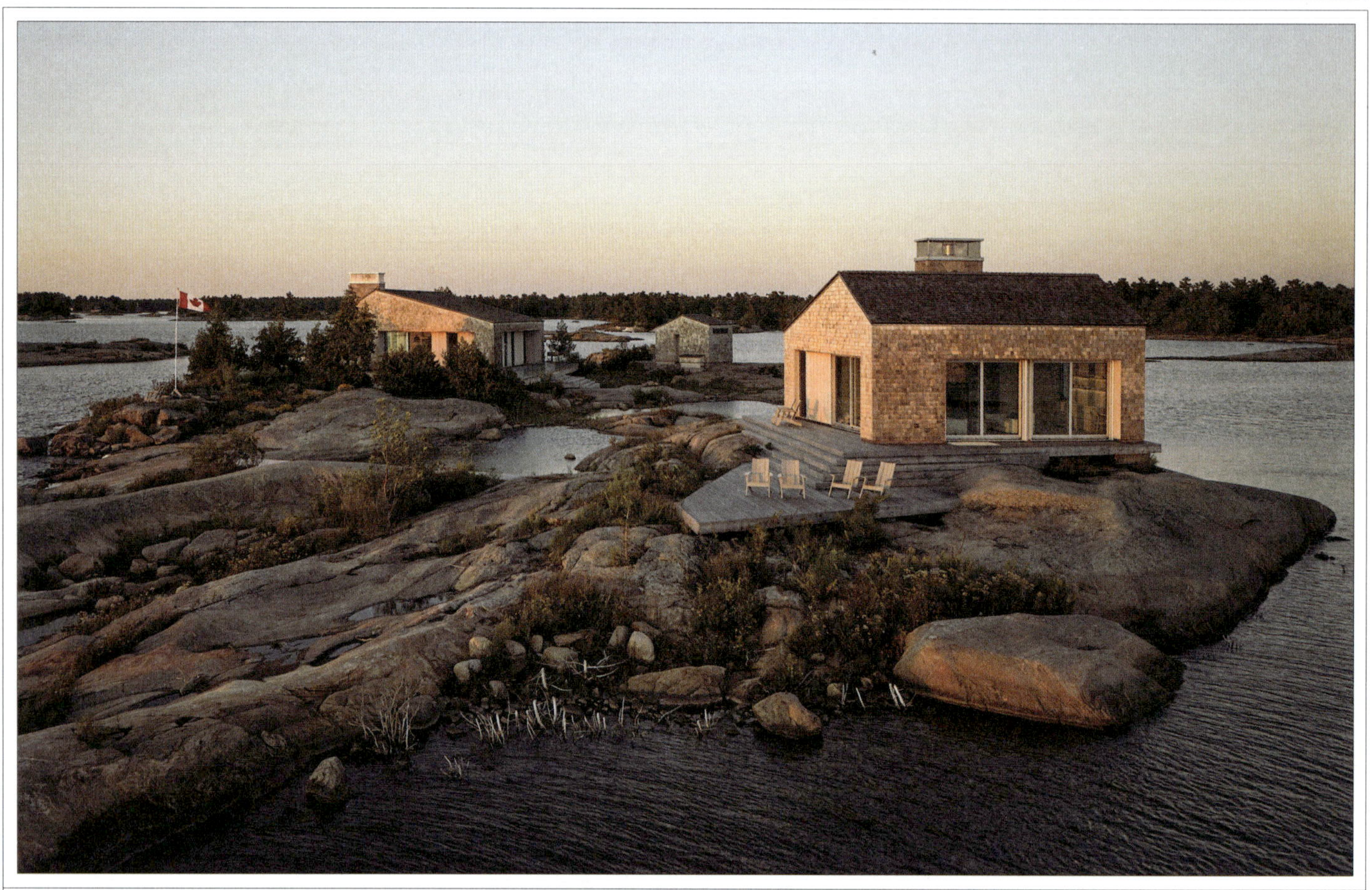

Whistling Wind Island Images by Doublespace

The sheer seclusion of Whistling Wind Island is nothing short of breathtaking. Four small structures perch atop one of the 30,000 craggy islands situated along the east coast of Ontario's Georgian Bay. From this island, few other buildings can be seen, with those looking humble in comparison to the outstandingly executed quartet of dwellings crafted by Akb Architects. Just to be clear, it's not that those homes are ugly. Far from it, in fact. It's just that Whistling Wind Island has the charming appearance of seeming like its own harmonious minuscule community, almost as if it were a work of art named "The World's Tiniest Model Village."

In addition to standing out from their surroundings, the buildings also paradoxically blend in with the vista. This contradictory element is partly thanks to the decision to use silver-weather cedar shingles as cladding in a shade that reflects the hues of the rocks that make up the island. These almost camouflaging tones invite the eye to focus on the minutiae of the project, which also aids in making the structures seem somewhat translucent. For example, wrap-around gangplank decking connects the four buildings, and these have been designed with steps that angle in harmony with the sedimentary rocks below to act as a transitional point, seeming almost as if the buildings had started to melt into the landscape.

Inside the primary building of Whistling Wind Island, the impression of idyllic rural living is also subtly reinforced, with the matching wood planks that line the cathedral ceiling being a modern reinterpretation of gabled wood forms often found in older cottage roofs. This roof shields a kitchen and dining space that also achieves an angular, contemporary impression of a classic style, with the traditional layout of cabin interiors being realized with minimalistic furnishing.

The importance of connecting with nature for the owner of Whistling Wind Island should be apparent already. But one small yet shocking fact demonstrates how they are pushing this goal to the extreme: On completion, Whistling Wind Island lacked either a bathtub or a shower, with the only bathing option being the surrounding Canadian lake water, which can get as cold as 32 degrees Fahrenheit (0 Celsius). Notably, Akb Architects does state that an exterior shower was eventually installed. What led to this decision is left to speculation. One theory could be that the shower came about after much nagging from the owner's partner. Unfortunately, for this possibly fictional person, the shower also uses water from the lake.

Many architectural projects in secluded environments set out with the goal of creating buildings that complement their natural landscapes. Often, these statements turn out to be jargon. Whistling Wind Island is an example of the claim ringing true, thanks to both the macro and micro choices that allow it to live in visual harmony with the immediate environs.

THE VISUAL SOLIDITY OF THESE BUILDINGS FOSTERS COMFORT IN KNOWING THESE DWELLINGS CAN WITHSTAND EXTREME WEATHER PATTERNS… WHILE THE MODEST SCALE AND TACTILE WARMTH OF THE INTERIORS PROVIDE COZY REFUGE. **Akb Architects**

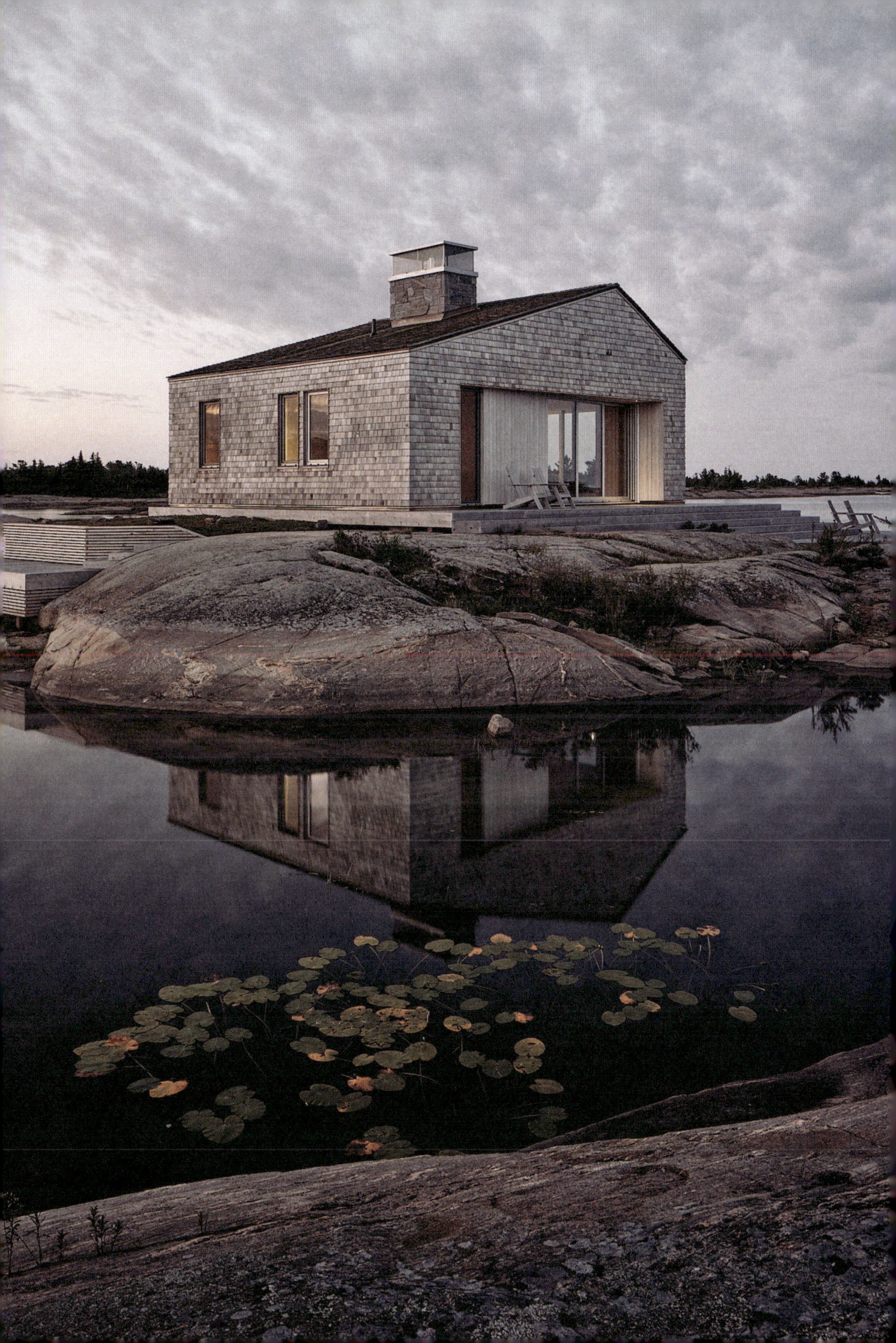

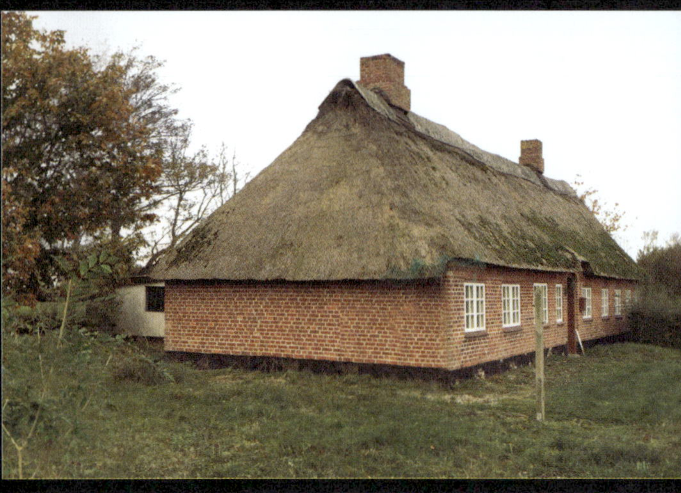
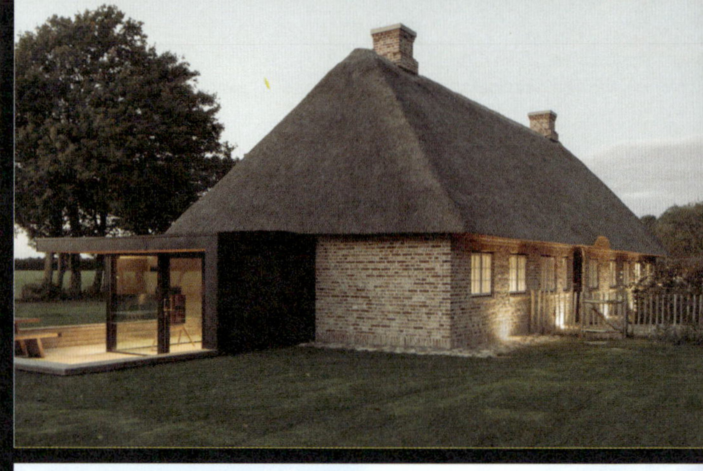
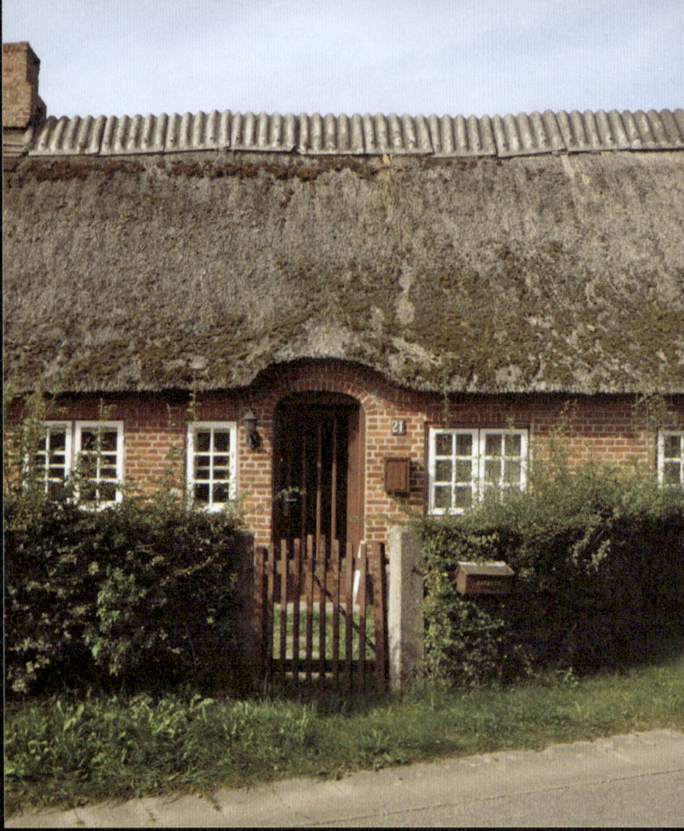
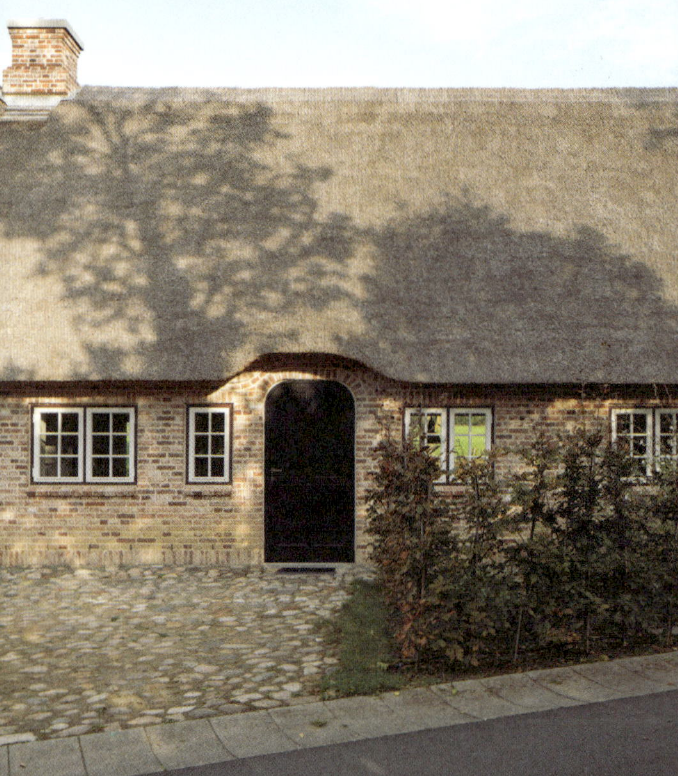
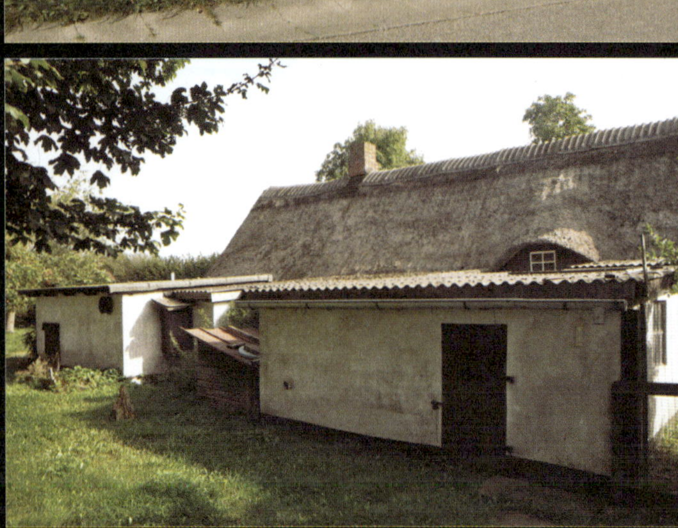
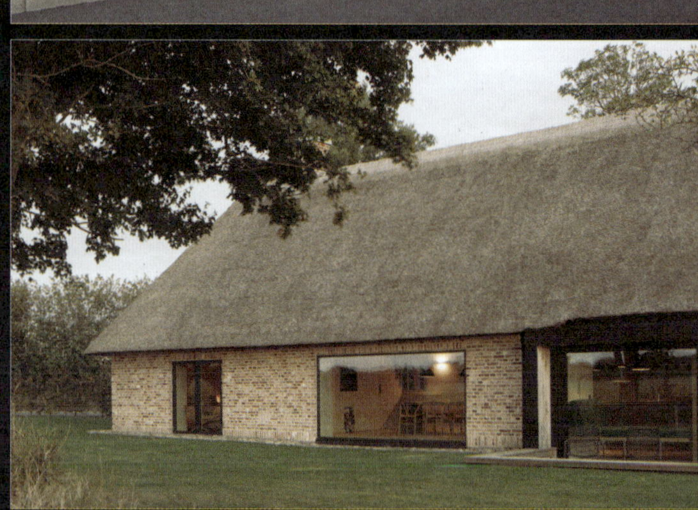

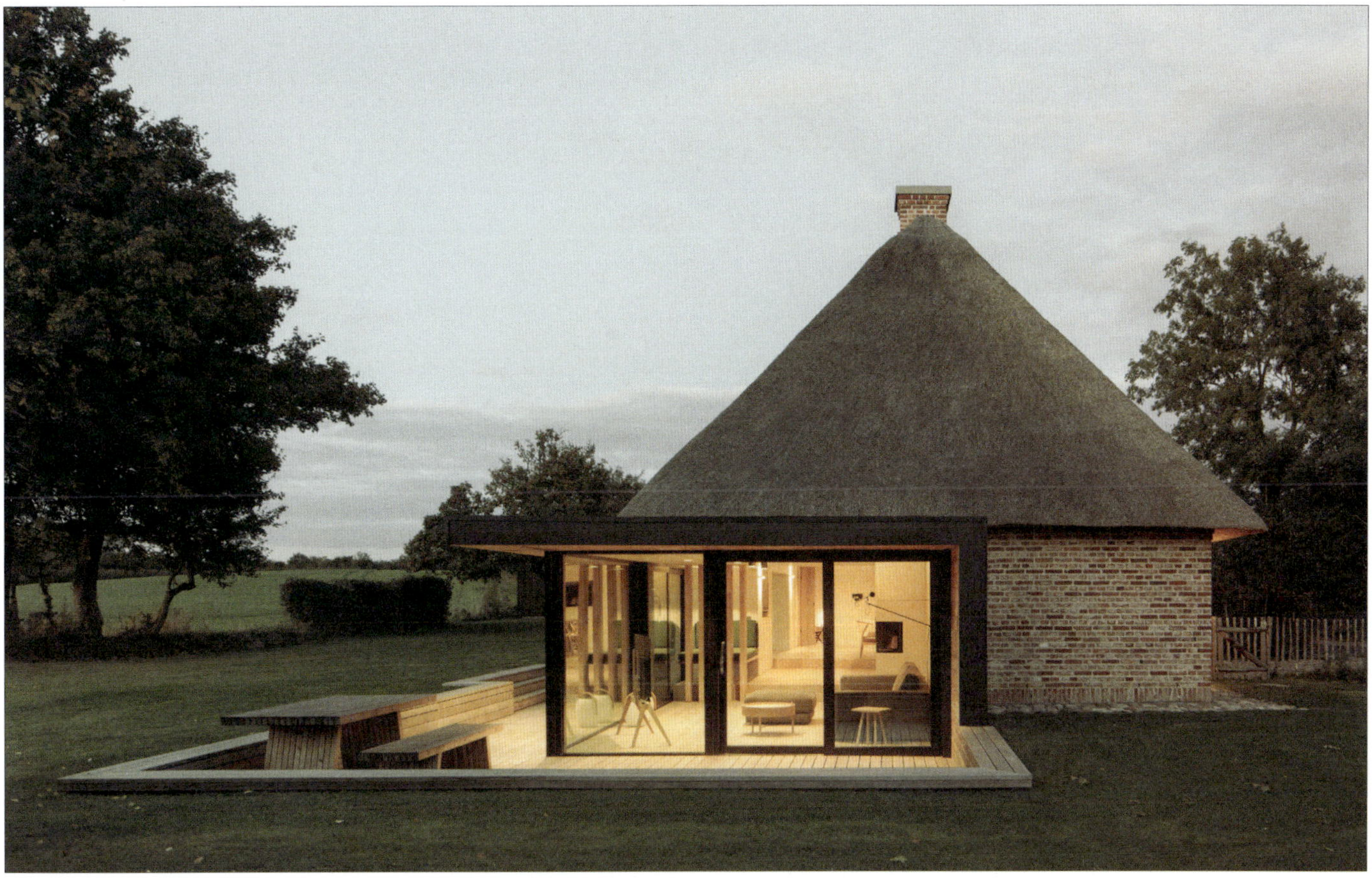

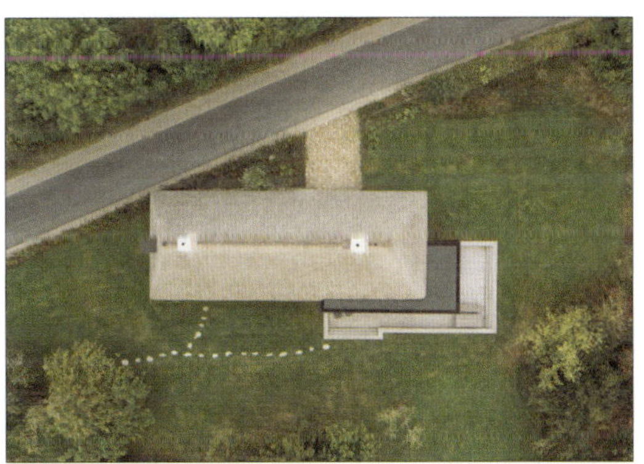

Nieby Crofters Cottage

At the turn of the 20th century, a charming brick cottage was built along the Baltic Coast of Germany by humble farmers. Over the next 120 years, this building withstood two world wars, ever more extreme weather, and the natural pressures of time. Finally, at the turn of the 21st century, the building was abandoned, falling into a state of disrepair, with the roof even partially collapsing.

Still, the character of the cottage remained. After another decade, Jan Henrik Jansen and Marshall Blecher's clients realized that the building was worth salvaging. The assignment was to create a contemporary country retreat without diminishing the essence of the original structure.

While other cottages in the area have been renovated beyond recognition, the architects were determined to maintain the historic nature of Nieby Crofters Cottage. From certain angles, this building appears to be perfectly preserved. This is certainly the case for the street view, with little other than modern window frames suggesting that any major changes have been made. However, from other angles, the scale of the project is revealed.

The most dramatic modern addition, from both the inside and the outside, is the airy living room, which, in concept, is similar to a glass conservatory, except with a square execu-tion and a single oak-lined wall and ceiling combination, giving the space a unique realization. This room leads out to a sunken timber terrace, which encompasses the three glass walls of the added structure.

Behind the living space, what was once 14 maze-like rooms have been combined into one large kitchen and dining area, with the showstopping item being a 20-foot (6-meter) long plinth acting as an island bench and dining table. This lengthy item, which appears to be a modern reworking of a grand medieval banquet table, was so immense that it could only be added to the building by lowering it through the roof during reconstruction.

In restoring Nieby Crofters Cottage, Jan and Marshall chose to work with instead of against some of the ravages of time that had impacted the building. For example, many of the new windows in the original structure were added in parts of the walls that had sustained significant damage. Similarly, the terrace area previously housed sheds and pigsties. In essence, this means that Nieby Crofters Cottage quite literally reflects the impacts of its lengthy existence into the present day. Few renovations can claim to have harnessed the original building's experiences in such a novel way!

THE INTERIOR COMBINES HISTORIC ELEMENTS, INCLUDING SMALL MULLIONED TIMBER WINDOWS AND EXPOSED OAK RAFTERS WITH SHARP, MINIMAL, AND MODERN INTERVENTIONS. Jan Henrik Jansen & Marshall Blecher

EDUCATION
126 PROFESSOR SIMON JO
EDUCATION

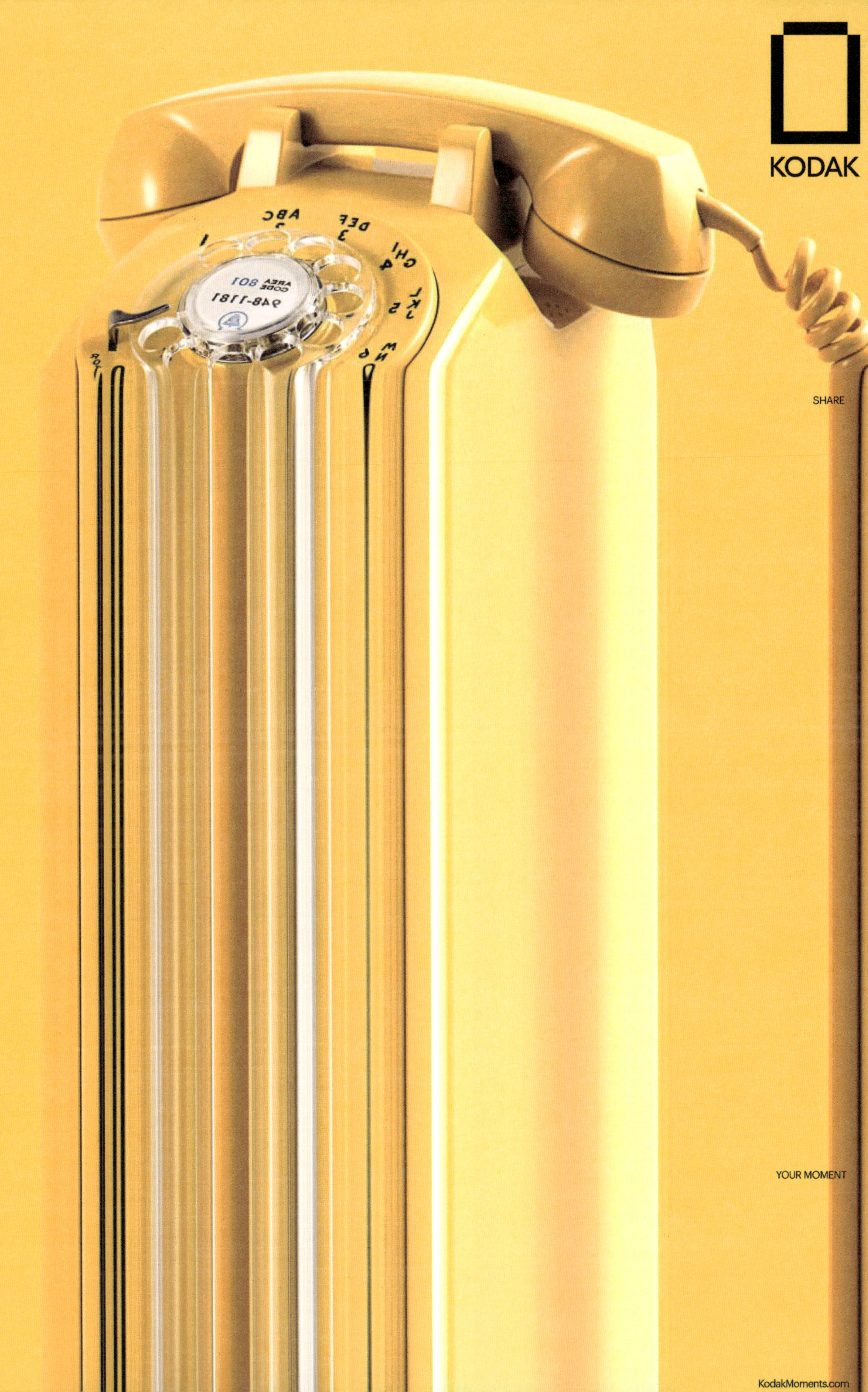
KODAK
SHARE
YOUR MOMENT
AREA CODE 801
948-1181
KodakMoments.com

SIMON'S LEGACY IS A MASTERCLASS IN BALANCING HISTORICAL FLUENCY WITH A CRITICAL AND SELF-REFLECTIVE CONCERN FOR LANGUAGE.

Austin Redman, *Former Student & Freelance Graphic Designer*

SIMON IS, WITHOUT A DOUBT, ONE OF THE BEST PROFESSORS I'VE EVER HAD. HIS PHILOSOPHY AND APPROACH TO DESIGN HAVE PROFOUNDLY SHAPED THE DESIGNER I'VE BECOME TODAY.

Alan Xu, *Former Student & Department Assistant, ArtCenter College of Design*

SIMON HELPED ME FIND ONE OF THE MOST POWERFUL TOOLS I HAVE—TYPOGRAPHY.

Ximena Amaya, *Former Student, Freelance Graphic Designer, & Typography Fellow, Hoffmitz Milken Center for Typography*

SIMON JOHNSTON IS AN INSPIRING MENTOR AND DESIGN LEGEND. TAKING HIS CLASS HAS BEEN A TRANSFORMATIVE EXPERIENCE.

Esther Yeseul Lee, *Former Student & Freelance Graphic Designer*

I AM GRATEFUL TO HAVE BENEFITED FROM HIS ORIGINAL, INSPIRED, YET DISCIPLINED APPROACH TO TEACHING TYPOGRAPHY AND DESIGN. IT WAS A PRIVILEGE TO STUDY WITH HIM.

Tim Bavington, *Former Student & Artist*

SIMON JOHNSTON HAS PLAYED A MAJOR ROLE IN ESTABLISHING ARTCENTER'S REPUTATION AS ONE OF THE TOP DESIGN SCHOOLS IN THE COUNTRY. MUCH RESPECT!

River Jukes-Hudson, *Professor, ArtCenter College of Design*

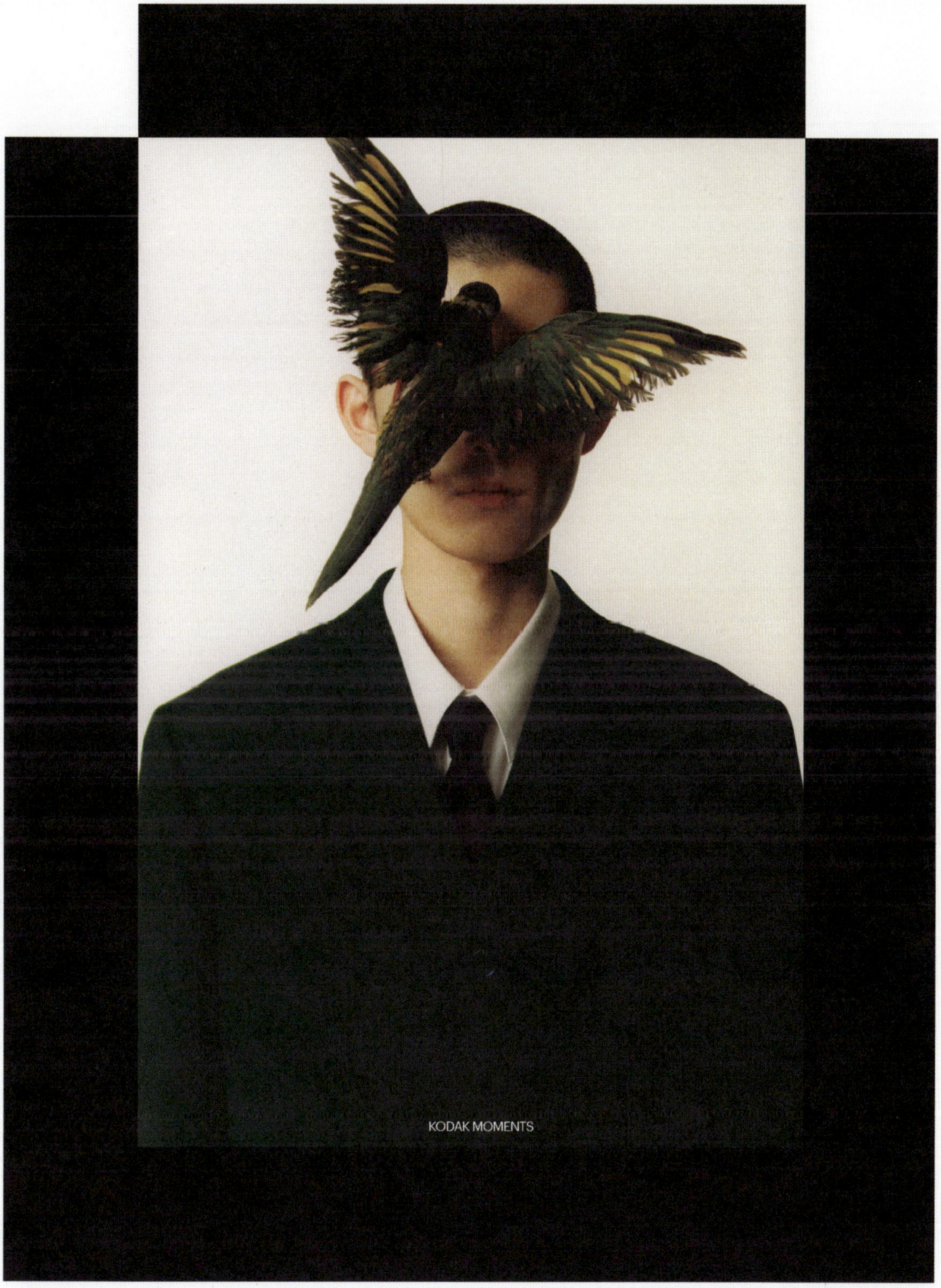

KODAK MOMENTS

KODAK

Introduction by Lavinia Lascaris *Designer, Professor, & Assoc. Director, Hoffmitz Milken Center for Typography*

Of the countless lessons Simon Johnston imparts in his classroom, two are my favorite: first, to think of type as music and to treat the negative space in typography as the space between the notes in a musical composition, and second, to recognize that typography shapes how we see and understand words, and so essential to mastering it is a deep love and respect for language. I am sure that each of the thousands of students he has taught has their own set of favorites among the many memorable metaphors and visual analogies he brings to his lessons. Simon has shaped a generation of graphic designers. In his 30+ years of teaching, he has developed a comprehensive curriculum for typography that combines technical skills with conceptual depth. His ability to inspire critical thinking and distill the essence of form defines his pedagogy and leaves an indelible mark on those who learn from him.

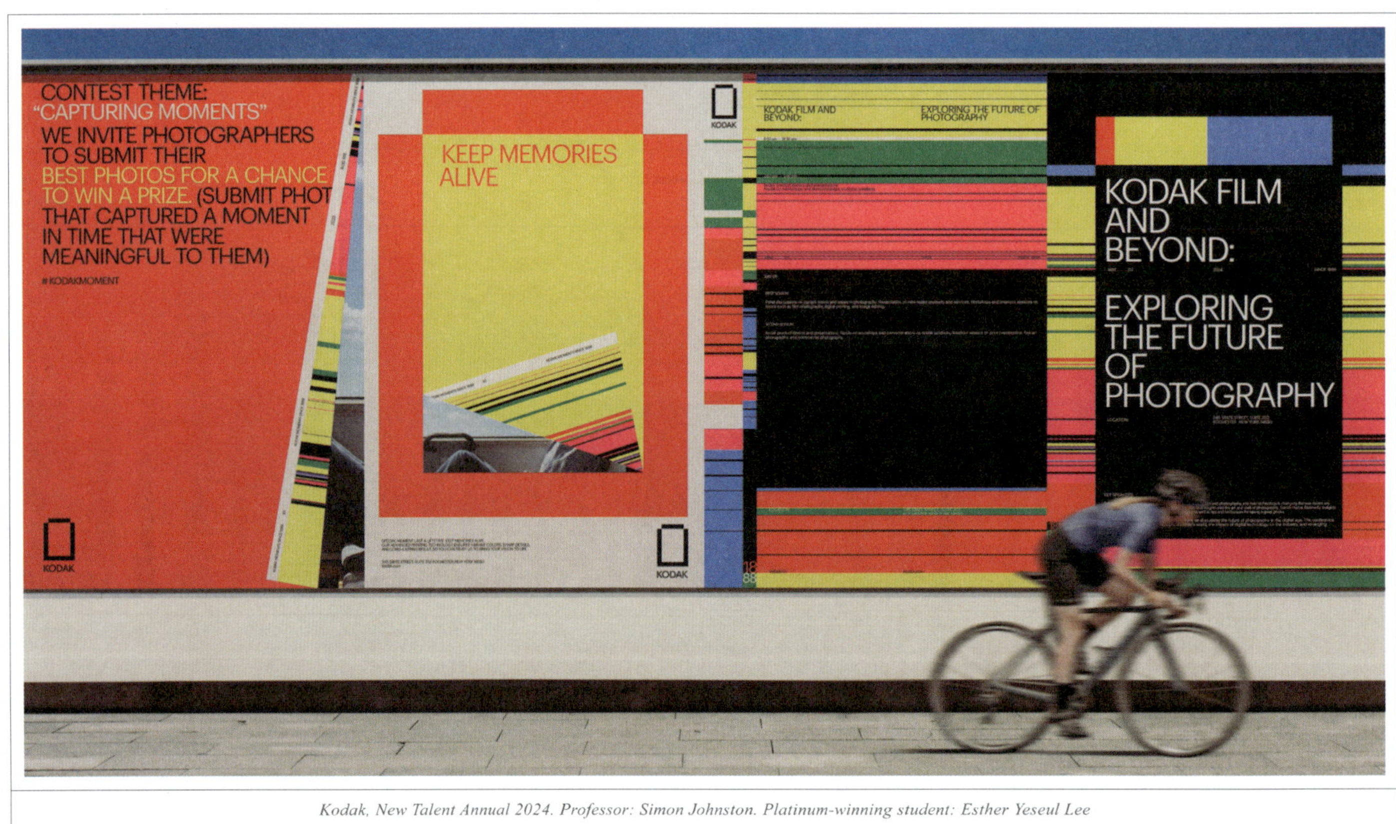

Kodak, New Talent Annual 2024. Professor: Simon Johnston. Platinum-winning student: Esther Yeseul Lee

SIMON'S EMPHASIS ON TYPOGRAPHIC PRAGMATISM AND LETTING THE PROJECT'S NEEDS SHAPE THE DESIGN DIRECTION HAVE BEEN THE CORNERSTONES OF MY ENTIRE CAREER.

Josh Finklea, *Former Student & Freelance Type Designer*

SIMON JOHNSTON'S TEACHINGS REVEAL HOW TYPOGRAPHY SHAPES PERCEPTION AND EMOTION, TRANSFORMING OUR UNDERSTANDING OF BRAND DESIGN INTO SOMETHING TRULY IMPACTFUL.

Elaine Gong, *Student*

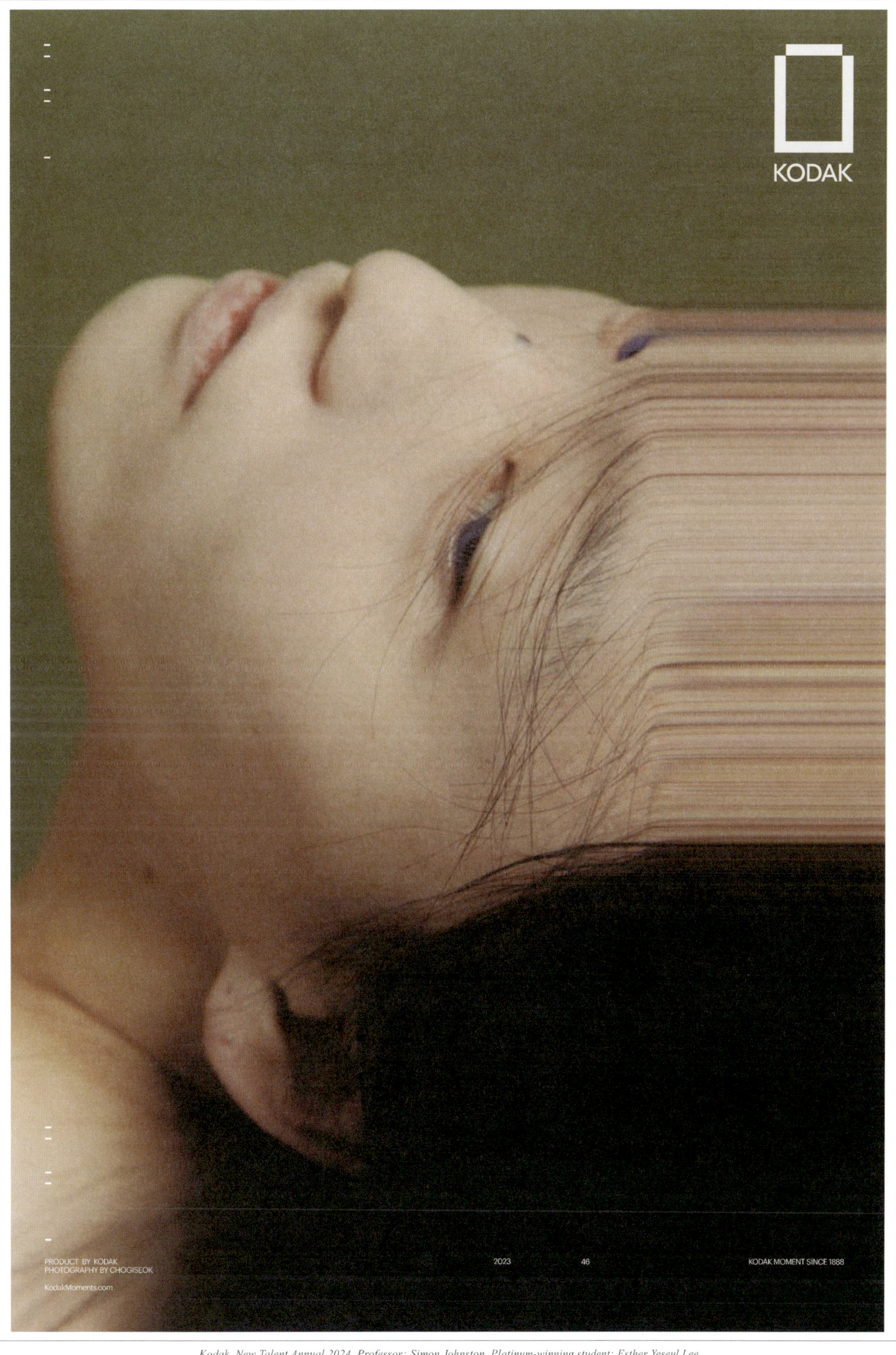

Kodak, New Talent Annual 2024. Professor: Simon Johnston. Platinum-winning student: Esther Yeseul Lee

What is your process for selecting a student for your class? Are there specific qualifications?

I don't select the students. They apply for one of my classes through the college's time-sensitive online application system. We have a progressive, cumulative curriculum which, as a faculty director, I have been involved in developing, so students applying for a Typography 3 class, for example, will have been required to take Type 1 and 2, or those applying for my Communication Design 4: Identity Systems class will have had to take the previous three classes in the CD sequence. Each class in the Type and CD sequences has its own required learning outcomes and builds on the previous one, with some overlap for reinforcement. Each is intended to progressively encourage and develop the student's conceptual and formal skills, hence the prerequisite classes.

What might be a typical first assignment?

Typically, I teach three classes: CD4: Identity Systems, Type 3, and then either Information Design or a Grad Type 3 class. CD4 is a term-long assignment where I give the students a choice between a cultural, commercial, or event-based identity. Research is always the first phase in any assignment. I don't want the students to start designing immediately; instead, I want them to become immersed in their research to get a deeper sense of the subject matter. That way, their design ideas will come from a place of knowledge. I refer to this as organic design because it is rooted in and grows from an understanding of the content. In Type 3, we usually begin with designing a text-heavy, eight-page plus cover booklet for a writer; the intention behind this is to enable the students to lose any fear they might have of dealing with grids and quantities of text, to refine their typeface choices, and to find an appropriate typographic voice for the content and context. A short initial information design project is typically black-and-white only and is based on an analysis of a narrow subject field, such as screen aspect ratios. The pedagogical thinking behind an assignment is very important. For instance, I would never set an assignment such as an identity for an Italian or Mexican restaurant, as the students typically would mimic pre-existing aesthetics, and it just becomes an exercise in producing a pastiche of what is already out there rather than an opportunity for innovation and experimentation. Some types of assignments are conducive to learning, but others are not.

Do you ever ask them to include something they're passionate about in their work for your class?

This can work for some graduate classes or upper-term students when they've acquired good formal skills, but for the most part, early-term projects need to be rigorously structured to develop thinking and formal skills. I find predetermined assignments to be most effective at that early phase, as they have particular required learning outcomes. But of course, you have to find ways in the classroom to engage the students and make them passionate about design and typography.

Do you work with students individually or in groups?

Initially, all critiques are group critiques with the work up on the wall so that the students can see one another's work developing on a week-to-week basis. They can learn as much from seeing their classmates' work develop as they can from listening to me. Group crits are the best way to expose students to different ways of analyzing and discussing their work. Students are encouraged to provide feedback, ask questions of their fellow students, and develop their critical faculties along with my guidance. In the latter half of the term, I will switch to a mixture of group and individual critiques in a more working studio environment. In CD4: Identity Systems, for example, this means that students will already have the main identity resolved by week seven, and the second half of the term is about making refinements to a range of graphic applications using their new identity. Individual crits are better suited to refinements of details later in the term.

How do you develop and raise your student's visual and verbal standards?

Regarding verbal standards, I talk to the students about the importance of what I refer to as "verbalizing the visual" and that they need to develop their skills in articulating visual concepts and approaches. They need to have a strong visual vocabulary and an analytical approach to discussing design matters that go beyond the language of someone who is not visually trained. A recently graduated student showed me a note she took in one of my classes where I banned the students from saying, "Just tweak it to make it pop." This is something a client might say, but designers need to learn to be more articulate than that. The better the students intelligently explain their concepts and design moves, the easier it is for a client or colleague to agree with the design direction. I also point out that the operational reality of the design is that it ultimately has to communicate on its own and be self-explanatory without anyone there to talk about it.

Regarding visual standards, I emphasize the importance of developing formal skills at every level. You can have the best concept in the world, but without good formal skills to express it, the idea will fall flat on its face. Students should be able to analyze and deconstruct a design in terms of concept, language, scale relationships, color, tonal values, hierarchies, alignments, eye movement, typographic voice, and so forth, rather like a mechanic can deconstruct an engine and put it back together after fixing a problem. I tell students that the design process takes several steps and that you cannot see the end result from the starting point. The final design is around the corner, and it might take 16 steps to get around that corner before you can see the final design direction. You must put in the time and create multiple iterations and variations before the final design reveals itself.

What percentage of a typical class goes on to create award-winning work?

Awards are not a focus at all in the process of teaching. Of course, they're a nice bonus after the work is done, but if you start a project thinking about awards, you'll take your eye off the ball and not have a good working process. Get the research, the initial concepts, the design development, and the refinement process right, and the results will follow.

What advice do you give the class at the end of the semester?

Often, I will recap the main points from the class that I want them to take away. I remind them that we are making visual equations and that the work will only be as strong as the weakest point in the equation, so analyze where that might be and improve it. I remind them that designing takes time and involves producing and refining many options. At the start of the project, there are 360 degrees of possible directions. Don't narrow it down too soon and just fall in love with your first idea. What is the opposite of your first idea? Give yourself reference points to navigate towards the most promising direction. Don't be afraid of simplicity or evident structure. Don't be scared to be brave and change something at the last minute if it comes from a late realization of what is needed. Order and structure are perceived as intelligence by a viewer. Ask yourself what intelligence can look like in a design. We don't talk about that enough. I want them to be greedy in the sense that I want to see intelligence AND beauty in their designs. For typography students, I tell them that learning typography is like learning a language—you can start with no knowledge of it but slowly learn to become fluent, by which I mean having control over it and making it say what you want it to say in an effective and appropriate tone of voice. I tell them to have the mindset

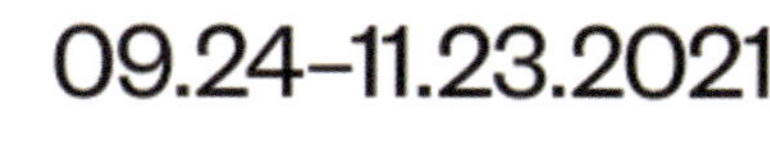

THE FAITH CELL

Shamanism and
Transcendental Experience:
Reaching for Beyond

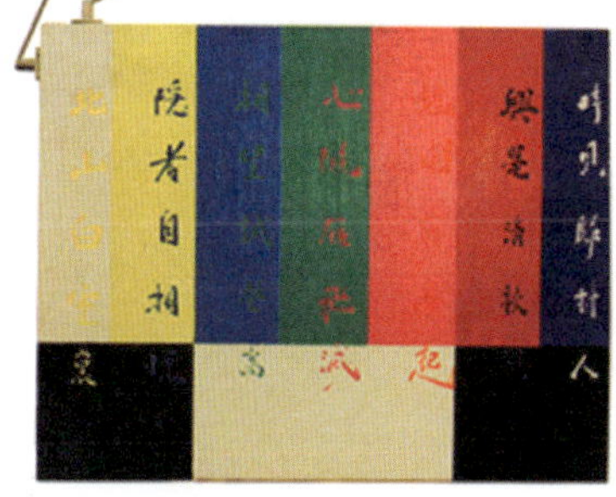

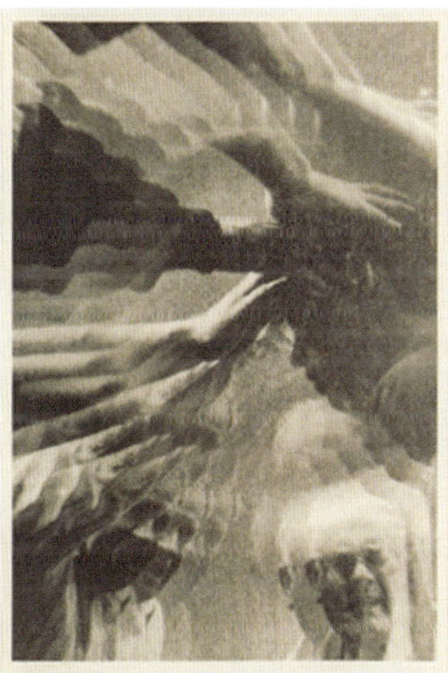

JEREMY
SHAW

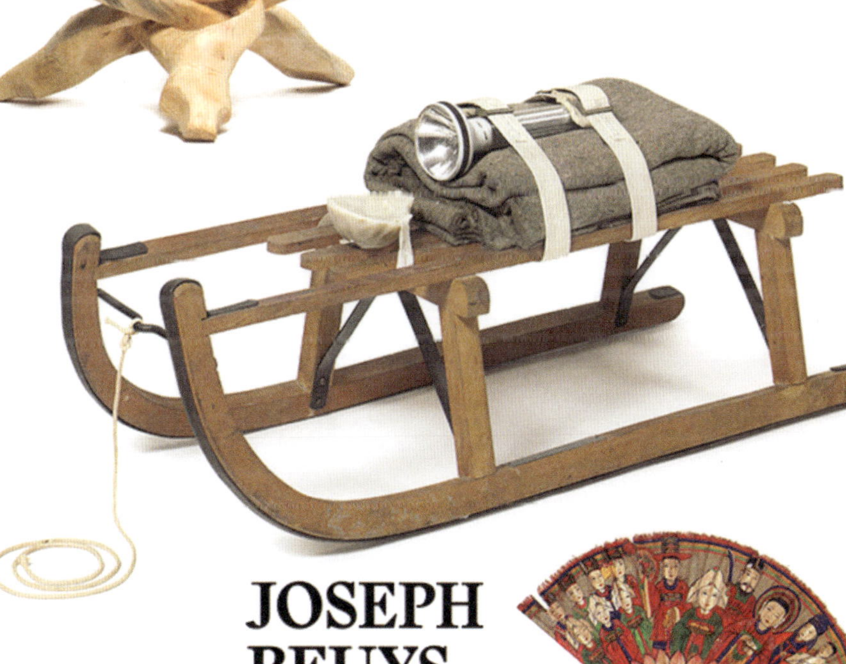

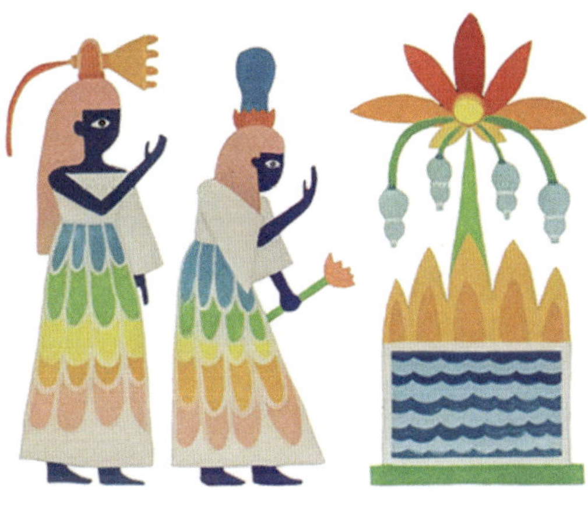

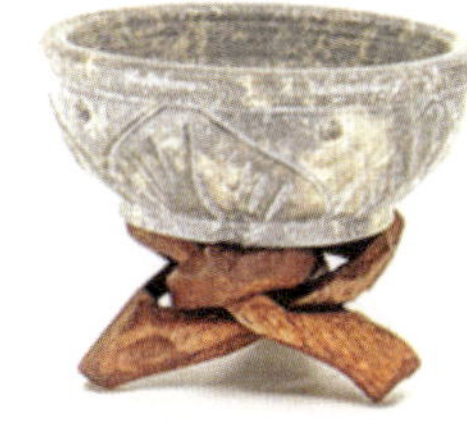

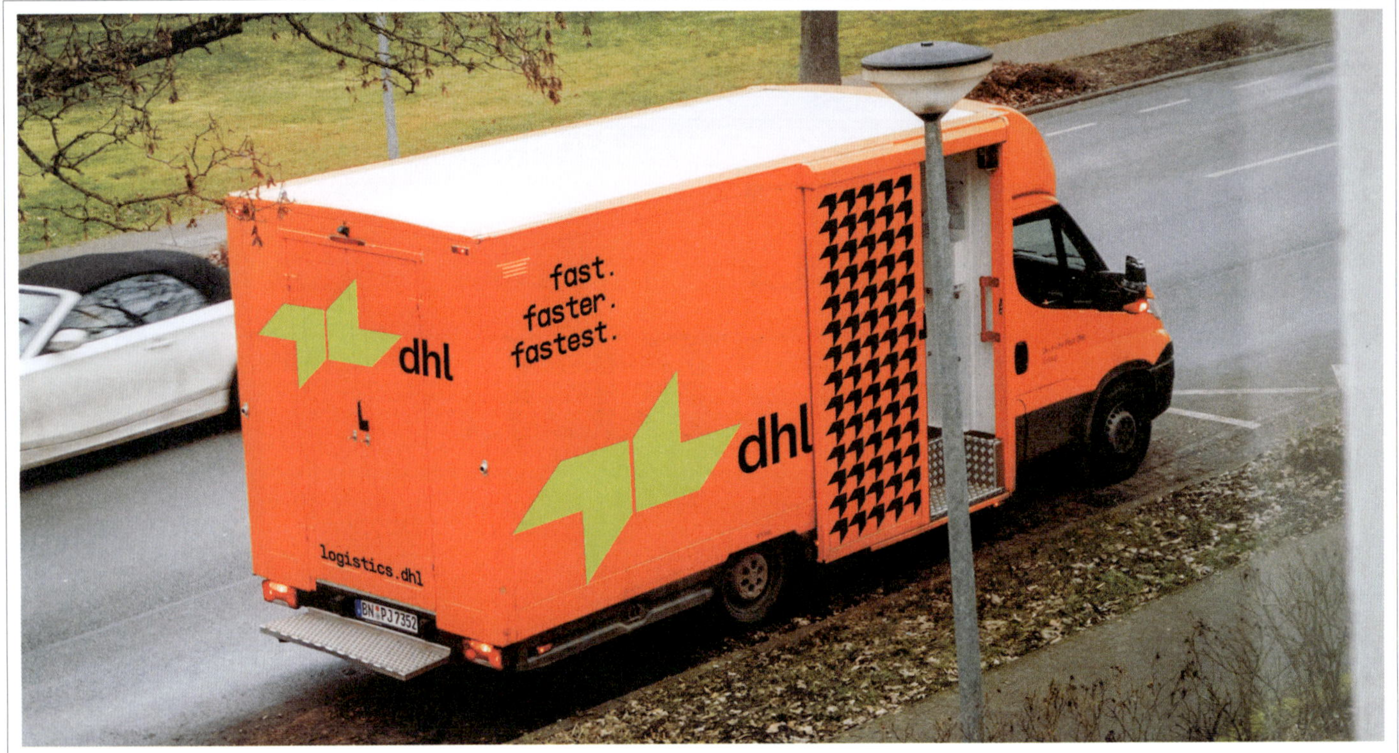

(Above & Opposite page) DHL Identity System, New Talent Annual 2021. Professor: Simon Johnston. Gold-winning student: Tiffany Shen

to make their next piece of work the best thing they have ever done and to keep that intention going throughout their career.

Can you name a few of your past students who have found success? If so, what are they doing now?
I am blessed to have taught so many great students over the years, some of whom I have also been able to mentor as teachers. In no particular order: Mike Abbink is executive creative director at IBM and designed the IBM Plex typeface; River Jukes-Hudson and Stephen Serrato run the design studio Ella in Los Angeles, and both now teach at ArtCenter; Elizabeth Azen Andia runs EA Projects in Brooklyn; Ben Schwartz collaborates with Laurenz Brunner and others and just published *Unlicensed: Bootlegging as Creative Practice*; Lavinia Lascaris is a director at the Hoffmitz Milken Center for Typography (HMCT) at ArtCenter and also teaches there; Ximena Amaya is a designer at HMCT; Tim Bavington is an artist based in Las Vegas; Josh Finklea is a typeface designer; Jorge Verdin was a graphic and sound designer (RIP); Thomas Mueller is global head of design at Accenture Song; Hank H. Huang; Austin Redman; Josh Moore; Pat Slack; and too many past students to name individually who work at Apple and Google. I am having flashbacks. There are too many to mention.

What attracted you to teaching at your current school?
I had moved from London to California to be with my girlfriend. The day after I landed, I was invited to teach at ArtCenter by Ramone Muñoz, a revered professor who knew of *Octavo*, the typographic journal I'd started in London with my 8vo studio colleagues in 1986. The college has a pragmatic edge to it, successfully educating students for employment in the creative industries by blending conceptual and formal rigor with experimentation and a sense of adventure. We are lucky to have highly motivated students who are prepared to put in the time and effort and are open to learning.

What do you think of how so many creative people are now without formal, never mind university-level, training?
The nature of graphic design practice is that it is a commissioned, socially engaged partnership where the designer has re-

sponsibilities to both the client and the viewer. As designers, we are in the middle of this tripartite relationship—we take raw, unformed communication materials and give them form appropriate to both the client and the end user. To do this well takes extensive training. Of course, some will get into creative fields based on their ability in one area, but they will likely have a narrow focus. Some may take internships and learn on the job, but nothing can replace a degree-level education in your chosen field. Even if you think of yourself as a creative rebel who wants to break the rules and make anti-structure, you will do a better job if you first learn about structure. A well-rounded design education is imperative if you want to keep growing and have a promising career. Its importance cannot be underestimated. Once, in a faculty meeting, a colleague used the phrase, "But in the real world…" I realize it is a commonly used cliché. Still, I felt obliged to point out to him that what he was referring to was the commercial world and that to use that phrase is to imply that education is somehow not part of the real world. The phrase downplays the importance of the very real world of education.

Can you tell us something about your background?
I studied in England at the Bath Academy of Art and then in Basel, Switzerland, where I studied with Armin Hofmann and Wolfgang Weingart. Then I returned to London, where I co-founded 8vo studio and *Octavo*, which was recently reprinted in the book *Octavo Redux* by Unit Editions. I have now been in California for over 30 years, dividing my time between teaching, my design studio (mainly designing books for galleries and museums), and my art and photography practice.

Teaching is giving. It is a sacred responsibility to effectively impart your knowledge and experience regarding the art of visual communication and then pass the torch to inspire the next generation. As I reach the end of my teaching journey, I remember that once, when I came home exhausted from teaching, my wife reminded me of a quote from the artist Joseph Beuys: "To be a teacher is my greatest work of art."

Simon Johnston www.simonjohnstondesign.com

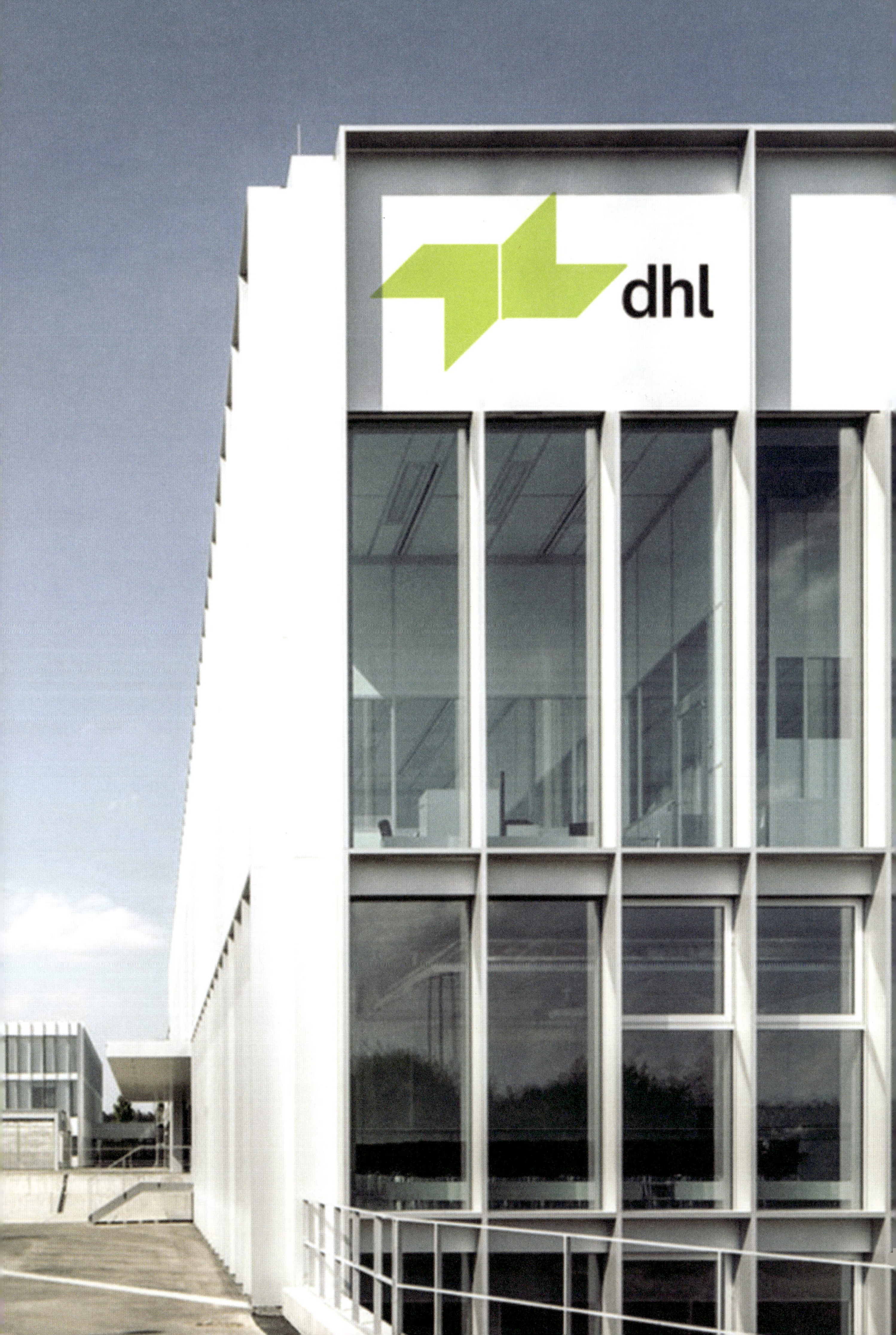

dhl

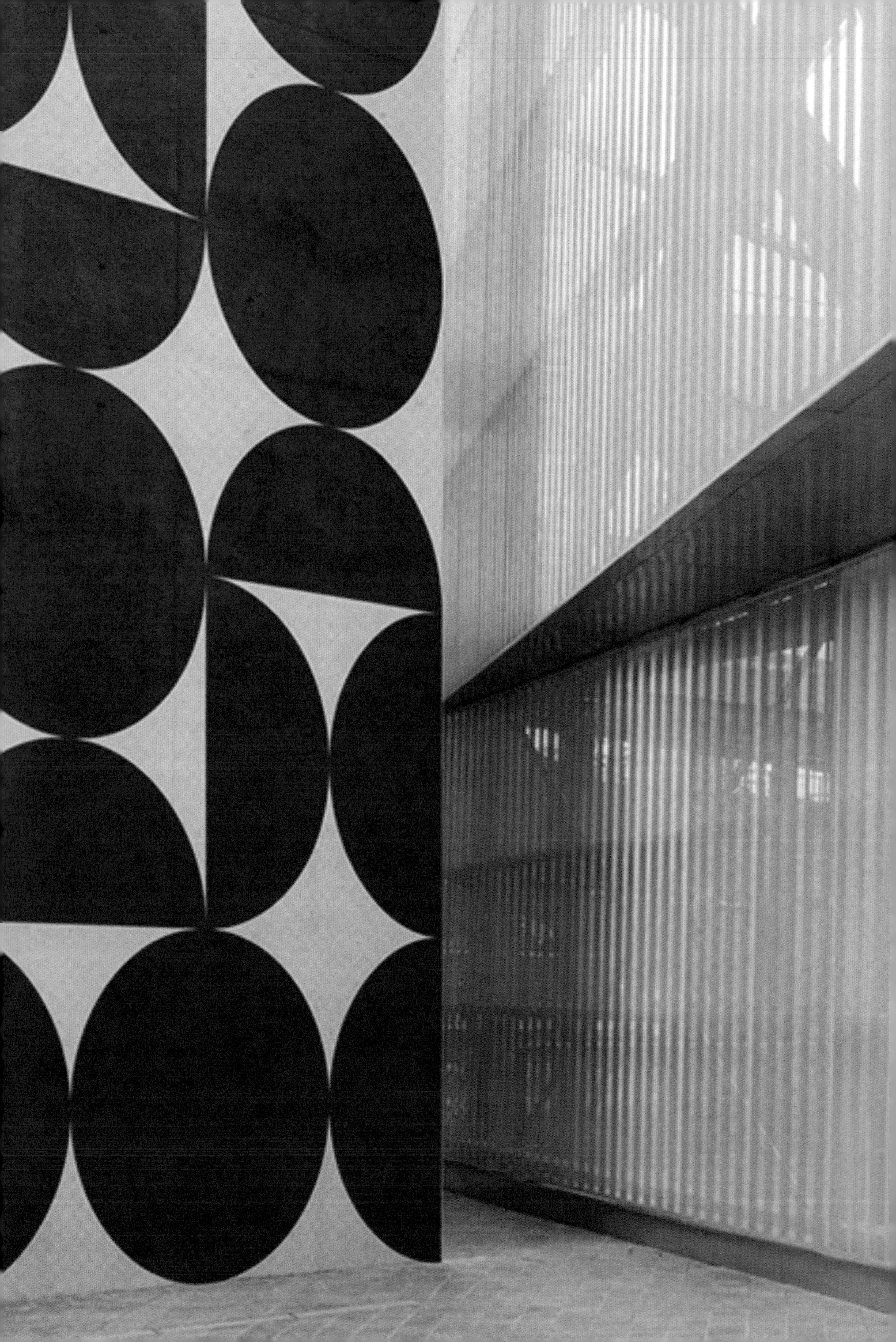

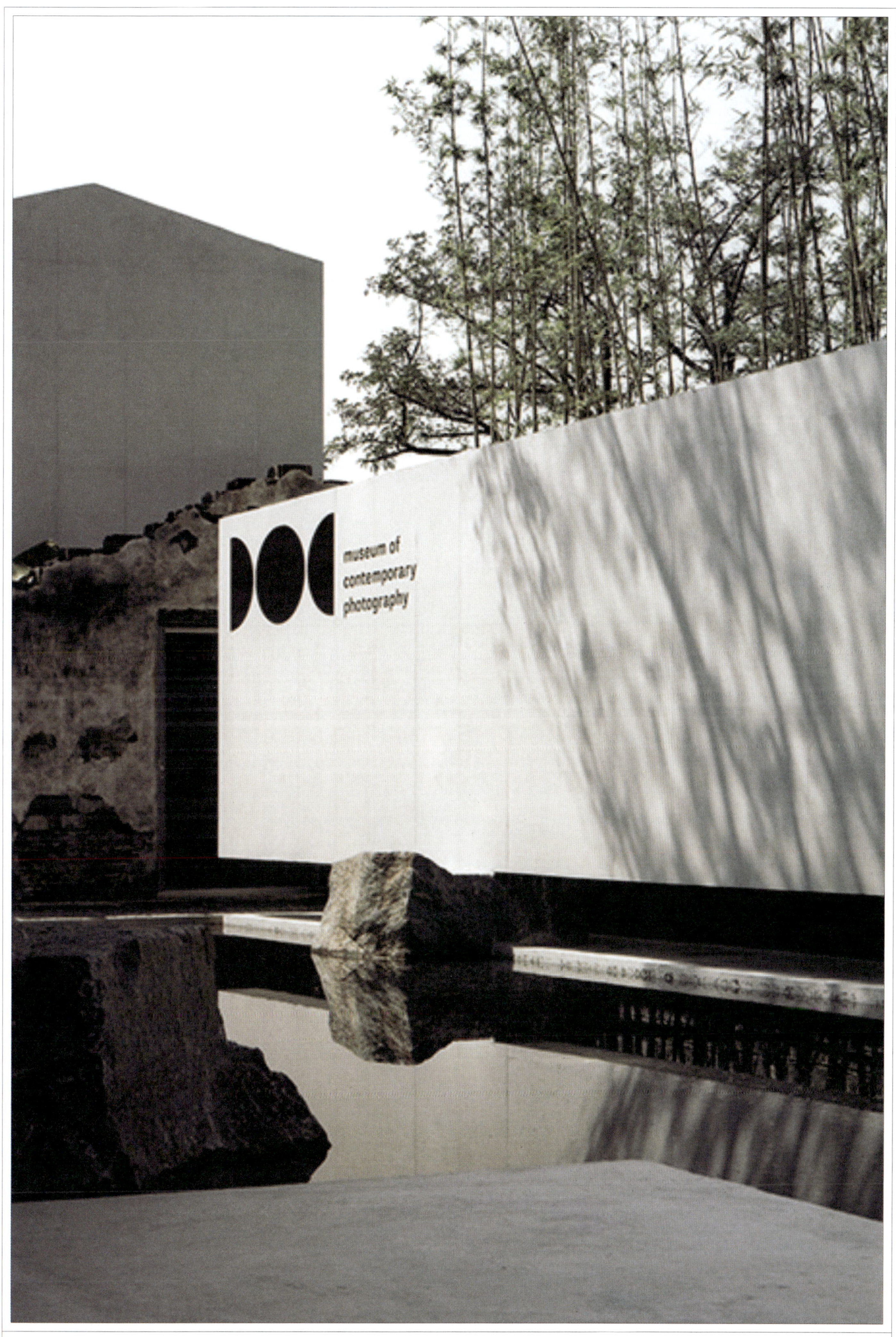

(Above & Opposite page) Museum of Contemporary Photography Rebrand Identity, New Talent Annual 2022. Professor: Simon Johnston. Gold-winning student: Sarah Oh

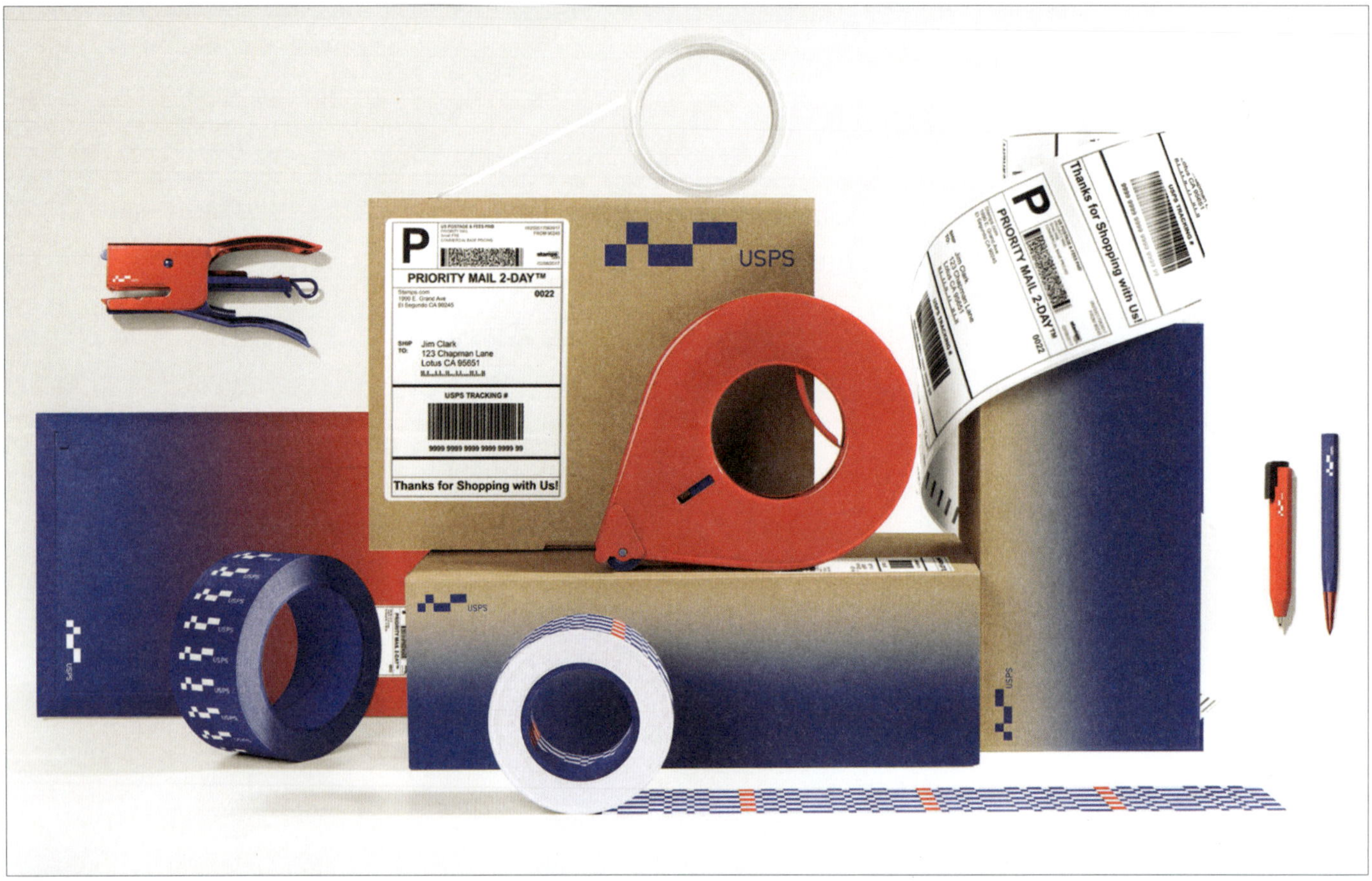

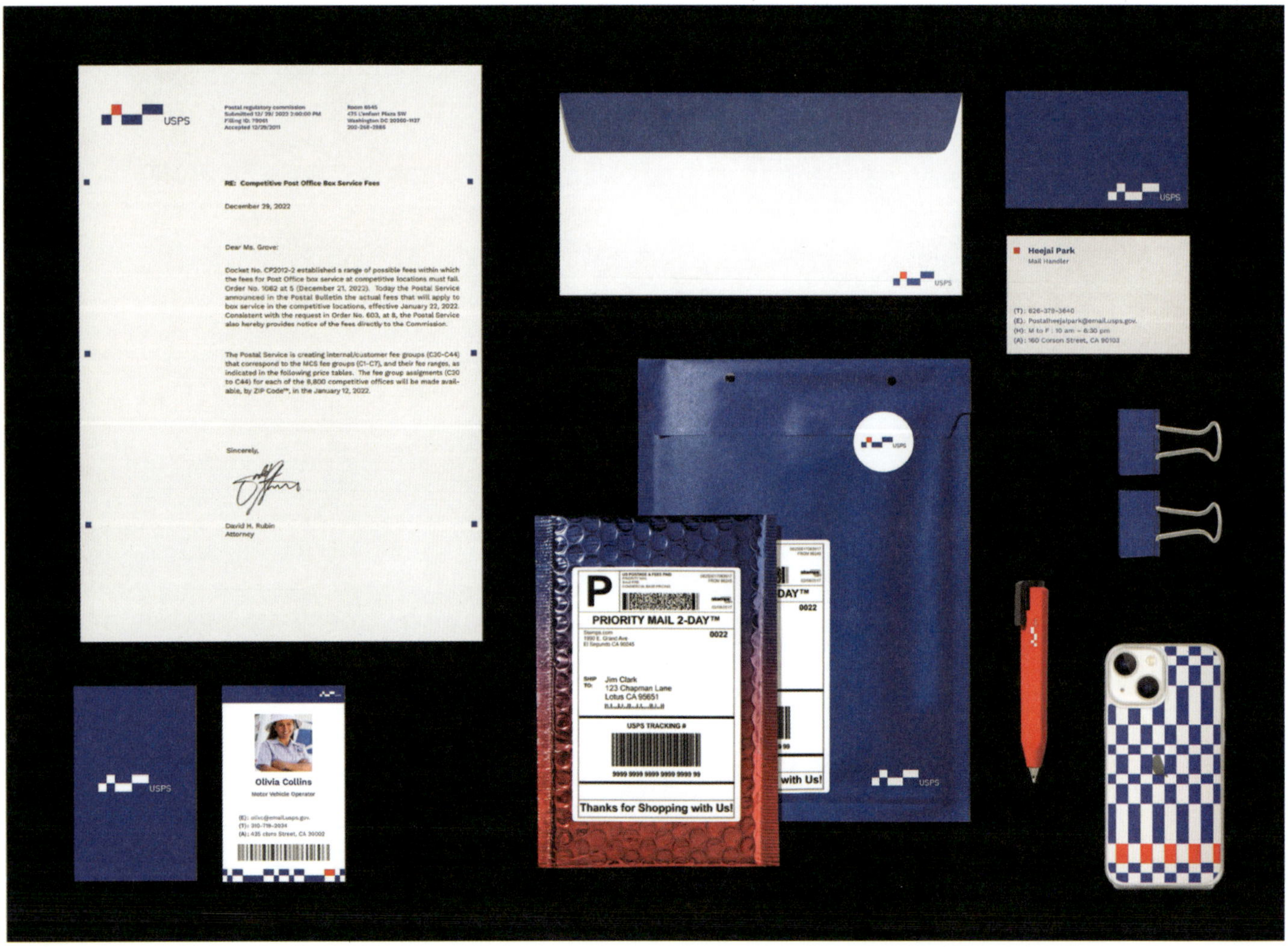

USPS Rebranding, New Talent Annual 2024. Professor: Simon Johnston. Silver-winning student: Heejai Park

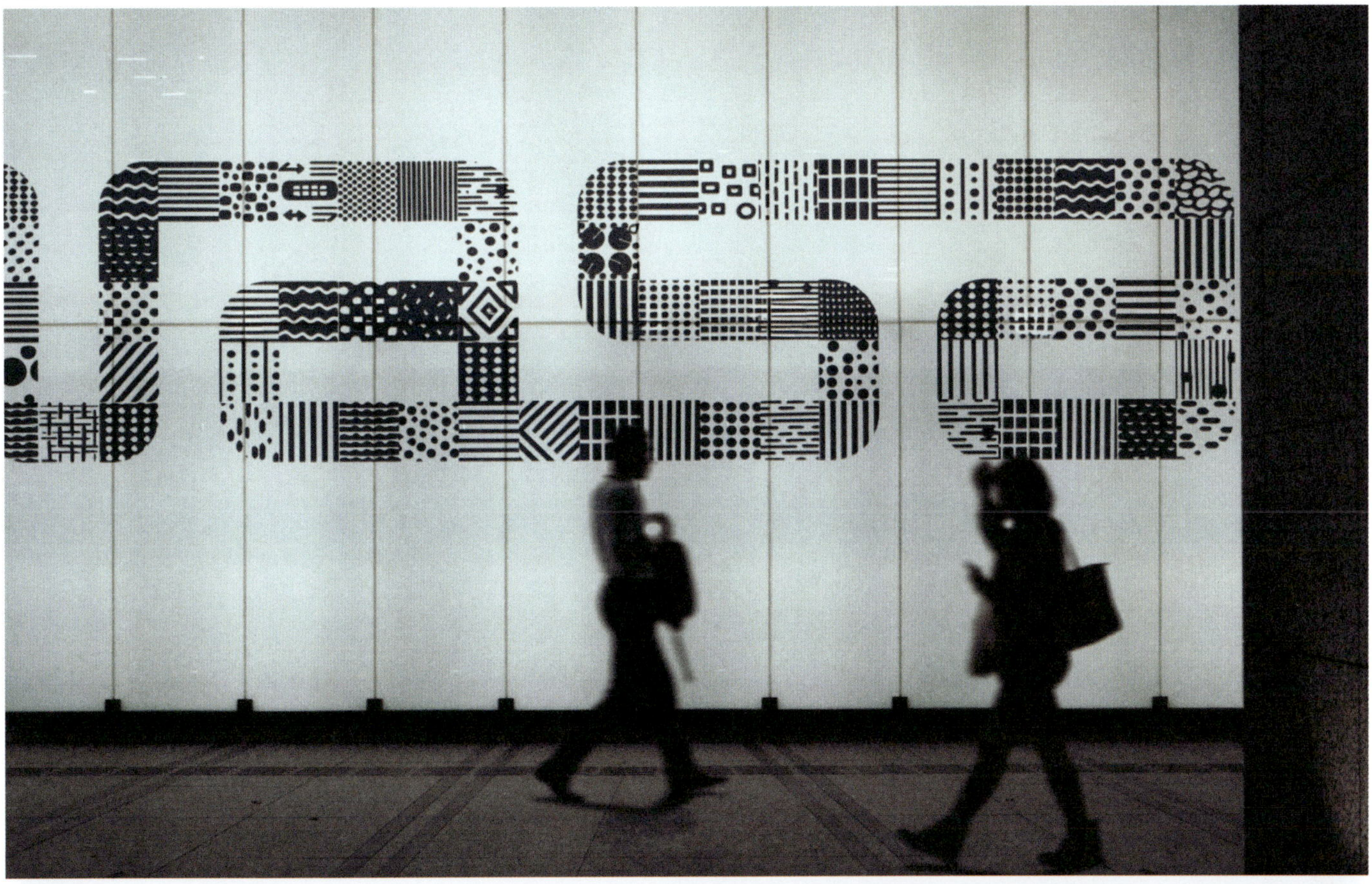

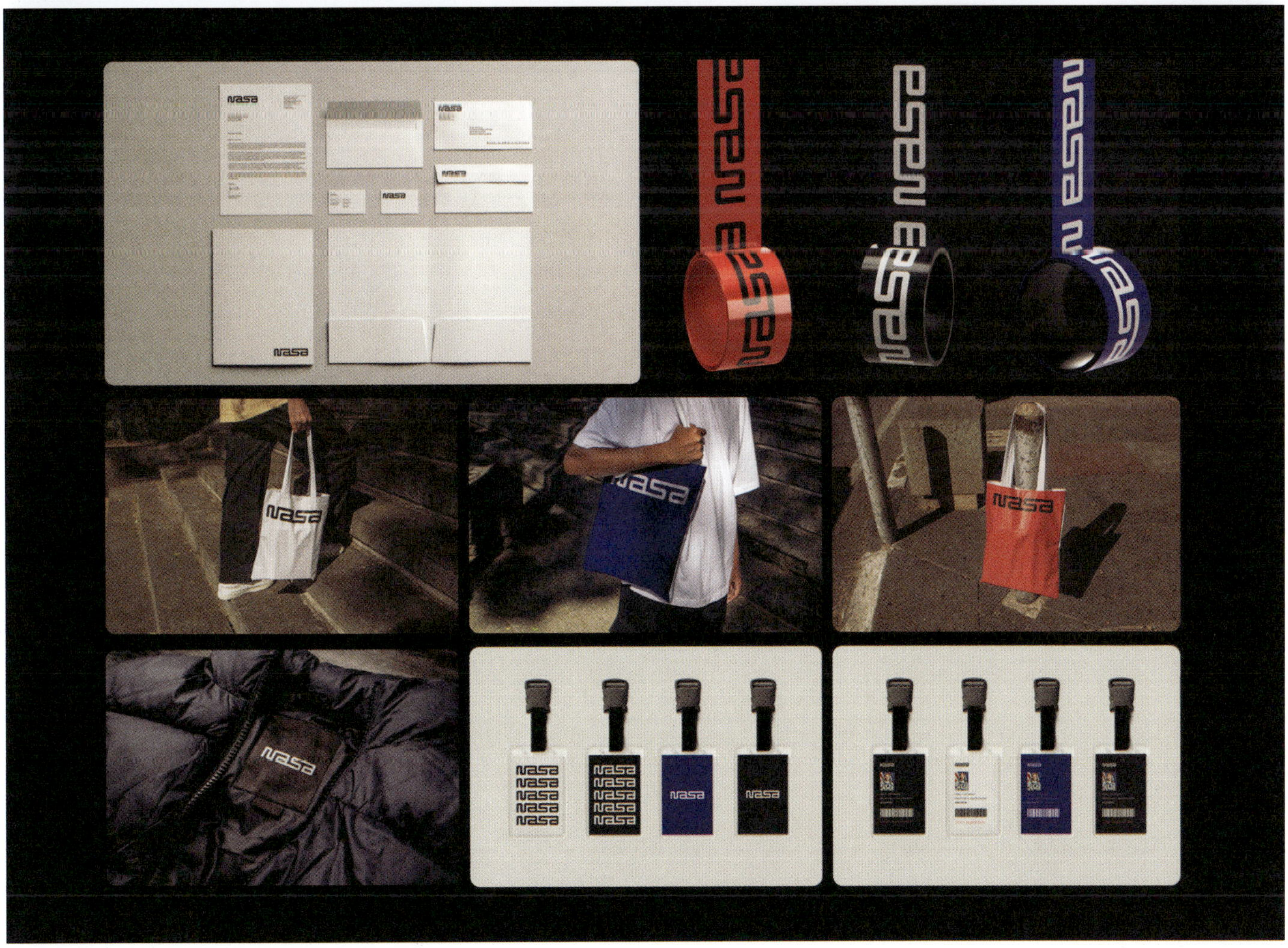

NASA Rebrand, New Talent Annual 2024. Professor: Simon Johnston. Silver-winning student: Elaine Gong

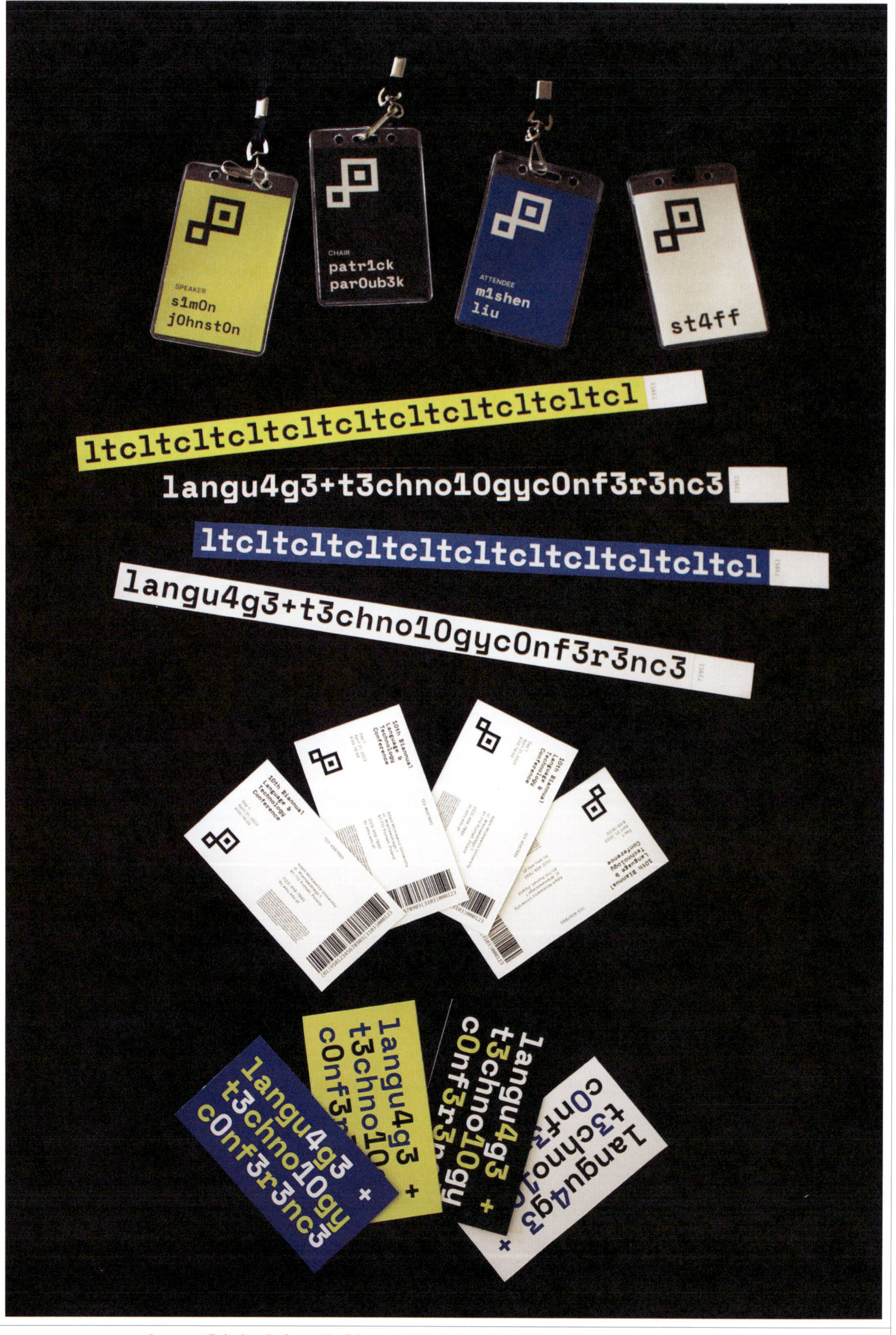

Language + Technology Conference, New Talent Annual 2024. Professor: Simon Johnston. Silver-winning student: Mishen Liu

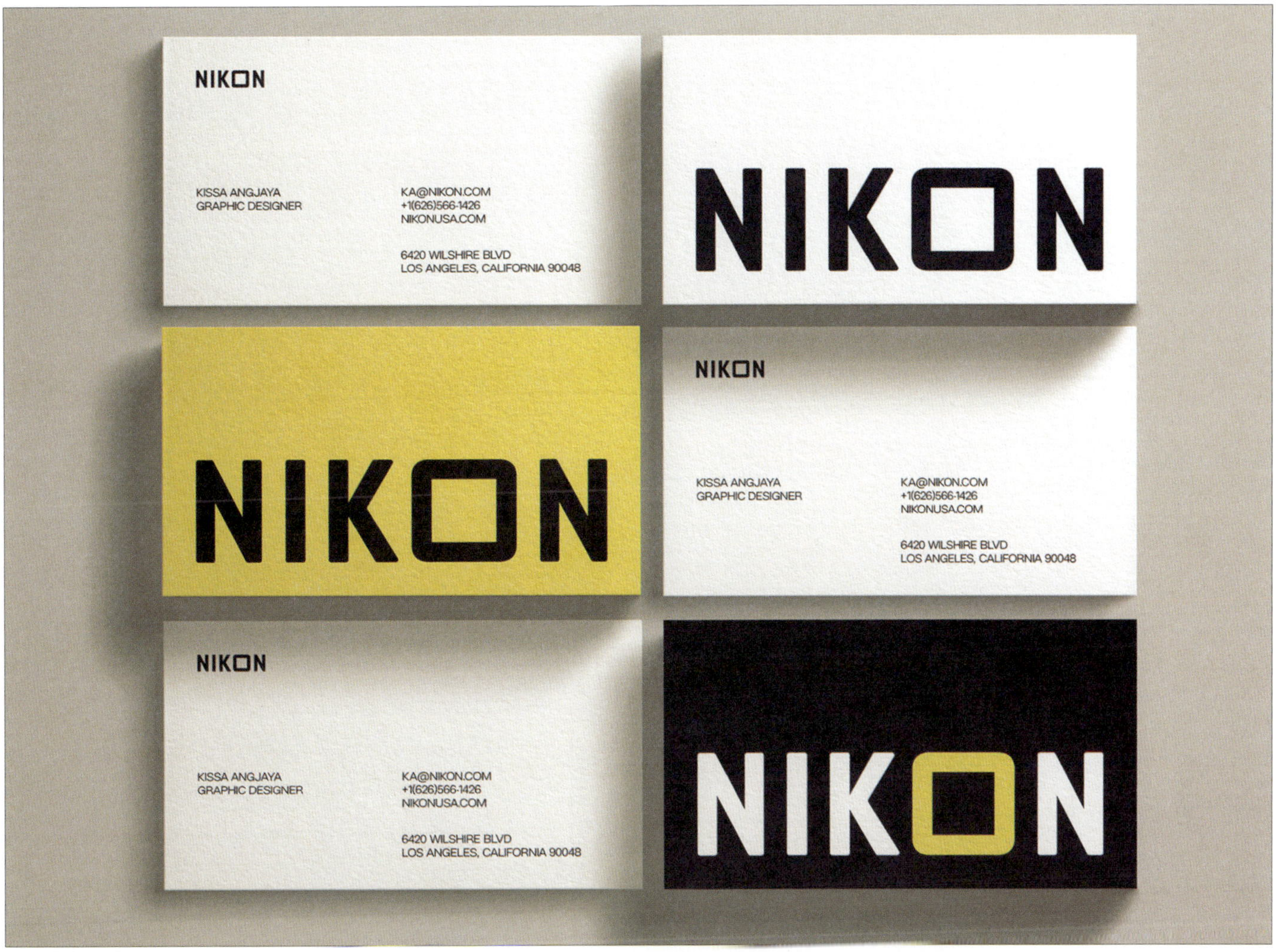

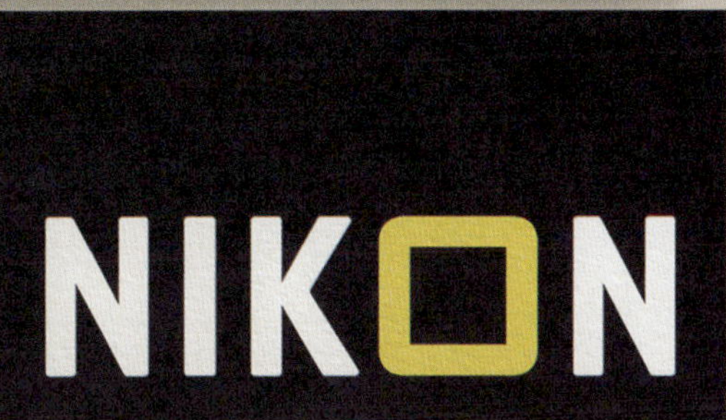

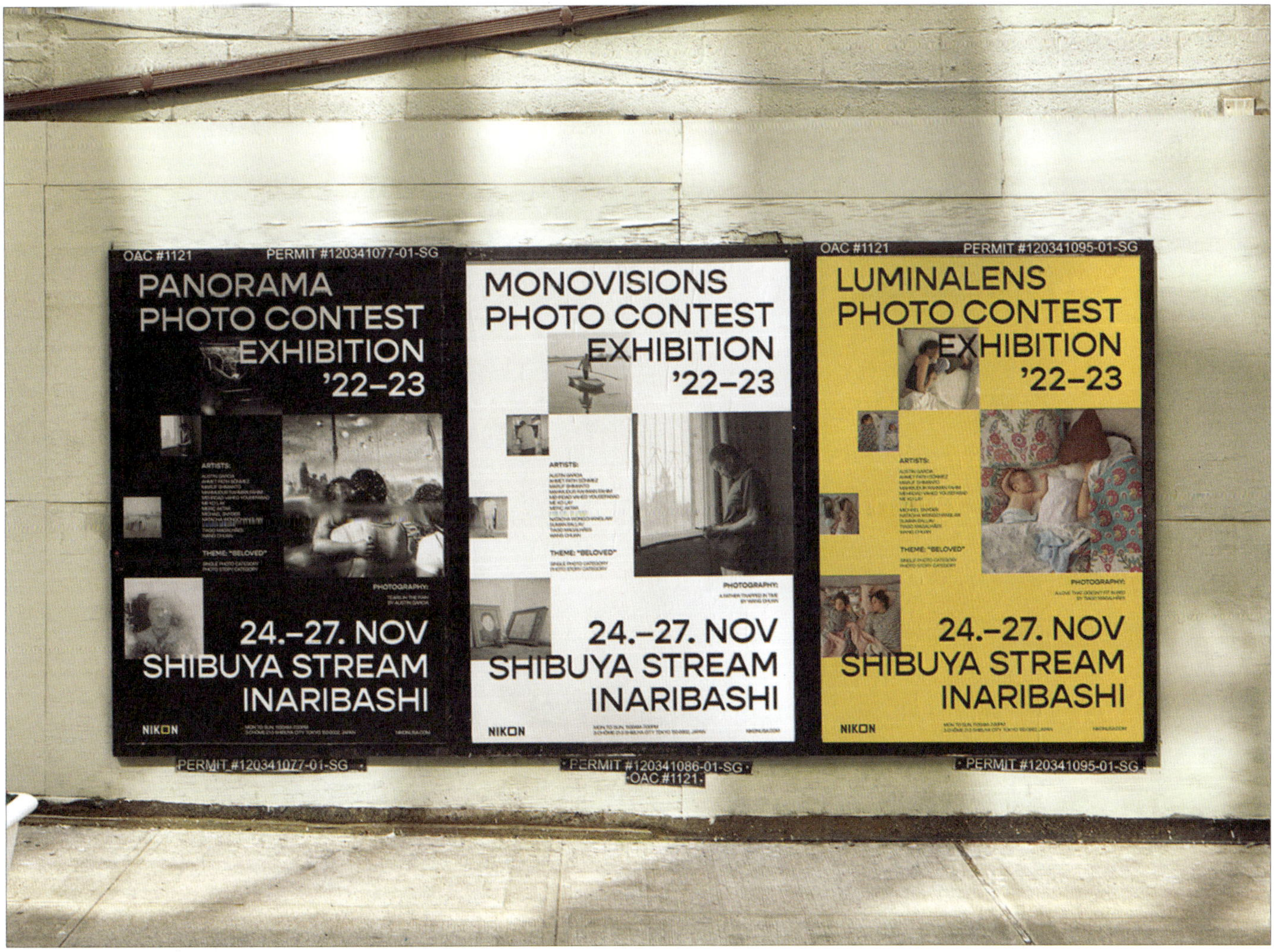

Nikon (Re)Brand Identity System, New Talent Annual 2024. Professor: Simon Johnston. Silver-winning student: Kissa Angjaya

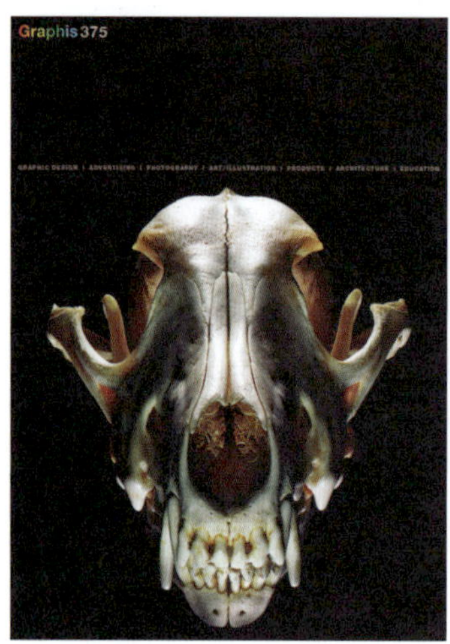

Graphis 375
GRAPHIC DESIGN | ADVERTISING | PHOTOGRAPHY | ART/ILLUSTRATION | PRODUCTS | ARCHITECTURE | EDUCATION

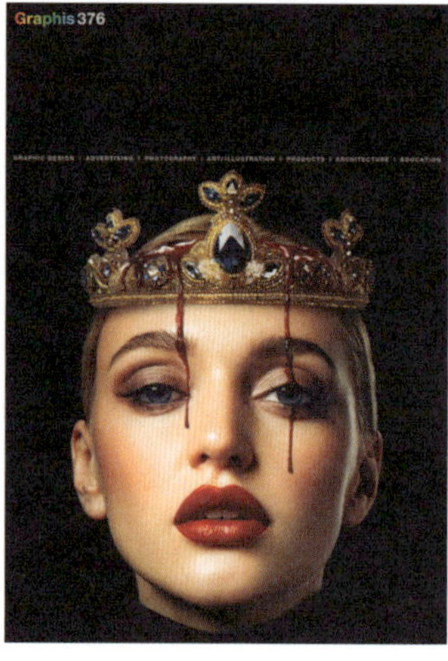

Graphis 376
GRAPHIC DESIGN | ADVERTISING | PHOTOGRAPHY | ART/ILLUSTRATION | PRODUCTS | ARCHITECTURE | EDUCATION

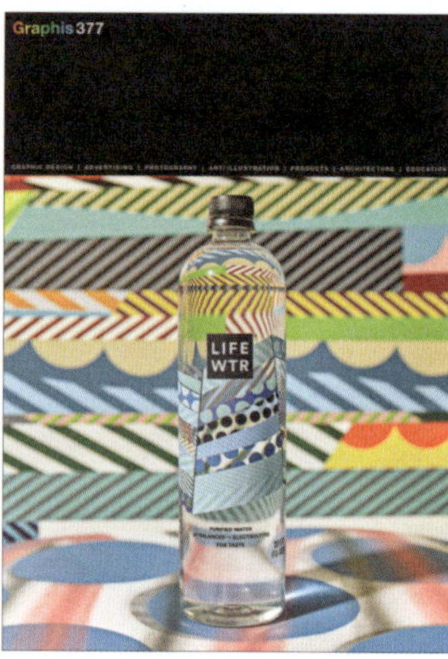

Graphis 377
GRAPHIC DESIGN | ADVERTISING | PHOTOGRAPHY | ART/ILLUSTRATION | PRODUCTS | ARCHITECTURE | EDUCATION
LIFE WTR

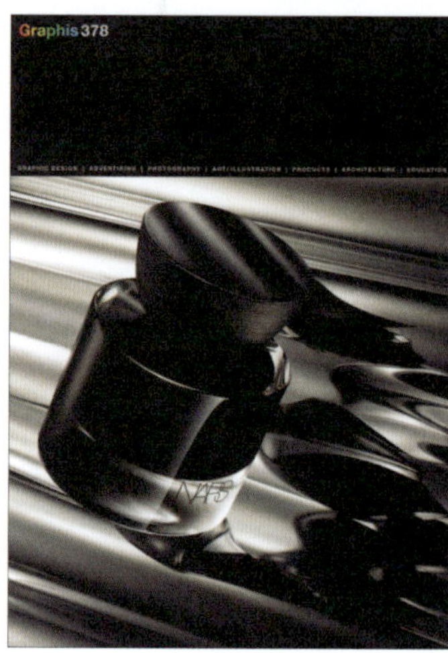

Graphis 378
GRAPHIC DESIGN | ADVERTISING | PHOTOGRAPHY | ART/ILLUSTRATION | PRODUCTS | ARCHITECTURE | EDUCATION
NARS

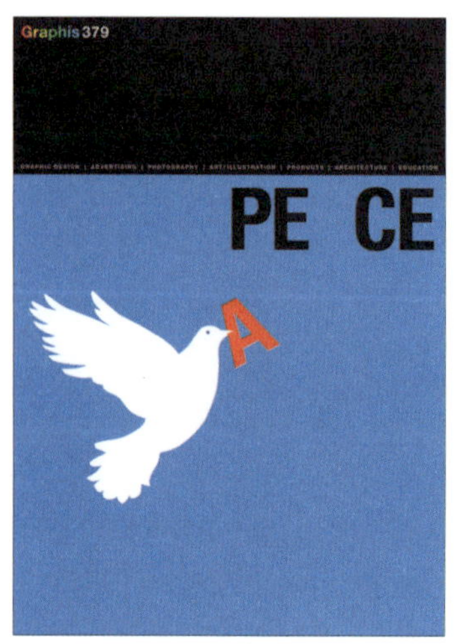

Graphis 379
GRAPHIC DESIGN | ADVERTISING | PHOTOGRAPHY | ART/ILLUSTRATION | PRODUCTS | ARCHITECTURE | EDUCATION
PE CE
A

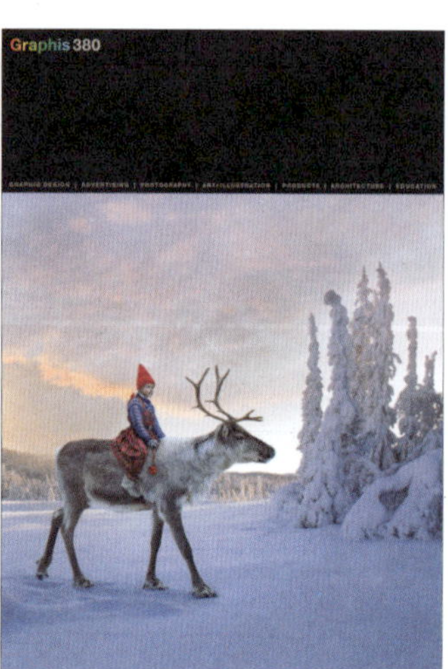

Graphis 380
GRAPHIC DESIGN | ADVERTISING | PHOTOGRAPHY | ART/ILLUSTRATION | PRODUCTS | ARCHITECTURE | EDUCATION

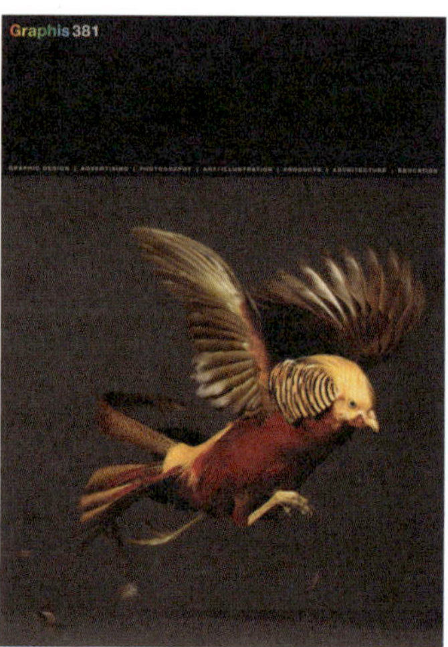

Graphis 381
GRAPHIC DESIGN | ADVERTISING | PHOTOGRAPHY | ART/ILLUSTRATION | PRODUCTS | ARCHITECTURE | EDUCATION

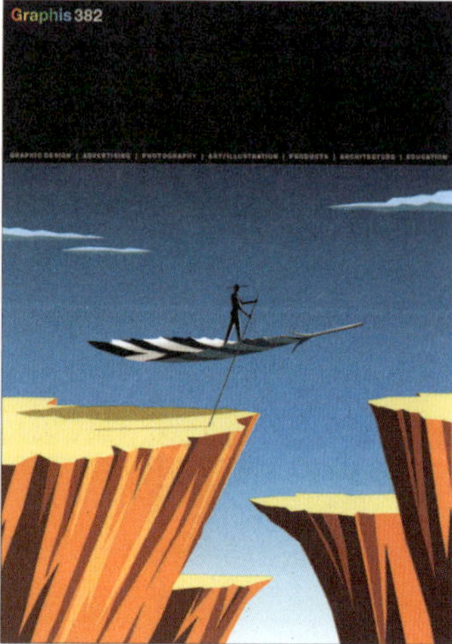

Graphis 382
GRAPHIC DESIGN | ADVERTISING | PHOTOGRAPHY | ART/ILLUSTRATION | PRODUCTS | ARCHITECTURE | EDUCATION

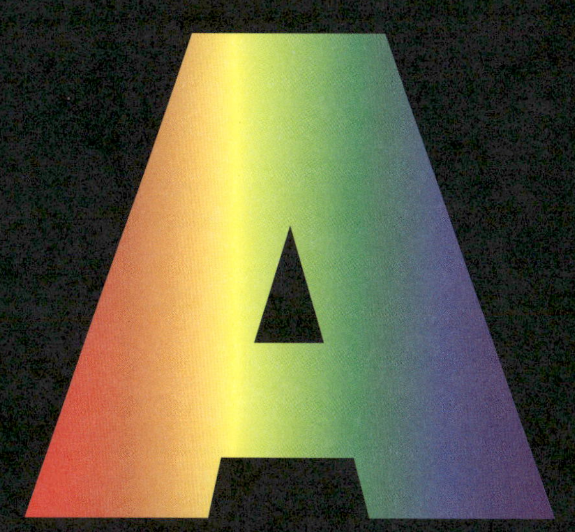

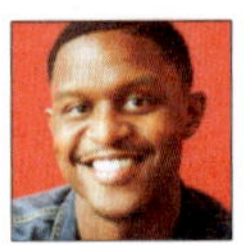

Quinnton Harris

Retrospect co-founder and chief executive officer, Quinnton J. Harris is a creative leader and entrepreneur living in Brooklyn, New York. His new venture focuses on building products and digital experiences that are radical, culturally nuanced, and more accessible for untapped or overlooked market opportunities. Previously, he served as Publicis Sapient Group's creative director within experience design as well as co-leader of global computational design, which focused on evolving the organization's design systems practice. He played a critical role in accelerating CXO John Maeda's vision for fostering a more inclusive, multi-dimensional, and cohesive experience design capability. He also served as head of experience for San Francisco. In early 2020, he completed a short tenure as John Maeda's chief of staff, finding much success in pushing critical CXO initiatives, implementing systems for global collaboration, and enhancing internal communication strategies. Quinnton also led the #hellajuneteenth movement and got over 600 companies committed to observing Juneteenth as a paid holiday for its employees. Prior to joining Publicis Sapient, he served as inaugural creative director at Blavity, Inc., and before that led design at Walker & Company Brands, a start-up consumer products and tech company notably acquired by Procter & Gamble. He is an MIT alum, graduating with a SB in mechanical engineering and dual minors in architecture and visual arts.

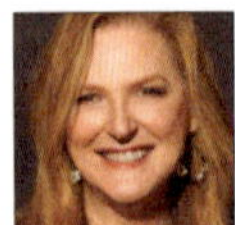

Patti Judd

Award-winning creative director, accomplished marketing and film executive, and co-founder of the San Diego International Film Festival, Patti joined Graphis as chief visionary officer. A key initiative was forming the Graphis Industry Advisory Board to promote greater industry insights and connections globally. Patti blends business savvy gained from twenty plus years at her agency with the entertainment biz acumen garnered from working in music and film. Her studio, Judd Brand Media, champions her passion for creating innovative work, receiving over 100 awards in design, advertising, and marketing. Her work includes notable global brands such as WME, Disney, Mattel, Montreux Jazz Festival, Century 21, Aramark, Service America, and Hilton, alongside numerous emerging brands, recording artists, and filmmakers. Her influence goes from helping launch a major live music venue, where she was a key player in its growth, to one of the top live jazz venues in the world, to co-founding the San Diego International Film Festival. She holds two executive producer credits for a children's TV series on Nickelodeon and a feature film in association with the BBC, which premiered at Sundance (acquired by Universal Pictures). Currently, she is in development as executive producer on an exciting new animated children's series. Patti's nonprofit work includes being a foster youth board member and a past president of an arts and culture board benefiting Balboa Park, the largest urban cultural park in the US. Recently, she was awarded as an Altruist Honoree by *Modern Luxury* magazine.

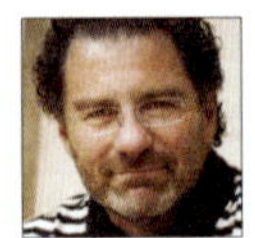

Michael Pantuso

As a multidisciplined graphic designer and artist, Michael Pantuso thrives at the intersection of creative thinking, artistic expression, and strategically inspired ideas. Throughout his career, Michael has managed his own design practice, partnered with the branding agency IDEAS360°, and held positions inside TBWA Worldhealth (formerly CAHG) and Discover Financial. Located in the Chicago area, Michael is focused on creating design and art for clients, collectors, and organizations that make a social impact—these include charities, not-for-profits, NGOs, educational and arts bodies, social enterprises, and for-profit businesses who want to do more good. Michael's practice creates all the usual outputs of a branding agency—design identities, advertising, social media, print literature, websites, email, e-newsletters, photography, etc. But he does so in the context of a bigger picture—a vision for what the brand is, and, more importantly, what it can become. It's a passion that comes from a desire to make things better. Michael's art is an extension of this passion, but it's revealed and expressed in a more visceral way. One example of this can be seen in his "Mechanical Integration" work, where he explores nature and humanity through a series of fine art illustrations that integrate natural life forms with the inner workings of mechanical components. Part of this collection was recently celebrated as a solo exhibition which began in Paris, France, followed by a tour of Europe that concluded in early 2020. Much of that work now remains in galleries and private collections.